AFRICAN
AMERICAN
AUTOBIOGRAPHY

AFRICAN AMERICAN AUTOBIOGRAPHY

A Collection of Critical Essays

Edited by
William L. Andrews

Prentice Hall, Englewood Cliffs, New Jersey 07632

Library of Congress Cataloging-in-Publication Data

African American autobiography : a collection of critical essays /
    edited by William L. Andrews.
        p.   cm.—(New century views)
    Includes bibliographical references.
    ISBN 0–13–019845–5
    1. American prose literature—Afro-American authors—History
and criticism.   2. Afro-American authors—Biography—History and
criticism.   3. Afro-Americans—Biography—History and criticism.
4. Autobiography.   I. Andrews, William L.   II. Series.
PS366.A35A37   1993
810.9′4920009296073—dc20   92–18226
                                                            CIP

Acquisitions editor: Phil Miller
Editorial assistant: Heidi Moore
Editorial/production supervision and interior design: Joan Powers
Copy editor: Sherry Babbitt
Cover design: Karen Salzbach
Prepress buyer: Herb Klein
Manufacturing buyer: Patrice Fraccio/Robert Anderson

© 1993 by Prentice-Hall, Inc.
A Simon & Schuster Company
Englewood Cliffs, New Jersey 07632

Printed in the United States of America
10 9 8 7 6 5 4 3 2 1

ISBN 0-13-019845-5

Prentice-Hall International (UK) Limited, *London*
Prentice-Hall of Australia Pty. Limited, *Sydney*
Prentice-Hall Canada Inc., *Toronto*
Prentice-Hall Hispanoamericana, S.A., *Mexico*
Prentice-Hall of India Private Limited, *New Delhi*
Prentice-Hall of Japan, Inc., *Tokyo*
Simon & Schuster Asia Pte. Ltd., *Singapore*
Editora Prentice-Hall do Brasil, Ltda., *Rio de Janeiro*

To Blyden Jackson,
who taught me

Contents

Introduction

William L. Andrews

Autobiography holds a position of priority, indeed many would say preeminence, among the narrative traditions of black America. African Americans had been dictating and writing first-person accounts of their lives for almost a century before the first black American novel appeared in 1853. It is significant that this novel, William Wells Brown's *Clotel*, was subtitled *A Narrative of Slave Life in the United States* and was authored by a man who had made his initial literary fame as a fugitive slave autobiographer. Ever since, the history of African American narrative has been informed by a call-and-response relationship between autobiography and its successor, the novel. Not until the modern era would the African American novel begin to match the rhetorical sophistication and social impact of autobiography. The number of important twentieth-century African American novels that read like or are presented as autobiographies confirms a recent black critic's contention that "ours is an extraordinarily self-reflexive tradition."[1]

It was the eighteenth-century slave narrator who first sang into print the "long black song" of black America's quest for freedom.[2] Since then African American autobiography has testified to the ceaseless commitment of people of color to realize the promise of their American birthright and to articulate their achievements as individuals and as persons of African descent. Perhaps more than any other literary form in black American letters, autobiography has been recognized and celebrated since its inception as a powerful means of addressing and altering sociopolitical as well as cultural realities in the United States. Nineteenth-century abolitionists sponsored the publication of the narratives of escaped slaves out of a conviction that first-person accounts of those victimized by and yet triumphant over slavery would mobilize white readers more profoundly than any other kind of antislavery discourse. A similar belief

---

[1]The idea of the African American narrative tradition as patterned by a call-and-response formula is set forth in Robert B. Stepto, *From Behind the Veil: A Study of Afro-American Narrative* (Urbana: University of Illinois Press, 1979). Henry Louis Gates, Jr., has emphasized the self-reflexivity of African American literature in both *Figures in Black: Words, Signs, and the "Racial" Self* (New York: Oxford University Press, 1987), and *The Signifying Monkey* (New York: Oxford University Press, 1988).

[2]The phrase "long black song" is taken from the title of Houston A. Baker, Jr., *Long Black Song: Essays in Black American Literature and Culture* (Charlottesville: University Press of Virginia, 1972).

in modern black American autobiography's potential to liberate white readers from racial prejudice, ignorance, and fear led Rebecca Chalmers Barton to publish *Witnesses for Freedom: Negro Americans in Autobiography* in 1948, the first book-length scholarly study of African American (or for that matter *any* form of American) autobiography.[3] It was the narratives of self-styled black revolutionaries in the 1960s and early 1970s that compelled the American academy to reconsider widespread assumptions about literature's transcendent relationship to social struggle. Since then, the fact that the antebellum slave narrative still receives more critical attention than any other subgenre of American autobiography points up the persistence of the conviction that black life-writing speaks powerfully to America's need to confront its history if it is ever to change it.

Since Barton's pioneering book, students and critics of African American autobiography have argued, with increasing emphasis and sophistication in the past twenty years, that this genre deserves to be regarded as a phenomenon of literary significance in its own right, in addition to its import as a social document. Described in terms of the three constituent elements of the word autobiography—*autos* (self), *bios* (life), and *graphe* (writing)—the recent history of readerly and scholarly interest in African American autobiography pivots on a shift from a traditional focus on the *bios* of the author, from whose example valuable insights about history and personal conduct might be gleaned, to investigations of the *autos* and *graphe* represented in and by the text. No doubt the civil rights and Black Power movements of the 1960s and 1970s, which posed profound questions about the kind of identity African Americans wished to create for themselves in the postcolonial era, spurred the concern with selfhood and modes of identification that reoriented so much African American autobiography criticism in the 1970s. The realization that selfhood is itself constituted by language, along with a poststructuralist wariness of granting any text—especially autobiography—the authority of an unmediated representation of a life or a self, has contributed to the insistence in the 1980s and 1990s on an interrogation of the modes of writing adopted by black autobiographers. To comprehend the rhetorical choices and dilemmas that have faced black autobiographers, scholars and critics have recently begun the most extensive excavation of the history of the genre ever attempted. A notable result of this effort has been the creation of new editions of texts that had been long forgotten or facilely dismissed as inauthentic or subliterary. The recovery and republication of such texts as Harriet Jacobs's *Incidents in the Life of a Slave Girl* and Zora Neale Hurston's *Dust Tracks on a Road* enable readers to reexamine what black writers actually wrote in a context informed by the best biographical, historical, and critical scholarship

---

[3]See Barton, *Witnesses for Freedom: Negro Americans in Autobiography* (1948; Oakdale, N.Y.: Dowling College Press, 1976).

that has ever been brought to bear on African American autobiography.[4] It may well be that criticism's determination to reclaim the words of black autobiographers will lead in turn to enhanced study of their lives, their times, and their sense of themselves.

Along with this wide-ranging intellectual reconnaissance of their field, scholars and critics of African American autobiography have become increasingly engaged in rethinking the methods by which they do criticism. More than a little effort has gone into the task of demonstrating that autobiographies such as the *Narrative of the Life of Frederick Douglass* and Richard Wright's *Black Boy* are works deserving of a high rank in the canon of American literature. But a countervailing trend in criticism has raised questions about the wisdom of evaluating black American autobiographies according to standard assumptions about how life, self, and writing interact in the tradition of Western autobiography. Much of the criticism of African American autobiography has thus been devoted to fashioning new, culturally specific ways of analyzing and judging texts. As a consequence, this criticism has not only reconstructed the viability of the study of black American autobiography as a discipline in and of itself but also has played a leading role in the deconstruction of myths that assume a universal Western standard by which all autobiographies could be measured. The doors opened by scholars and critics of African American autobiography have seen the arrival of students of women's, Native American, Hispanic, and Third World life-writing, each with a significant contribution to the burgeoning field of autobiography studies.

Given these developments in African American autobiography study, it seems useful to reflect on the critical history of this field. This book may be regarded as an effort to bring together certain significant critical essays that have addressed some of the most important texts and traditions in African American autobiography. The editor does not claim that the pieces collected in *African American Autobiography* are *the* essential critical essays on African American autobiography. No single book could hold that many essays. But the editor does believe that no serious student of African American autobiography can afford to miss the essays collected here, especially if her or his aim is to gain a fair and full reckoning of where criticism of autobiography has come from and what its key concerns have been.

From Henry Louis Gates, Jr.'s, opening essay on eighteenth-century African American autobiography to Albert E. Stone's survey of trends in the tradition during the five decades since W. E. B. Du Bois's *Dusk of Dawn* and Wright's *Black Boy*, the contents of this volume are ordered chronologically to give the

---

[4]See Harriet "Linda Brent" Jacobs, *Incidents in the Life of a Slave Girl, Written by Herself*, ed. Jean Fagan Yellin (1861; Cambridge, Mass.: Harvard University Press, 1987), and Zora Neale Hurston, *Dust Tracks on a Road*, 2nd ed., ed. Robert Hemenway (Urbana: University of Illinois Press, 1984). The most ambitious excavation work in the history of African American autobiography is The Schomburg Library of Nineteenth-Century Black Women's Writing in thirty volumes (1988), with a ten-volume supplement (1991), published by the Oxford University Press under the general editorship of Henry Louis Gates, Jr.

reader a sense of the historical development and scope of the genre. Within this structure, the reader can discern major trends in the history of African American autobiography from the slave narrative to the recent efflorescence of various kinds of women's spiritual autobiography represented by such texts as Pauli Murray's *Song in a Weary Throat* and Audre Lorde's *Zami: A New Spelling of My Name*. The last two essays in this volume examine aspects of two first-person traditions—those of West Indians and of Africans—whose importance to a proper and complete understanding of the genre in North America is only beginning to be studied.

The first four essays in *African American Autobiography* posit central themes and issues in the American slave narrative. Gates's "James Gronniosaw and the Trope of the Talking Book" singles out what may be the earliest common trope of African American autobiography, in which an African attempts to understand a Western book by listening to it, a scene that appears strikingly in five narratives by native-born Africans published in the late eighteenth and early nineteenth centuries. Gates argues that the intertextual presence of the trope of the talking book demonstrates that from its inception black American life-writing has been profoundly concerned with making the language and conventions of the Western literary tradition speak to and through the voice of black oral culture. This view of the slave narrative as a site of negotiation between black and white voices and discourses is further developed in Robert B. Stepto's "Narration, Authentication, and Authorial Control in Frederick Douglass' *Narrative* of 1845." In this essay, Stepto outlines the complex dynamic between black storytelling and white authenticating documents in slave narratives, using Douglass's classic text as a case in point. To Stepto, Douglass's *Narrative* is distinguished by the fact that the author's voice sets the terms for the dialogue that occurs among the documents that compose the *Narrative*. This achievement of "authorial control" identifies Douglass as the archetypal "articulate hero" of the antebellum slave narrative, a figure who has won not only his physical freedom but also the power to determine the text of his own life.

Reviewing Douglass from a feminist perspective, Deborah E. McDowell raises serious doubts about the degree to which Douglass got free of a gendered view of selfhood that privileges manhood at the expense of a nonobjectified view of women. McDowell's extensive inquiry into the positioning of women in both the *Narrative* and *My Bondage and My Freedom* challenges not only the idea of Douglass's priority and predominance in the canon of nineteenth-century African American literature, but also the very notion that some *one* writer, male or female, should be given this honorific status in contemporary criticism. Hazel V. Carby also questions the idea that the quest for freedom and literacy on the part of the slave narrator can be effectively epitomized in Douglass's act of wresting his manhood from political and intellectual bonds. In " 'Hear My Voice, Ye Careless Daughters,' " a study of antebellum black women's narratives, Carby shows how Harriet Jacobs used her autobiography to address the peculiar conditions of black women under slavery in the South and quasifreedom in the North and to articulate a concept of freedom liberated from the dominant ideology of "true womanhood."

The vast middle period in the history of African American autobiography, from the end of the slavery era to the beginning of the Great Depression, claims the attention of two essayists in this volume. I survey developments in the slave narrative in the post–Civil War era in "The Representation of Slavery and the Rise of Afro-American Literary Realism, 1865–1920." Joanne M. Braxton identifies Ida B. Wells's posthumously published autobiography *Crusade for Justice* as a transitional text that both revoices the message of the slave narrative's "outraged mother" and anticipates challenges to the split between the public and the private in modern black women's autobiography. In my article, I point out a pragmatic perspective among postbellum black autobiographers that culminates in Booker T. Washington's *Up from Slavery* and its celebration of the man of action over the man of words. Washington's brand of realism undermined the faith built up by such writers as Douglass and Jacobs in the power of the word to effect change in the world. The Ida B. Wells of Braxton's analysis wrote her memoirs to serve as a history of antiracist struggle for an uninformed posterity, but her determination to "set the record straight" about her era does not ignore the potential of rhetoric to claim the future while repossessing the past. Yet the most thoughtful challenge to Tuskegee realism in early twentieth-century African American letters may have come from pseudo-autobiographical fiction, such as James Weldon Johnson's novel *The Autobiography of an Ex-Colored Man* (1912), which blurs the line between fact and fiction, and thus dismantles the opposition between effective acts and mere words that Washington tried so hard to impress upon black American consciousness.

The difficulty of distinguishing fact from fiction in modern African American autobiography has presented critics with a number of interpretive and evaluative problems, as Françoise Lionnet's study of Zora Neale Hurston's *Dust Tracks on a Road* and Charles T. Davis's essay on Richard Wright's *Black Boy* demonstrate. In response to questions raised about the reliability of Hurston's representation of herself and about the failure of her autobiography to conform to patterns authorized by the black American literary tradition, Lionnet argues that the key to Hurston's effort lies in her "an-archic style," not in the statements about self and society often rendered ironic, exaggerated, and playful through that style. What underlies Hurston's highly individualized style is her attitude toward life-writing as "autoethnography," which enables her to bring her anthropological training to bear not only on the representation of her experience but also on her status as creator of meaning out of that experience. Ultimately, in Lionnet's view, Hurston does reveal herself in her autobiography, but only through a process of self-construction involving a highly personalized "braiding" of daughter and mother, personal history and cultural myth, to yield a truth of its own making authorized by the writer as a kind of female *griot*. Similarly, by examining the "gray area" between autobiography and fiction represented by *Black Boy*, Davis shows how Wright progressed "from experience to eloquence," thereby turning his autobiography into a work of art, indeed, in Davis's view, Wright's "supreme artistic achievement." Taking a biographical approach to *Black Boy*, Davis explains how the discrepancies between life and text reveal Wright's austere design. Like *Dust Tracks, Black Boy* achieves distinction as a deliberately multivocalic text because the narrator's voices ultimately blend into that of the artist who transforms a grim, lonely survival tale into a metaphor of liberation.

The two most widely read and studied autobiographies of the 1960s have been *The Autobiography of Malcolm X* and Maya Angelou's *I Know Why the Caged Bird Sings*. In the critical essays by Paul John Eakin on the former and George E. Kent on the latter, a careful effort is made to situate these unprecedented texts in appropriate literary traditions, partly as a basis for showing what makes them so original. In Eakin's "Malcolm X and the Limits of Autobiography," the critic reveals powerful tensions between Malcolm's initial intention to create a conversion narrative and his evolving realization in the last months of his life that he could no longer subscribe to the "fiction of the completed self" that the traditional conversion narrative maintains. What Malcolm's autobiography becomes, as a consequence, is a highly personal testament to both Malcolm's increasingly open-ended sense of himself and the black autobiographer's ability to write himself out of the enclosing limitations of his form. Kent sees Angelou as equally adept in negotiating and ultimately reconciling the demands of tradition, particularly the black autobiographical tradition. Kent notes that the conflicting positive and negative attitudes toward American institutions that underlie such canonical autobiographies as *Up from Slavery* on the one hand and *Black Boy* on the other are clearly registered in *I Know Why*. But Angelou's triumph stems from her ability to strike a balance between the communalism of her grandmother's religious ideals and the individualism of her mother's streetwise code to produce an autobiography that reclaims the American Dream according to an African American woman's needs, rather than the other way around.

In 1978 Albert E. Stone published "After *Black Boy* and *Dusk of Dawn*: Patterns in Recent Black Autobiography," in which he offered for the first time a survey and a taxonomy of major narratives and narrative modes in modern African American autobiography. Stone's argument—that the historically focused memoir on the one hand and the novelized private confession on the other constitute the two "polar modes of self-representation" in African American autobiography of the modern era—has yet to receive a strong critical challenge. As he points out in his postscript to the essay, written expressly for this volume, several critics have built upon the basic classification scheme that Stone proposed in 1978. Indeed, as he examines trends in African American autobiography during the last decade and a half, Stone shows how the fictional and the historical, the individual and the collaborative, and other dialectical influences that he identified in 1978 underlie contemporary experiments in autobiography. It is also important to find Stone in his postscript revising his earlier notion of a strict polarity of autobiographical modes; he no longer leaves his reader with the assumption that the distinctions between modes are stark or unmediated. As cross-fertilization among the various traditions of African American autobiography steadily increases, Stone helps us see how few hard and fast generic or modal distinctions really hold up any more.

As criticism of African American autobiography continues to develop, its circle inexorably expands to include not only those North American voices hitherto muted but also pan-American and pan-African traditions from which we can learn much about what is African and what is American about African American autobiography. The increasing recognition of the international context in which African American autobiography studies can be situated is strikingly evident in Sandra Pouchet Paquet's ground-breaking essay on West Indian autobiography, and James Olney's comparatist study of Wright's *Black Boy* and Camara Laye's *L'enfant noir*. Paquet focuses on the first-person narratives of George Lamming, C. L. R. James, Derek Walcott, and Vidia Naipaul, arguing that they were present at the creation of West Indian literature in the 1950s. These men were highly conscious of their obligation to create through their self-portraits what Paquet calls "cultural archetypes" of their decolonized homeland. Just as these West Indians were determined to endow their life stories with the maximum collective, even mythic, significance, so, as Olney points out, Laye followed his African traditions in identifying himself according to the cultural myths, rituals, and communal ideals he inherited, subscribed to, and represents as the ground of his own sense of selfhood. How different, Olney suggests, is Richard Wright's highly personal myth of selfhood tempered by his rejection of a stifling community and celebration of a radically alienated sense of self. Whether Wright's *Black Boy* should be estimated in an exclusively "Western" context, or whether it should be taken as representative of larger differences between African American and African first-person narratives are among the many provocative questions that Olney's essay, as well as others in this volume, are likely to stimulate for readers and students of black American autobiography. It is my hope that what follows in *African American Autobiography: A Collection of Critical Essays* will promote an increasingly well-informed critical dialogue about the linchpins of African American autobiography: selfhood and the community of historical precedents, social identifications, and literary-cultural traditions that constitute it.

James Gronniosaw and the Trope of the Talking Book

Henry Louis Gates, Jr.

[A] disingenuous and unmanly *Position* had been formed; and privately (*and as it were in the dark*) handed to and again, which is this, that the *Negro's*, though in their Figure they carry some resemblances of Manhood, yet are indeed *no Men*.

The consideration of the shape and figure of our *Negro's* Bodies, their Limbs and Members; their Voice and Countenance, in all things according with other Mens; together with their *Risibility* and *Discourse* (Man's *peculiar* Faculties) should be sufficient Conviction. How should they otherwise be capable of Trades, and other no less Manly imployments; as also of *Reading and Writing*; . . . were they not truly Men?

—Morgan Godwin, 1680

Let us to the Press Devoted Be,
Its *Light* will *Shine* and *Speak Us Free.*
—David Ruggles, 1835

Language, for the individual consciousness, is on the borderline between oneself and the other. The word in language is someone else's.

—Mikhail Bakhtin

I

The literature of the slave, published in English between 1760 and 1865, is the most obvious site to explore to determine the usage of tropes of race in Anglo-African texts as an ultimate sign of difference. Indeed, "race," writing, and difference comprised a nexus of issues that informed the shaping of all black texts published in this period. Between 1770 and 1815, black writers

From Henry Louis Gates, Jr., *Southern Review* 22 (April 1986), 252–72. Reprinted with permission of Henry Louis Gates, Jr.

figured "race," writing, and difference in the trope of the Talking Book.[1] After 1815, "freedom and literacy" became the trope that revises that of the text that speaks in the literature of the slave.

"The literature of the slave" is an ironic phrase, at the very least, and is an oxymoron at its most literal level of meaning. "Literature," as Samuel Johnson used the term, denoted an "acquaintance with 'letters' or books," according to *The Oxford English Dictionary.* It also connoted "polite or humane learning" and "literary culture." While it is self-evident that the ex-slave who managed, as Frederick Douglass put it, to "steal" some learning from his or her master and the master's texts, was bent upon demonstrating to a sceptical public an acquaintance with letters or books, we cannot honestly conclude that slave literature was meant to exemplify either polite or humane learning or the presence in the author of literary culture. Indeed, it is more accurate to argue that the literature of the slave consisted of texts that represent *impolite* learning and that these texts collectively railed against the arbitrary and *inhumane* learning which masters foisted upon the slave to reinforce a perverse fiction of the "natural" order of things. The "slave," by definition, possessed at most a liminal status within the human community.[2] To read and to write was to transgress this nebulous realm of liminality. The slave's texts, then, could not be taken as specimens of a black "literary culture." Rather, the texts of the slave could only be read as testimony of defilement: the slave's *representation* of the master's attempt to transform a human being into a commodity, and the slave's simultaneous verbal witness of the possession of a "humanity" shared in common with Europeans. The slave wrote not primarily to demonstrate humane letters, but to demonstrate her or his own membership in the human community.

This intention cannot be disregarded as a force extraneous to the production of a text, a common text that I like to think of as the "text of blackness." If we recall Ralph Ellison's apt phrase by which he defines what I am calling "tradition," "a sharing of that 'concord of sensibilities' which the group *expresses*," then what I wish to suggest by the "text of blackness" perhaps is clearer. Black writers to a remarkable extent have created texts that express the broad "concord of sensibilities" shared by persons of African descent in the Western hemisphere. Texts written over two centuries ago address what we might think of as common "subjects of condition" that continue to be strangely resonant, and "relevant," as we approach the twenty-first century.

---

[1]The trope appeared in Garcilasso de la Vega's 1617 edition of *Historia General del Peru*, in an account of the confrontation between Pizzaro and the great Inca king, Atuahualpa. This is probably the black tradition's source of the figure. See Garcilasso de la Vega, *The Royal Commentaries of Peru*, Part II: *General History of Peru*, trans. Sir Paul Rycaut (London: Miles Flesler, for Samuel Hendrick, 1688), pp. 456–57. Jose Piedra located this reference for me.

[2]My understanding of "liminality" arises from Robert Pelton's usages in *The Trickster in West Africa.* Houston A. Baker's usage is also relevant here, as taken from Victor Turner's work. See Houston Baker's *Blues, Ideology, and Afro-American Literature: A Vernacular Theory* (Univ. of Chicago Press, 1984).

Just as there are remarkably few literary traditions whose first century's existence is determined by texts created by *slaves,* so too are there few traditions that claim such an apparent unity from a fundamental political *condition* represented for over two hundred years in such strikingly similar patterns and details.

Has a common experience, or more accurately, the shared *sense* of a common experience, been largely responsible for the sharing of this text of blackness? It would be foolish to argue against an affirmative response to this rhetorical question. Nevertheless, shared experience of black people vis-à-vis white racism is not sufficient "evidence" upon which to argue that black writers have shared patterns of *representation* of their common subject for two centuries—unless one wishes to argue for a "genetic" theory of literature, which the biological sciences do not support. Rather, shared modes of figuration result only when writers *read* each other's texts and seize upon topoi and tropes to revise in their own texts. This form of revision is a process of *grounding* and has served to create curious formal lines of continuity between the texts that, together, comprise the shared text of blackness, the discrete "chapters" of which scholars are still establishing.

What seems clear upon reading eighteenth-century texts created by black writers in English or the critical texts that responded to these black writings is that the production of "literature" was taken to be the central arena in which persons of African descent could, or could not, establish and redefine their status within the human community. Black people, the evidence suggests, had to represent themselves as "speaking subjects" before they could even begin to destroy their status as "objects," as commodities, within Western culture. In addition to all of the myriad reasons for which human beings write books, this particular reason seems to have been paramount for the black slave. At least since 1600, Europeans had wondered aloud whether or not the African "species of men," as they most commonly put it, *could* ever create formal literature, could ever master "the arts and sciences." If they could, then, the argument ran, the African variety of humanity and the European variety were fundamentally related. If not, then it seemed clear that the African was destined by nature to be a slave.

Why was the *creative writing* of the African of such importance to the eighteenth-century's debate over slavery? I can briefly outline one thesis: after Descartes, *reason* was privileged, or valorized, among all other human characteristics. *Writing,* especially after the printing press became so widespread, was taken to be the *visible* sign of reason. Blacks were "reasonable," and hence "men," if—and only if—they demonstrated mastery of "the arts and sciences," the eighteenth-century's formula for writing. So, while the Enlightenment is famous for establishing its existence upon man's ability to reason, it simultaneously used the absence and presence of "reason" to delimit and circumscribe the very humanity of the cultures and people of color which Europeans had been discovering since the Renaissance. The urge towards the systematization of all human knowledge, by which we characterize the Enlightenment, in other words led directly to the relegation of black people to a lower rung on the Great Chain of Being, an eighteenth-century metaphor that arranged all of creation on a vertical scale from animals and plants and insects through man to the angels and God himself. By 1750, the Chain had become individualized; the human scale slid from "the lowliest Hottentot" (black South Africans) to "glorious Milton and Newton." If blacks could write and publish imaginative literature, then they could, in effect, take a few Giant Steps up the Chain of Being, in a pernicious game of "Mother, May I?" As the Rev. James W. C. Pennington, an ex-slave who wrote a slave narrative and who was a prominent black abolitionist, summarized this curious idea in his prefatory note "To the Reader" that authorizes Ann Plato's 1841 book of essays, biographies, and poems: "The history of the arts and sciences is the history of individuals, of individual nations." Only by publishing books such as Plato's, he argues, can blacks demonstrate "the fallacy of that stupid theory, *that nature has done nothing but fit us for slaves, and that art cannot unfit us for slavery!*"

Not a lot changed, then, between Phillis Wheatley's 1773 publication date of her *Poems* (complete with a prefatory letter of authenticity signed by eighteen of "the most respectable characters in Boston") and Ann Plato's, except that by 1841 Plato's attestation was supplied by a black person. What we might think of as the black text's mode of being, however, remained pretty much the same during these sixty-eight years. What remained consistent was that black people could become "speaking" subjects only by inscribing their "voices" in the written word. If this matter of recording an authentic "black" voice in the text of Western letters was a matter of widespread concern in the eighteenth century, then how did it affect the production of black texts, if indeed it affected them at all? It is not enough simply to trace a line of shared argument as "context" to show that blacks regarded this matter as crucial to their texts; rather, evidence for such a direct relationship of text to context must be found in the black texts themselves.

The most salient indication that this idea informed the writing of black texts is found in a topos that appears in five black texts published in English by 1815. This topos assumed such a central place in the black use of figurative language that we can call it a trope. This trope is the trope of the Talking Book, which first occurs in James Gronniosaw's 1770 slave narrative and was then revised in other narratives published by John Marrant in 1785, Cugoano in 1787, Equiano in 1789, and John Jea in 1815. Not only does this shared but revised trope argue forcefully that blacks were intent upon placing their individual and collective "voices," as it were, in the text of Western letters, but also that even the earliest writers of the Anglo-African tradition *read* each other's texts and "grounded" these texts in what soon became a "tradition."

The trope of the Talking Book is the "ur-trope" of the Anglo-African tradition. Bakhtin's metaphor of "double-voiced" discourse, figured within the black tradition most literally in representational sculptures of *Esu-Elegbara's* twin mouths and implied in the Signifying Monkey's function as the *rhetoric* of a vernacular literature, comes to bear in black texts through the trope of the Talking Book. In the slave narrative that I shall explicate in this essay, making the (white) written text "speak" with a (black) voice is the initial mode of inscription of the metaphor of the double-voiced. This metaphor has proven to be of such fundamental import to the Afro-American literary tradition that it can usefully be thought of as the central informing metaphor of that tradition, its hidden "figure in the carpet," its speaking voice from within the woodpile. In Zora Neale Hurston, the concept of a doubled voice is complex, oscillating as representation among direct discourse, indirect discourse, and a unique form of free indirect discourse that serves to privilege the speaking voice. In Ishmael Reed's novel, *Mumbo Jumbo,* the double-voiced text emerges as the text of ultimate critique and revision of the rhetorical strategies at work in the canonical texts of the tradition. Finally, in Alice Walker's *The Color Purple,* the double-voiced text assumes the form of the epistolary novel in which revision manifests itself as a literal representation of a protagonist creating herself by finding her voice, but finding this voice in the act of *writing.* The written representation of this "voice" is a rewriting of the speaking voice that Hurston created for her protagonist of *Their Eyes Were Watching God.* Walker, in this brilliant act of "grounding" herself in the tradition by *Signifyin(g) upon* Hurston's rhetorical strategy, "tropes" Hurston's trope by "capping" *(metalepsis)* and *inverts* Hurston's effect of creating an "invisible" writing that "speaks" by creating an "invisible" speaking voice that, as it were, can only *write!*

The explication of the trope of the Talking Book enables us to witness the extent of intertextuality and presupposition at work in the first discrete "period" in Afro-American literary history. But it also reveals, rather surprisingly, that the curious tension between the black vernacular and the literate "white" text, the spoken and the written word, between the oral and the printed forms of literary discourse, has been represented and thematized in black letters at least since slaves and ex-slaves met the challenge of the Enlightenment to their humanity by writing themselves, literally, into being through carefully crafted representations in language of "the black self." Literacy, the very literacy of the printed book, stood as the ultimate parameter by which to "measure" the "humanity" of authors struggling to define the African self in Western letters. It was to establish a collective black "voice," through the sublime example of an individual text, and thereby to register a black presence in letters that most clearly motivated black writers from the Augustan Age to the Harlem Renaissance. Voice and presence, silence and absence, then, have been the resonating terms of a four-part homology in our literary tradition for well over two hundred years.

The trope of the Talking Book became the first repeated and revised trope of the tradition, the first trope to be Signified upon. The paradox of representing, of "containing" somehow, the oral within the written, *precisely* when oral black culture was transforming itself into a *written* culture, proved to be of sufficient concern for five of the earliest black autobiographers to repeat the same figure of the Talking Book that fails to speak, appropriating the figure accordingly with embellished rhetorical differences. Whereas Gronniosaw, Marrant, and Jea employ the figure as an element of plot, Cugoano and Equiano, with an impressive sense of their own relation to these earlier texts, bracket the tale in ways that direct attention to its status as a figure. The tension between the spoken and written voice, for Cugoano and Equiano, is a matter they problematize as a rhetorical gesture, included in the text for its own sake, "voicing," as it were, for the black literary tradition a problematic of speaking and writing. John Jea's use of this curious figure has become decadent in the repetition, with the god in the machine here represented literally as the God who springs from the text to teach the illiterate slave to read in a primal, or supernatural, scene of instruction.

This general question of the voice in the text is compounded in any literature, such as the Afro-American literary tradition, in which the oral and written literary traditions comprise separate and distinct discursive universes, discursive universes that, on occasion, overlap, but often do not. Precisely because successive Western cultures have privileged written art over oral or musical forms, the writing of black people in Western languages has, at all points, remained "political," implicitly or explicitly, regardless of its intent or its subject. Then, too, since blacks began to publish books they have been engaged in one form of direct political dialogue or another, consistently to the present. The very proliferation of black written voices, and the concomitant political import of these, led fairly rapidly in our literary history both to demands for the coming of a "black Shakespeare or Dante," as one critic put it in 1925, and for an authentic black printed voice of deliverance, whose presence would, by definition, put an end to all claims of the black person's subhumanity. In the black tradition, writing became the visible sign, the commodity of exchange, the text and technology of Reason.

II

The first text in which the trope of the Talking Book appears is James Albert Ukawsaw Gronniosaw's first edition of *A Narrative of the Most Remarkable Particulars in the Life of James Albert Ukawsaw Gronniosaw, An African Prince, As Related By Himself*. Gronniosaw's narrative of enslavement and delivery had by 1811 been published in seven editions, including American editions in 1774 and 1810 and a Dublin edition in 1790. In 1840, another edition was published simultaneously in London, Manchester, and Glasgow. It is this edition to which I refer.

Reading and writing were of signal import to the shaping of James Gronniosaw's text, as presences and absences refigured throughout his twenty-four-page narrative. While the 1770 edition bears as its subtitle the fact that Gronniosaw "related" his tale "himself," the 1774 edition, "reprinted" at Newport, Rhode Island, claims that his narrative was "written by himself." When referred to in editions subsequent to 1840, "related" or "dictated" replace "written by himself." It is the narrator's concern with literacy that is of most interest to our argument here.

Gronniosaw's curious narrative has not enjoyed a wide reading among critics, or at least has not engendered many critical readings, unlike the works of his eighteenth-century colleagues, John Marrant and Olaudah Equiano. What we know of him stems only from his slave narrative, generally thought to be the second example of the genre, after the 1760 *Narrative of the Uncommon Sufferings and Surprizing Deliverance of Briton Hammon, A Negro Man, ...* While the two texts are narratives of bondage and "deliverance," and while they both use the figure of the "return to my Native Land," it is Gronniosaw's that most clearly inaugurates the genre of the slave narrative, from its "I was born" opening sentence to the use of literacy training as a repeated figure that functions to unify the structure of his tale.

Who does Gronniosaw claim to be? Gronniosaw states that he was born "in the city of Bournou," which is the "chief city" of the Kingdom of Zaara. Gronniosaw's mother was the oldest daughter of the "reigning King of Zaara," and he was the youngest of six children. Gronniosaw stresses his intimate relationship with his mother, and to a lesser extent with his maternal grandfather, but rarely mentions his father, who we presume was not born to royalty but wed royalty. Gronniosaw's identification of himself in his narrative's title as "An African Prince" helps to explain the significance of this rhetorical gesture. Gronniosaw, by representing himself as a "Prince," implicitly tied his narrative to the literary tradition of the Noble Savage, and to its subgenre, the Noble Negro.

Gronniosaw, in other words, represents himself as no mere common Negro slave, but as one nurtured, indulged, and trained in the manner of royalty everywhere. Faced with what must have seemed a deafening silence in black literary antecedents, Gronniosaw turned to the fictions of the Noble Savage to ground his text within a tradition. He also turned to the tradition of the Christian confession, referring to the import of works of Bunyan and Baxter upon his quest to learn the identity of "some great Man of Power," as he proudly tells us. James Albert Ukawsaw Gronniosaw, in other words, represents himself as an ebony admixture of Oroonoko and the Lord's questing Pilgrim.

One of the ironies of representation of the Noble African Savage is that he or she is rendered noble through a series of contrasts with his or her black countrymen. Oroonoko, we recall, bears aquiline features, has managed through some miraculous process to straighten his kinky hair, and speaks French fluently, among other languages. Oroonoko, in other words, looks like a European, speaks like a European, and thinks and acts like a European—or, more properly, like a European king. Unlike the conventions of representing most other Noble Savage protagonists, then, Oroonoko and his fellow black princes-in-bondage are made "noble" by a *dissimilarity* with their native countrymen. He is *the* exception, and not in any way the rule. Several Africans gained notoriety in eighteenth-century England and France by claiming royal lineage and even attending performances of *Oroonoko* on stage, weeping loudly as they were carried from the theatre.

Gronniosaw seized upon this convention of Noble Savage literature, but with a critical difference. To ground himself in the tradition of Bunyan, Gronniosaw figures his sense of difference as the only person in his grandfather's kingdom who understood, "from my infancy," that "some great Man of Power, . . . resided above the sun, moon, and stars, the objects of our [African] worship." Gronniosaw's salient sign of difference is his inherent knowledge that there existed one God, rather than the many worshipped by all and sundry in the Kingdom of Zaara.

The youngest prince's noble beliefs led, as we might suspect, to an estrangement from his brothers and sisters and even, eventually, from his father, his grandfather, and his devoted mother. Gronniosaw represents his discourse with his mother thusly:

> My dear mother, said I, pray tell me who is the great Man of Power that makes the thunder. She said that there was no power but the sun, moon, and stars; that they made all our country. I then inquired how all our people came. She answered me, from one another; and so carried me to many generations back. Then, says I, who made the *first man,* and who made the first cow, and the first lion, and where does the fly come from, as no one can make him? My mother seemed in great trouble; for she was apprehensive that my senses were impaired, or that I was foolish. My father came in, and seeing her in grief, asked the cause; but when she related our conversation to him, he was exceedingly angry with me, and told me that he would punish me severely if ever I was so troublesome again; so that I resolved never to say anything more to her. But I grew unhappy in myself.

Gronniosaw tells us that "these wonderful impressions" were unique in all of the Kingdom of Zaara, a situation "which affords me matter of admiration and thankfulness." But his alienation increased to such an uncomfortable extent that when "a merchant from the Gold Coast" offered to take young James to a land where he "should see houses with wings to them walk upon the water" and "see the white folks," he beseeched of his parents the freedom to leave. The only family tie that he regretted severing was that with his sister, Logwy, who was "quite white and fair, with fine light hair, though my father and mother were black."

Gronniosaw's affection for his "white" sister is one of three curious figures that he uses to represent his inherent difference from other black people. On one occasion, he describes "the devil" as "a black man" who "lives in hell," while he by contrast seeks to be washed clean of the blackness of sin. Moreover, the woman ordained by God for him to marry turns out to be white, echoing his bond with his "white" sister. Gronniosaw's color symbolism privileges whiteness, as we shall see, at the expense of his blackness.

The young prince, of course, is traded into slavery, and sails to "Barbadoes" where he is purchased by a Mr. Vanhorn of New York. His subsequent adventures, motivated by a desire to live among the "holy" inhabitants of England ("because the authors of the books that had been given me were Englishmen"), take him to "St. Domingo," "Martinco," "Havannah," and then to London and to Holland, only to return to marry and raise a family in England. The remainder of his *Narrative* depicts the economic hardships he suffers from racism and from evil people generally, and his fervent devotion to the principles of Christian dogma.

What is of concern to us about James Gronniosaw's *Narrative* are his repeated references to reading and writing. His second master in New York, a Mr. Freelandhouse, and his wife "put me to school," he writes, where he "learnt to read pretty well." His master and mistress, wishing to help him to overcome his spiritual dilemma about the nature of this One God ("the Author of all my comforts") whom he discovered at New York, gave him copies of "John Bunyan on the Holy War" and "Baxter's 'Call to the Unconverted.'" As an example of the "much persecution" that he received from "the sailors," Gronniosaw writes that "I cannot help mentioning one circumstance that hurt me more than all the rest." Even this scene of cruelty turns upon the deprivation of a book:

> I was reading a book that I was very fond of, and which I frequently amused myself with, when this person snatched it out of my hand, and threw it into the sea. But, which was very remarkable, he was the first that was killed in our engagement. I do not pretend to say that this happened because he was not my friend; but I thought it was a very awful providence, to see how the enemies of the Lord were cut off.

It is his ability to read and write and speak the Word of the Lord which motivates Gronniosaw's pilgrimage to England, as it did Phillis Wheatley's, to "find out Mr. [George] Whitefield." Since Gronniosaw informs his readers late in his text that "I could not read English," and since he describes his eloquent discourse on religion with "thirty-eight ministers, every Tuesday, for seven weeks together" in Holland, and since his two masters at New York bore Dutch names, it is probable that he was literate in Dutch. By the age of "sixty," which W. Shirley in his "Preface" estimates to be his age at the time of publication, he spoke fluent English, in which, like Caliban, he learned first "to curse and swear surprisingly."

If Gronniosaw, like Caliban, first learned the master's tongue to curse and swear, he quickly mended his ways. Indeed, almost from the beginning of his capture, Gronniosaw seems to have been determined to allow nothing to come between his desire to know the name of the Christian God and its fulfillment. Gronniosaw represents this desire within an extended passage in which he uses the trope of the Talking Book. He first describes his pleasure at disregarding the principle *material* sign of his African heritage, an extensive gold chain which must have been remarkably valuable, judging by its description:

> When I left my dear mother, I had a large quantity of gold about me, as is the custom of our country. It was made into rings, and they were linked one into another, and formed into a *kind of chain,* and so put round my neck, and arms, and legs, and a large piece hanging at one ear, almost in the shape of a pear. I found all this troublesome, and was glad when my new master [a Dutch captain of a ship] took it from me. I was now washed, and clothed in the Dutch or English manner. [emphasis mine]

Gronniosaw admits to being "glad" when his royal chain, a chain of gold that signified his cultural heritage, was removed from him, to be replaced, after a proverbial if secular "baptism" by water, with the "Dutch or English" clothing of a ship's crew. That which signified his African past, a veritable signifying chain, Gronniosaw eagerly abandons, just as he longs to abandon his other signifying chain, the language that his European captors "did not understand."

Gronniosaw's signifying gold chain is an ironic prefigurement of Brother Tarp's link to *his* cultural heritage, a prison gang, in Ralph Ellison's *Invisible Man.* When Tarp tells Ellison's narrator that his chain "had a whole lot of signifying wrapped up in it," and that "it might help you remember what we're really fighting against," we not only recall Gronniosaw's willingness to relinquish his signifying chain, but we also begin to understand why. James Albert Ukawsaw Gronniosaw has absolutely no desire "to remember what we're really fighting against." As Tarp continues, such a signifying chain "signifies a heap more" than the opposition between "*yes* and *no*" that it connotes, on a first level of meaning, for the escaped prisoner. It is these significations that Gronniosaw seeks to forget.

If Gronniosaw willingly abandons his signifying chain of gold, then he also is willing to discard that chain of signifiers that comprise whatever African discourse in which he greets his Dutch enslavers. This desire he represents in the black tradition's first use of the trope of the Talking Book, which follows the unchaining ceremony in the same paragraph:

> [My master] used to read prayers in public to the ship's crew every Sabbath day; and when I first saw him read, I was never so surprised in my life, as when I saw the book talk to my master, for I thought it did, as I observed him to look upon it, and move his lips. I wished it would do so with me. As soon as my master had done reading, I followed him to the place where he put the book, being mightily delighted with it, and when nobody saw me, I opened it, and put my ear down close upon it, in great hopes that it would say something to me; but I was very

sorry, and greatly disappointed, when I found that it would not speak. This thought
immediately presented itself to me, that every body and every thing despised me
because I was black.

What can we say of this compelling anecdote? The book has no voice for
Gronniosaw; the book—or, perhaps I should say the very concept of "book"—
constitutes a silent *primary* text, a text, however, in which the black man
finds no echo of his own voice. The silent book does not reflect or acknowledge the black presence before it. The book's rather deafening silence
renames the received tradition in European letters that the mask of blackness
worn by James Albert Ukawsaw Gronniosaw and his countrymen was a trope
of *absence.*

Gronniosaw can speak to the text only if the text first speaks to him. The
text does not, not even in the faintest whisper, a decibel level accounted for
by the black man's charming gesture of placing his "ear down close upon it."
Gronniosaw cannot address the text because the text *will* not address Gronniosaw. The text does not "recognize" his presence and so refuses to share its
secrets or decipher its coded message. Gronniosaw *and* the text are silent; the
"dialogue" that he records that he had observed between book and master
eludes him. To explain the *difference* between his master's relations to this
text, and the slave's relation to the same text, Gronniosaw seizes upon one
explanation and only one: the salient difference was his blackness, the very
blackness of silence.

Gronniosaw explains the text's silence by resorting to an oxymoronic figure,
a figure in which voice and presence, (black) face and absence are conflated.
Perhaps a more accurate description of the figure is that Gronniosaw conflates
an oral figure ("voice") with a visual figure (his black face). In other words,
Gronniosaw's explanation of the silence of the text allows for no other
possibility but one; and it, he tells us, suggested itself on the spot: "This
thought immediately presented itself to me, that every body and every thing
despised me because I was black."

Gronniosaw's conflation of the senses, of the oral and the visual—the book
refused to speak to me because my face was black—was a curiously arbitrary
choice for figural substitution. After all, a more "natural" explanation might
have been that the book refused to speak to him because he could not speak
Dutch, especially if we remember that this scene occurs on the ship that
transports the newly captured slave from the Gold Coast to Barbados, the
ship's destination. This more logical or natural explanation, however, did not
apparently occur to the African. Rather, the curse of silence that the text
yielded could only be accounted for by the curse of blackness that God had
ostensibly visited upon the dusky sons of Ham. The text's *voice,* for Gronniosaw, presupposed a *face,* and a black face, in turn, presupposed the text's
silence since blackness was a sign of absence, the remarkably ultimate absence
of face *and* voice. Gronniosaw could achieve no recognition from this canonical text of Western letters—either the Bible, or else a prayer book—because

the text could not *see* him or hear him. Texts can only address those whom they can see. *Cognition,* or the act of "knowing" as awareness and judgment, presupposes the most fundamental form of *(re)cognition* in Gronniosaw's text. It was his black face that interrupted this most basic, if apparently essential, mode of recognition, thereby precluding communication.

This desire for recognition of his "self" in the text of Western letters motivates Gronniosaw's creation of a text, in both a most literal and a most figurative manner. Literally, this trope of the (non)Talking Book becomes the central scene of instruction against which this black African's entire autobiography must be read. The text refuses to speak to Gronniosaw, so some forty-five years later, Gronniosaw "writes" a text that "speaks" his face into existence among the authors and texts of the Western tradition. As I have shown above, no less than five subsequent scenes of instruction (in a twenty-four-page text) are represented in the *Narrative* through tropes of reading and writing, including the curious scene in which Gronniosaw (with admirable control, if obvious pleasure) explains to us that the white man who "snatched" his favorite book from his hands and "threw it into the sea" proved to be "the first that was killed in our [first military] engagement." Gronniosaw represents a sixty-year life in a brief text that depends for the shape of its rhetorical strategy upon six tropes of reading and writing. Gronniosaw narrates a text, the rhetorical patterning of his autobiography forces us to conclude, to satisfy the desire created when his first master's seminal text, the prayer book, refuses to address him. Gronniosaw, in other words, narrates a text that simultaneously *voices, contains,* and *reflects* the peculiar contours of his (black) face. Given the fact that by 1770, only four black people are thought to have published "books" in Western languages (Juan Latino, Jacobus Capitein, Wilhelm Amo, and Briton Hammon), Gronniosaw's gesture was a major one, if its motivation as inscribed in his central trope is ironic.

But is his a "black" face as voiced in his text? When I wrote above that the ship captain's text and its refusal to speak to the slave motivated the slave to seek recognition in other Western texts (as figured in his several scenes of literacy instruction), I argued that this motivation was both literal and metaphorical. By metaphorical, I mean that the "face" of the author at sixty is fundamentally altered from that (black) African face that the adolescent Gronniosaw first presented in his initial encounter with his first Western text. Gronniosaw is a careful narrator and is especially careful to state what he means. We recall that the trope of the Talking Book occurs in the same paragraph as does his description of his eager abandonment of the gold chain that signifies his African heritage. Indeed, he presents his face before the ship captain's speaking text only after he has been "washed, and clothed in the Dutch or English manner." The text represents this procedure as if it were a rite of baptism, but a secular or cultural cleansing or inundation that obliterates (or is *meant* to obliterate) the traces of an African past that Gronniosaw is eager to relinquish, as emblematized in his gold chain: "I found all this troublesome, and was glad when my new master took it from me."

In the sentence that follows immediately upon this one, Gronniosaw tells us, "My master grew fond of me, and I loved him exceedingly," unlike the mutual disdain and mistrust that he had obtained between him and his "first" master and his partner. We recall that it was the first master who, along with this partner, had persuaded the unhappy adolescent to leave the Kingdom of Bournou to seek the land of "the white folks," where "houses with wings to them walk upon the water." His second master "grew fond" of the "new" Gronniosaw, the Gronniosaw who had willingly submitted to being "washed, and clothed in the Dutch or English manner." His old master had related to an "old" Gronniosaw, an unregenerated (black) African Gronniosaw whose alienation from his traditional belief system and from most of the members of his family had, in retrospect, persuaded him to seek "the white folks" in the first place. Gronniosaw, in other words, was now capable of being regarded "fondly" by his second master because he was no longer the "pure" cultural African that he was when enticed to leave his village.

If he was, at this point in his *Narrative,* no longer the African that he once was, he was not yet the Anglo-African that he would become and that he so wished to be. "Clothes," and we might add, a good washing, "do not make the man," the ship captain's text in its silent eloquence informs the "new" Gronniosaw. He was merely an African, sans signifying chain, cloaked in European garb. His dress may have been appropriately European, but his face retained the blackness of his willingly abandoned African brothers. Gronniosaw, as he placed his ear close upon the text, was a *third-term,* neither fish nor fowl: no longer the unadulterated African, he was not yet the "European" that he would be. The text of Western letters could not accommodate his liminal status, and therefore refused to speak to him, because Gronniosaw was not yet *this,* while clearly he was no longer *that.* It was not enough, the text in its massive silence informs him, to abandon his signifying gold chain in order to be able to experience the sublime encounter with the European text's chain of signifiers. Much, much more "washing" and "re-clothing" would be demanded of him to make the text speak.

Forty-five years later, Gronniosaw registered his presence and figured the contours of his face in the text of his autobiography. At sixty, he was fluent in *two* European languages, Dutch and English, he was a freed man, he was sufficiently masterful of the "Calvinist" interpretation of Christianity to discourse "before thirty-eight [Dutch] ministers every Tuesday, for seven weeks together, and they were all very satisfied," and he was the husband of an English wife and the father of both her child (by an English first marriage) and their "mulatto" children. The Christian text that had once refused to acknowledge him, he had by sixty mastered sufficiently not only to "satisfy" and "persuade" others by his eloquence "that I was what I pretended to be," but also to interweave within the fabric of his autobiographical text the warp and the woof of Protestant Christianity and the strange passage from black man to white. The presence found in Gronniosaw's own text is generated by the voice, and face, of assimilation. What is absent, of course, is the African's black mask of humanity, a priceless heritage discarded as readily as was a priceless gold chain. Indeed, Gronniosaw's text is free of what soon became in the slave narratives the expected polemic against the ungodly enslavement of blacks. It is also free of descriptions of any other black characters, except for the "old black servant that lived in the [Vanhorn] family," Gronniosaw's first masters in New York, and except for his reference to "a black man called the devil." It was the "old black servant" who taught Gronniosaw about the devil's identity, and who, we presume (along with other servants), taught him to curse. No longer could Gronniosaw claim that "every body and every thing despised me because I was black."

Gronniosaw's important text in the history of black letters Signifies upon, in its trope of the Talking Book, two texts of the Western tradition. The first text is that of William Bosman, entitled *A New and Accurate Description of the Coast of Guinea.* Bosman's account of his travels in Africa was published in Dutch in 1704 and was published in English at London in 1705. By 1737, four Dutch editions had been published, as well as translations in French and German, as well as English. In 1752, an Italian translation appeared. At least two more English editions have been published in this century.

Bosman was the Dutch "Chief Factor" at the Fort of Elmira, on the coast of West Africa (popularly called "Guinea" at the time) in what is now Ghana. Bosman is thought to have been the "second most important Dutch official on the coast of Guinea from about 1688 to 1702." Bosman's tenth "Letter" is devoted to "the Religion of the *Negroes*" at "Guinea," another name for the "Gold Coast" that appears in James Albert Gronniosaw's *Narrative.* Indeed, it is probable that Gronniosaw's Dutch ship captain set sail from the Fort of Elmira. It is just as probable that Gronniosaw and Bosman were at Elmira within twenty-three years of each other, if W. Shirley's estimate of Gronniosaw's age in 1770 is correct. If he has *underestimated* Gronniosaw's age, then it is conceivable that the two men could have been at Elmira at the same time. What is more probable is that Gronniosaw knew Bosman's Dutch text, especially "Letter X."

Bosman's "Letter X," according to Robert D. Richardson, has had an extraordinary influence upon the development of the concept of "fetishism" in modern anthropology, by way of Pierre Bayle's *Historical and Critical Dictionary* (1697, 1734–1738) and Charles de Brosses' *Du culte des dieux fetiches* (1760), the latter of which asserted the theory that fetishism, as practiced by blacks in West Africa, was the most fundamental form of religious worship. Auguste Comte's declaration that a "primary, fetishistic, or theological stage" was central to the development of a society depended upon de Brosses' 1760 theory of fetishism. Bosman's observations, then, have proven to be central to the discourse on religion so fundamental to the development of anthropology in this century (M. T. Hodgen, *Early Anthropology in the Sixteenth and Seventeenth Centuries*).

Bosman's "Letter" begins with an assertion that "all the Coast *Negroes* believe in one true God, to whom they attribute the Creation of the World." This claim, of course, at first appears to be at odds with Gronniosaw's claim that he alone of all of the people in the Kingdom of Zaara held this belief. But Bosman quickly adds that for this belief in the *one* God the coastal blacks "are not obliged to themselves nor the Tradition of their Ancestors." Rather, the source of this notion is "their daily conversation with the *Europeans*, who from time to time have continually endeavoured to emplant this notion in them." The initial sense of *difference* that Gronniosaw strives so diligently to effect between himself and his African kinsman (his monotheism as opposed to their polytheism) is prefigured in Bosman's second paragraph.

What is even more relevant here is that Bosman's account of the Ashanti people's myth of creation *turns upon* an opposition between *gold*, on one hand, and "Reading and Writing," on the other. As Bosman recounts this fascinating myth:

> . . . a great part of the *Negroes* believe that man was made by *Anansie*, that is, a great Spider: the rest attribute the Creation of Man to God, which they assert to have happened in the following manner: They tell us, that in the beginning God created Black as well as White Men; thereby not only hinting but endeavouring to prove that their race was as soon in the World as ours; and to bestow a yet greater Honour on themselves, they tell us that God having created these two sorts of Men, offered two sorts of Gifts, *viz*, Gold, and the Knowledge of Arts of Reading and Writing, giving the Blacks, the first Election, who chose Gold, and left the Knowledge of Letters to the White. God granted their Request, but being incensed at their Avarice, resolved that the Whites should for ever be their Masters, and they obliged to wait on them as their Slaves.

Gold, spake God to the African, or the Arts of Western Letters: *choose!* The African, much to his regret, elected Gold and was doomed by his avarice to be a slave. As a footnote to Bosman's first edition tells us, the African's avarice was an eternal curse and his punishment was the doom of never mastering the Western arts and letters.

If the African at the Creation was foolish enough to select Gold over "Reading and Writing," James Albert Ukawsaw Gronniosaw, African man but European-in-the-making, would not repeat that primal mistake. Rather, Gronniosaw eschewed the temptation of his gold chain and all that it signified and sought a fluency in Western languages through which he could remake the features, and color, of his face.

If Gronniosaw echoes Bosman, probably self-consciously, then he also echoed Kant, probably not aware of Kant's 1764 German text. Writing in *Observations on the Feelings of the Beautiful and Sublime*, Kant prefigures Gronniosaw's equation of his black skin with the text's refusal to speak to him. Kant, drawing upon Hume's note on blacks in "Of National Characters," argues that "so fundamental is the difference between these two races of man, [that] it appears to be as great in regard to mental capacities as in color." Two pages later, responding to a black man's comment to Jean Baptiste Labat about male-female relations in Europe, Kant delivers this supposedly *natural* relation between blackness and intelligence: "And it might be that there was something in this which perhaps deserved to be considered; but in short, this fellow was quite black from head to foot, a clear proof that what he said was stupid." Gronniosaw, after Kant, presupposes a *natural* relation between blackness and being "despised" by "every body and every thing," including the Dutch ship captain's silent primary text. To undo this relation, Gronniosaw devoted his next forty-five years, until he was fully able to structure the events of his life into a pattern that "speaks" quite eloquently, if ironically, to readers today.

III

After 1815, the trope of the Talking Book disappeared from the black literary tradition.[3] John Jea's extended revision, *The Life, History, and Unparalleled Sufferings of John Jea, the African Preacher,* in which God answers the slave's desperate prayers by emerging from the Bible and teaching him to read, is the final usage of the trope. After Jea's revision, or "erasure" as I am thinking of it, the trope of the Talking Book disappears from the other slave narratives published in the nineteenth century. No longer is this sign of the *presence* of literacy, and all that this sign adumbrates in the life of the black slave, available for revision after Jea has "erased" its figurative properties by his turn to the supernatural. Rather, the trope of the Talking Book now must be displaced in a second-order revision in which the absence and presence of the *speaking* voice is refigured as the absence and presence of the *written* voice. Jea's scene of instruction, or midnight *dream* of instruction (did it *actually* happen, he wonders aloud as we his readers wonder, or was it "only a dream?" he asks), represents the "dream" of freedom as the "dream" of literacy, a dream realized as if by a *miracle* of literacy. Jea's "dream" is composed of elements common to the usages of his black antecedents, but the central content of the trope has been expanded *disproportionately* from its figurative associations to its most literal level, wherein an "angel" teaches the slave how to read and thus to escape the clutches of the "devil" that keeps the slave in chains. Equiano's "angel" was a young white boy; Frederick Douglass' "guardian angel" was the white woman married to his master. Many of the post-1830 slave narrator's "guardian angels" are also white women or children, related directly or indirectly by a marriage bond to the master.

[3]Rebecca Cox Jackson, in an autobiographical manuscript (1830–32) not published until 1981, revises John Jea's figure of the primal scene of literary instruction.

These representations of the mastery of letters (literally, the "A, B, C's") are clearly transferences and displacements of the "dream" of freedom figured for the tradition by Jea's text, again in the most literal way. Whereas Jea's Signifyin(g) relation to Gronniosaw, Marrant, Cugoano, and Equiano is defined by a disproportionate expansion and elaboration upon the contents of their tropes, to such an extent that we are led to conclude that these narrators could have saved themselves loads of trouble had they only prayed to God intensely for six weeks to make the text speak, Jea's revision "erased" the trope (or Signified upon it by reducing it to the absurd) for the slave narrators who follow him in the tradition. They no longer *can* revise the trope merely by displacing or condensing its contents. Rather, Jea's supernatural *naming* demands that a completely new trope be figured to represent that which Jea's revision has made "unrepresentable" without some sort of "censorship," *if* the narrator is to be "believed" and "believable" as one who is capable of, and entitled to, the enjoyment of the *secular* idea of liberty that obtains in a text of a life such as Frederick Douglass'. Because Douglass and his black contemporaries wish to "write" their way to a freedom epitomized by the abolition movement, they cannot afford Jea's luxury of appealing, in his representation of his signal scene of instruction, primarily to the Christian converted. Douglass and his associates long for a secular freedom *now.* They can ill afford to represent even their "previous" selves—the "earlier" self that is transformed, as we read their texts, into the speaking subjects who *obviously* warrant full equality with white people—as so naïve as to believe that books "speak" when their masters "speak" to them. Instead, the post-Jea narrators *refigure* the trope of the Talking Book by the secular equation of the mastery of slavery through the "simple" mastery of letters. Their "dream" of freedom, figured primarily in tropes of *writing* rather than *speaking,* constitutes a displacement of the eighteenth-century trope of the Talking Book, wherein the "presence" of the human voice "in" the text is only implied by its absence as we read these narratives and especially their tropes of writing "against" the trope that we have been examining here.

These narrators, linked by revision of a trope into the very first black chain of signifiers, implicitly Signify upon another "chain," the metaphorical Great Chain of Being. Blacks were most commonly represented on the Chain either as the "lowest" of the human races, or as first cousin to the ape. Since writing, according to Hume, was the ultimate sign of difference between animal and human, these writers implicitly were Signifyin(g) upon the figure of the Chain itself, simply by publishing autobiographies that were indictments of the received order of Western culture of which slavery, to them, by definition stood as the most salient sign. The writings of Gronniosaw, Marrant, Equiano, Cugoano, and Jea served as a critique of the sign of the Chain of Being and the black person's figurative "place" on the Chain. This chain of black signifiers, regardless of their intent or desire, made the first political gesture in the Anglo-African literary tradition "simply" by the act of writing, a collective act that gave birth to the black literary tradition and defined it as the "other's chain," the chain of black being as black people themselves would have it. Making the book speak, then, constituted a motivated, and political, engagement with and condemnation of Europe's fundamental figure of domination, the Great Chain of Being.

The trope of the Talking Book is not a trope of the presence of voice at all, but of its absence. To speak of a "silent voice" is to speak in an oxymoron. There is no such thing as a silent voice. Furthermore, as Juliet Mitchell has put the matter, there is something untenable about the attempt to represent what is not there, to represent that which is *missing* or absent. Given that this is what these five black authors sought to do, we are justified in wondering aloud if the sort of subjectivity that they seek can be realized through a process that is so very ironic from the outset. Indeed, how can the black subject posit a full and sufficient self in a language in which blackness is a sign of absence? Can writing, the very "difference" it makes and marks, mask the blackness of the black face that addresses the text of Western letters, in a voice that "speaks English" in an idiom that contains the irreducible element of cultural difference that shall always separate the white voice from the black? Black people, we know, have not been "liberated" from racism by their writings and have accepted a false premise by assuming that racism would be destroyed once white racists became convinced that they were human, too. Writing stood as a complex "certificate of humanity," as Paulin J. Hountondji, in *African Philosophy: Myth and Reality*, put it. Black writing, and especially the literature of the slave, served not to obliterate the difference of "race," as a would-be white man such as Gronniosaw so ardently desired; rather, the inscription of the black voice in Western literatures has preserved those very cultural differences to be preserved, imitated, and revised in a separate Western literary tradition, a tradition of black difference.

Narration, Authentication, and Authorial Control in Frederick Douglass' *Narrative* of 1845

Robert B. Stepto

The strident, moral voice of the former slave recounting, exposing, appealing, apostrophizing, and above all, *remembering* his ordeal in bondage is the single most impressive feature of a slave narrative. This voice is striking not only because of what it relates but because the slave's acquisition of that voice is quite possibly his only permanent achievement once he escapes and casts himself upon a new and larger landscape. In their most elementary form, slave narratives are, however, full of other voices that are frequently just as responsible for articulating a narrative's tale and strategy. These other voices may be those of various "characters" in the "story," but mainly they are those found in the appended documents written by slaveholders and abolitionists alike. These documents—and voices—may not always be smoothly integrated with the former slave's tale, but they are nevertheless parts of the narrative. Their primary function is, of course, to authenticate the former slave's account; in doing so, they are at least partially responsible for the narratives being accepted as historical evidence. However, in literary terms, the documents collectively create something close to a dialogue—of forms as well as of voices—which suggests that in its primal state or first phase the slave narrative is an eclectic narrative form.

When the various forms (letters, prefaces, guarantees, tales) and their accompanying voices become integrated in the slave narrative text, we are presented with another type of basic narrative which I call an integrated narrative. This type of narrative represents the second phase of narration in the slave narrative and usually yields a more sophisticated text, wherein most of the literary and rhetorical functions previously performed by several texts and voices (the appended prefaces, letters, and documents as well as the tale) are now rendered by a loosely unified single text and voice. In this second phase, the authenticating documents "come alive" in the former slave's tale as speech and even action; and the former slave—often while assuming a deferential posture toward his white friends, editors, and guarantors—carries

Reprinted by permission of the Modern Language Association of America from Dexter Fisher and Robert B. Stepto, eds. *Afro-American Literature: The Reconstruction of Instruction* (New York: MLA, 1979), 178–91.

much of the burden of introducing and authenticating his own tale. In short, a second-phase narrative is a more sophisticated narrative because the former slave's voice assumes many more responsibilities than that of recounting the tale.

Because an integrated or second-phase narrative is less a collection of texts and more a unified narrative, we may say that, in terms of narration, the integrated narrative is in the process of becoming—irrespective of authorial intent—a generic narrative, by which I mean a narrative of discernible genre such as history, fiction, essay, or autobiography. This process is no simple "gourd vine" activity: An integrated narrative does not become a generic narrative "overnight," and, indeed, there are no assurances that in becoming a new type of narrative it is transformed automatically into a distinctive generic text. What we discover, then, is a third phase to slave narrative narration wherein two developments may occur: The integrated narrative (Phase II) is dominated either by its tale or by its authenticating strategies. In the first instance, the narrative and moral energies of the former slave's voice and tale so resolutely dominate those of the narrative's authenticating machinery (voices, documents, rhetorical strategies) that the narrative becomes in thrust and purpose far more metaphorical than rhetorical. When the integrated narrative becomes in this way a figurative account of action, landscape, and heroic self-transformation, it is so close generically to history, fiction, and autobiography that I term it a generic narrative.

In the second instance, the authenticating machinery either remains as important as the tale or actually becomes, usually for some purpose residing outside the text, the dominant and motivating feature of the narrative. Since this is also a sophisticated narrative phase, figurative presentations of action, landscape, and self may also occur, but such developments are rare and always ancillary to the central thrust of the text. When the authenticating machinery is dominant in this fashion, the integrated narrative becomes an authenticating narrative.

As these remarks suggest, one reason for investigating the phases of slave narrative narration is to gain a clearer view of how some slave narrative types become generic narratives and how, in turn, generic narratives—once formed, shaped, and set in motion by certain distinctly Afro-American cultural imperatives—have roots in the slave narratives. This bears as well on our ability to distinguish between narrative modes and forms and to describe what we see. When, for example, a historian or literary critic calls a slave narrative an autobiography, what he *sees* is, most likely, a narrative told in the first person that possesses literary features distinguishing it from the ordinary documents providing historical and sociological data. But a slave narrative is not necessarily an autobiography. We need to know the finer shades between the more easily discernible categories of narration, and we must discover whether these stops arrange themselves in progressive, contrapuntal, or dialectic fashion—or whether they possess any arrangement at all. As the scheme described above and diagrammed below suggests, I believe there are

at least four identifiable modes of narration within the slave narrative, all of
which have a direct bearing on the development of subsequent Afro-American
narrative forms.

Phase I: basic narrative (a): "eclectic narrative"—authenticating documents
and strategies (sometimes including one by the author of the tale)
appended to the tale

Phase II: basic narrative (b): "integrated narrative"—authenticating documents and strategies integrated into the tale and formally becoming voices and/or characters in the tale

Phase III:

(a) "generic narrative"—authenticating documents and strategies
are totally subsumed by the tale;
the slave narrative becomes an
identifiable generic text, e.g., autobiography, etc.

(b) "authenticating narrative"—the
tale is subsumed by the authenticating strategy; the slave narrative
becomes an authenticating document for other, usually generic,
texts, e.g., novel, history

II

What we observe in the first two phases of slave narrative narration is the
former slave's ultimate lack of control over his own narrative occasioned
primarily by the demands of audience and authentication. This dilemma is not
unique to the authors of these narratives; indeed, many modern black writers
still do not control their personal history once it assumes literary form. For
this reason, Frederick Douglass' *Narrative of the Life of Frederick Douglass
an American Slave Written by Himself* (1845) seems all the more a remarkable
literary achievement. Because it contains several segregated narrative texts—
a preface, a prefatory letter, the tale, an appendix—it appears to be, in terms
of the narrative phases, a rather primitive slave narrative. But each of the
ancillary texts seems to be drawn to the tale by some sort of extraordinary
gravitational pull or magnetic attraction. There is, in short, a dynamic energy
between the tale and each supporting text; the Douglass narrative is an
integrated narrative of a very special order. While the integrating process
does, in a small way, pursue the conventional path of creating characters out

of authenticating texts (Wm. Lloyd Garrison silently enters Douglass' tale at the very end), its new and major thrust is the creation of that aforementioned energy that binds the supporting texts to the tale while at the same time removing them from participation in the narrative's rhetorical and authenticating strategies. In short, Douglass' tale dominates the narrative and does so because it alone authenticates the narrative.

The introductory texts to the tale are two in number: a Preface by Wm. Lloyd Garrison, the famous abolitionist and editor of *The Liberator;* and a "Letter from Wendell Phillips, Esq.," who was equally renowned as an abolitionist, a crusading lawyer, and a judge. In theory, each of these introductory documents should be a classic guarantee written almost exclusively to a white reading public, concerned primarily and ritualistically with the white validation of a new-found black voice, and removed from the tale in such ways that the guarantee and tale vie silently and surreptitiously for control of the narrative as a whole. But these entries simply are not fashioned that way. To be sure, Garrison offers a conventional guarantee when he writes:

> Mr. DOUGLASS has very properly chosen to write his own Narrative, in his own style, and according to the best of his ability, rather than to employ some one else. It is, therefore, entirely his own production; and . . . it is, in my judgment, highly creditable to his head and heart.

And Phillips, while addressing Douglass, most certainly offers a guarantee to "another" audience as well:

> Every one who has heard you speak has felt, and, I am confident, every one who reads your book will feel, persuaded that you give them a fair specimen of the whole truth. No one-sided portrait,—no wholesale complaints,—but strict justice done, whenever individual kindliness has neutralized, for a moment, the deadly system with which it was strangely allied.

But these passages dominate neither the tone nor the substance of their respective texts.

Garrison is far more interested in writing history (specifically that of the 1841 Nantucket Anti-Slavery Convention and the launching of Douglass' career as a lecture agent for various antislavery societies) and recording his own place in it. His declaration, "I shall never forget his [Douglass'] first speech at the convention," is followed shortly thereafter by "*I rose,* and declared that Patrick Henry of revolutionary fame, never made a speech more eloquent in the cause of liberty. . . . *I reminded* the audience of the peril which surrounded this self-emancipated young man. . . . *I appealed* to them, whether they would ever allow him to be carried back into slavery,—law or no law, constitution or no constitution" [italics added]. His Preface ends, not with a reference to Douglass or to his tale, but with an apostrophe very much like one he would use to exhort and arouse an antislavery assembly. In short, with the following cry, Garrison hardly guarantees Douglass' tale but reenacts his own abolitionist career instead:

Reader! are you with the man-stealers in sympathy and purpose, or on the side of their down-trodden victims? If with the former, then are you the foe of God and man. If with the latter, what are you prepared to do and dare in their behalf? Be faithful, be vigilant, be untiring in your efforts to break every yoke, and let the oppressed go free. Come what may—cost what may—inscribe on the banner which you unfurl to the breeze, as your religious and political motto—NO COMPRO-MISE WITH SLAVERY! NO UNION WITH SLAVEHOLDERS!"

In the light of this closure and (no matter how hard we try to ignore it) the friction that developed between Garrison and Douglass in later years, we might be tempted to see Garrison's Preface at war with Douglass' tale for authorial control of the narrative as a whole. Certainly, there is a tension, but that tension is stunted by Garrison's enthusiasm for Douglass' tale:

> This *Narrative* contains many affecting incidents, many *passages* of great eloquence and power; but I think the most thrilling one of them all is the *description* DOUGLASS gives of his feelings, as he stood soliloquizing respecting his fate, and the chances of his one day being a free man. . . . Who can read that passage, and be insensible to its pathos and sublimity? [italics added]

What Garrison does, probably subconsciously, is an unusual and extraordinary thing—he becomes the first guarantor we have seen who not only directs the reader to the tale but also acknowledges the tale's singular rhetorical power. Thus, Garrison enters the tale by being at the Nantucket Convention with Douglass in 1841 and by authenticating the impact of the tale, not its facts. He fashions his own apostrophe, but finally he remains a member of Douglass' audience far more than he assumes the posture of a competing or superior voice. In this way, Garrison's Preface stands outside Douglass' tale but is steadfastly bound to it.

This is even more so the case for Wendell Phillips' "Letter." It contains passages that seem to be addressed to credulous readers in need of a "visible" authority's guarantee, but by and large the "Letter" is directed to Frederick Douglass alone. It opens with "My Dear Friend," and there are many extraliterary reasons for wondering initially if the friend is actually Frederick. Shortly thereafter, however, Phillips declares, "I am glad the time has come when the 'lions write history,'" and it becomes clear that he not only addresses Douglass but also writes in response to the tale. These features, plus Phillips' specific references to how Douglass acquired his "ABC" and learned of "where the 'white sails' of the Chesapeake were bound," serve to integrate Phillips' "Letter" into Douglass' tale. Above all, we must see in what terms the "Letter" is a cultural and linguistic event: Like the Garrison document, it presents its author as a member of Douglass' audience, but the act of letterwriting, of correspondence, implies a moral and linguistic parity between a white guarantor and black author that we have not seen before and that we do not always see in American literary history *after* 1845. In short, the tone and posture initiated in Garrison's Preface are completed and confirmed in Phillips' "Letter," and while these documents are integrated into Douglass' tale, they remain segregated outside the tale in the all-important sense that they yield Douglass sufficient narrative and rhetorical space in which to render personal history in—and as—a literary form.

What marks Douglass' narration and control of his tale is his extraordinary ability to pursue several types of writing with ease and with a degree of simultaneity. The principal types of writing we discover in the tale are syncretic phrasing, introspective analysis, internalized documentation, and participant-observation. Of course, each of these types has its accompanying authorial posture, the result being that even the telling of the tale (as distinct from the content of the tale) yields a portrait of a complex individual marvelously facile in the tones, shapes, and dimensions of his voice.

Douglass' syncretic phrasing is often discussed, and the passage most widely quoted is probably "My feet have been so cracked with the frost, that the pen with which I am writing might be laid in the gashes." The remarkable clarity of this language needs no commentary, but what one admires as well is Douglass' ability to startlingly conjoin past and present and to do so with images that not only stand for different periods in his personal history but also, in their fusion, speak of his evolution from slavery to freedom. The pen, symbolizing the quest for literacy fulfilled, actually takes measure of the wounds of the past, and this measuring process becomes a metaphor in and of itself for the artful composition of travail transcended. While I admire this passage, the syncretic phrases I find even more intriguing are those that pursue a kind of acrid punning upon the names of Douglass' oppressors. A minor example appears early in the tale, when Douglass deftly sums up an overseer's character by writing, "Mr. Severe was rightly named: he was a cruel man." Here, Douglass is content with "glossing" the name; but late in the tale, just before attempting to escape in 1835, Douglass takes another oppressor's name and does not so much gloss it or play with it as *work upon* it to such an extent that, riddled with irony, it is devoid of its original meaning:

> At the close of the year 1834, Mr. Freeland again hired me of my master, for the year 1835. But by this time, I began to want to live *upon free land* as well as *with Freeland*; and I was no longer content, therefore, to live with him or any other slaveholder.

Of course, this is effective writing—far more effective than what is found in the average slave narrative—but the point I wish to make is that Douglass seems to fashion these passages for both his readership and himself. Each example of his wit and increasing facility with language charts his evershortening path to literacy; thus, in their way, Douglass' syncretic phrases reveal his emerging comprehension of freedom and literacy and are another introspective tool by which he may benchmark his personal history.

But the celebrated passages of introspective analysis are even more pithy and direct. In these, Douglass fashions language as finely honed and balanced as an aphorism or Popean couplet, and thereby orders his personal history with neat, distinct, and credible moments of transition. When Mr. Auld forbids Mrs. Auld to instruct Douglass in the ABC, for example, Douglass relates:

> From that moment, I understood the pathway from slavery to freedom. . . . Whilst I was saddened by the thought of losing the aid of my kind mistress, I was gladdened by the invaluable instruction which, by the merest accident, I gained from my master.

The clarity of Douglass' revelation is as unmistakable as it is remarkable. As rhetoric, the passage is successful because its nearly extravagant beginning is finally rendered quite acceptable by the masterly balance and internal rhyming of "saddened" and "gladdened," which is persuasive because it is pleasant and because it offers the illusion of a reasoned conclusion.

Balance is an important feature of two other equally celebrated passages that quite significantly open and close Douglass' telling of his relations with Mr. Covey, an odd (because he worked in the fields alongside the slaves) but vicious overseer. At the beginning of the episode, in which Douglass finally fights back and draws Covey's blood, he writes:

> You have seen how a man was made a slave; you shall see how a slave was made a man.

And at the end of the episode, to bring matters linguistically and narratively full circle, Douglass declares:

> I now resolved that, however long I might remain a slave in form, the day had passed forever when I could be a slave in fact. I did not hesitate to let it be known of me, that the white man who expected to succeed in whipping, must also succeed in killing me.

The sheer poetry of these statements is not lost on us, nor is the fact of why the poetry was created in the first place. One might suppose that in another age Douglass' determination and rage might take a more effusive expression, but I cannot imagine that to be the case. In the first place, his linguistic model is obviously scriptural; and in the second, his goal is the presentation of a historical self, not the record of temporary hysteria. This latter point persuades me that Douglas is about the business of discovering how personal history may be transformed into autobiography. Douglass' passages of introspective analysis almost single-handedly create fresh space for themselves in the American literary canon.

Instead of reproducing letters and other documents written by white guarantors within the tale or transforming guarantors into characters, Douglass internalizes documents that, like the syncretic and introspective passages, order his personal history. For example, Douglass' discussion of slave songs begins with phrases such as "wild songs" and "unmeaning jargon" but concludes, quite typically for him, with a study of how he grew to "hear" the songs and how the hearing affords yet another illumination of his path from slavery to freedom:

> I did not, when a slave, understand the deep meaning of those rude and apparently incoherent songs. I was myself within the circle; so that I neither saw nor heard as those without might see and hear. They told a tale of woe which was then altogether beyond my feeble comprehension. . . . Every tone was a testimony against slavery, and a prayer to God for deliverance from chains. The hearing of those wild notes always depressed my spirit, and filled me with ineffable sadness. I have frequently found myself in tears while hearing them. The mere recurrence to those songs, even now, afflicts me; and while I am writing these lines, an expression of feeling has already found its way down my cheek.

The tears of the past and present interflow, and Douglass not only documents his saga of enslavement but also, with typical recourse to syncretic phrasing and introspective analysis, advances his presentation of self.

Douglass' other internalized documents are employed with comparable efficiency as we see in the episode where he attempts an escape in 1835. In this episode, the document reproduced is the pass or "protection" Douglass wrote for himself and his compatriots in the escape plan:

> "This is to certify that I, the undersigned, have given the bearer, my servant, full liberty to go to Baltimore, and spend the Easter holidays. Written with mine own hand, &c., 1835.
>
> > "WILLIAM HAMILTON,
>
> "Near St. Michael's, in Talbot county, Maryland."

The protection exhibits Douglass' increasingly refined sense of how to manipulate language—he has indeed come a long way from that day Mr. Auld halted his ABC lessons—but even more impressive, I believe, is the act of reproducing the document itself. We know from the tale that when their scheme was thwarted, each slave managed to destroy his pass, so Douglass reproduces his language from memory, and there is no reason to doubt a single jot of his recollection. My point here is simply that Douglass can draw so easily from the wellsprings of memory because the protection is not a mere scrap of memorabilia but rather a veritable road sign on his path to freedom and literacy. In this sense, his protection assumes a place in Afro-American letters as a key antecedent to such documents as the fast-yellowing notes of James Weldon Johnson's Ex-Coloured Man and "The Voodoo of Hell's Half Acre" in Richard Wright's *Black Boy*.

All of the types of narrative discourse discussed thus far reveal features of Douglass' particular posture as a participant-observer narrator. But the syncretic phrases, introspective studies, and internalized documents only exhibit Douglass as a teller and doer, and part of the great effect of his tale depends upon what Douglass does not tell, what he refuses to reenact in print. Late in the tale, at the beginning of Chapter xi, Douglass writes:

> I now come to that part of my life during which I planned, and finally succeeded in making, my escape from slavery. But before narrating any of the peculiar circumstances, I deem it proper to make known my intention not to state all the facts connected with the transaction. . . . I deeply regret the necessity that impels me to suppress any thing of importance connected with my experience in slavery. It would afford me great pleasure indeed, as well as materially add to the interest of my narrative, were I at liberty to gratify a curiosity, which I know exists. . . . But I must deprive myself of this pleasure, and the curious gratification which such a statement would afford. I would allow myself to suffer under the greatest imputations which evil-minded men might suggest, rather than exculpate myself, and thereby run the hazard of closing the slightest avenue by which a brother slave might clear himself of the chains and fetters of slavery.

It has been argued that one way to test a slave narrative's authenticity is by gauging how much space the narrator gives to relating his escape as opposed to describing the conditions of his captivity. If the adventure, excitement, and perils of the escape seem to be the raison d'être for the narrative's composition, then the narrative is quite possibly an exceedingly adulterated slave's tale or a bald fiction. The theory does not always work perfectly: Henry "Box" Brown's narrative and that of William and Ellen Craft are predominantly recollections of extraordinary escapes, and yet, as far as we can tell, these are authentic tales. But the theory nevertheless has great merit, and I have often wondered to what extent it derives from the example of Douglass' tale and emotionally, if not absolutely rationally, from his fulminations against those authors who unwittingly excavate the underground railroad and expose it to the morally thin mid-nineteenth-century American air. Douglass' tale is spectacularly free of suspicion, because he never tells a detail of his escape to New York, and it is this marvelously rhetorical omission or silence that both sophisticates and authenticates his posture as a participant-observer narrator. When a narrator wrests this kind of preeminent authorial control from the ancillary voices "circling" his narrative, we may say that he controls the presentation of his personal history and that his tale is becoming autobiographical. In this light the last few sentences of Douglass' tale take on special meaning:

> But, while attending an anti-slavery convention at Nantucket, on the 11th of August, 1841, I felt strongly moved to speak. . . . It was a severe cross, and I took it up reluctantly. The truth was, I felt myself a slave, and the idea of speaking to white people weighed me down. I spoke but a few moments, when I felt a degree of freedom, and said what I desired with considerable ease. From that time until now, I have been engaged in pleading the case of my brethren—with what success, and what devotion, I leave those acquainted with my labors to decide.

With these words, the narrative, as many have remarked, comes full circle, taking us back, not to the beginning of the tale, but rather to Garrison's prefatory remarks on the Convention and Douglass' first public address. This return may be pleasing in terms of the sense of symmetry it affords, but it is also a remarkable feat of rhetorical strategy: Having traveled with Douglass through his account of his life, we arrive in Nantucket in 1841 to hear him speak and, in effect, to become, along with Mr. Garrison, his audience. The final effect is that Douglass reinforces his posture as an articulate hero while supplanting Garrison as the definitive historian of his past.

Even more important, I think, is the final image Douglass bestows of a slave shedding his last fetter and becoming a man by first finding his voice and then, as sure as light follows dawn, speaking "with considerable ease." In one brilliant stroke, the quest for freedom and literacy implied from the start even by the narrative's title is resolutely consummated.

The final text of the narrative, the Appendix, is a discourse by Douglass on his view of Christianity and Christian practice as opposed to what he exposed in his tale to be the bankrupt, immoral faith of slaveholders. As rhetorical strategy, the discourse is effective generally because it lends weight and substance to what passes for a conventional complaint of slave narrative narrators and because Douglass' exhibition of faith can only enhance his already considerable posture as an articulate hero. But more specifically, the discourse is most efficacious because at its heart lies a vitriolic poem written by a Northern Methodist minister, which Douglass introduces by writing

> I conclude these remarks by copying the following portrait of the religion of the south, (which is, by communion and fellowship, the religion of the north,) which I soberly affirm is "true to life," and without caricature or the slightest exaggeration.

The poem is strong and imbued with considerable irony, but what we must appreciate here is the effect of the white Northerner's poem conjoined with Douglass' authentication of the poem. The tables are clearly reversed. Douglass has controlled his personal history and at the same time fulfilled the prophecy suggested in his implicit authentication of Garrison's Preface: He has explicitly authenticated what is conventionally a white Northerner's validating text. Douglass' narrative thus offers what is unquestionably our best portrait in Afro-American letters of the requisite act of assuming authorial control. An author can go no further than Douglass did without writing all the texts constituting the narrative himself.

References

Blassingame, John W. *The Slave Community.* New York: Oxford Univ. Press, 1971.

Cox, James. "Autobiography and America." *Virginia Quarterly Review,* 47 (1971), 252–77.

Douglass, Frederick. *Narrative of the Life of Frederick Douglass an American Slave Written by Himself.* 1845; rpt. Cambridge: Belknap-Harvard Univ. Press, 1960.

Reed, Ishmael. *Mumbo Jumbo.* New York: Doubleday, 1972.

Stone, Albert E. "Identity and Art in Frederick Douglass' 'Narrative.'" *CLA Journal,* 17 (1973), 192–213.

In the First Place: Making Frederick Douglass and the Afro-American Narrative Tradition

Deborah E. McDowell

Beginning is principally an activity of reconstruction, repetition, restoration, redeployment.

—Edward Said, *Beginnings*

The fragmenting of knowledge into periods—firsts—is humanly necessary, but the fragments are by no means intrinsically inevitable or experientially real.

—Cathy Davidson, *Revolution and the Word*

I regarded the selection of myself as being somewhat remarkable. There were a number of slave children that might have been sent from the plantation to Baltimore. There were those younger, those older, and those the same age. I was chosen from among them all, and was *the first, last*, and *only choice*. [Emphasis added]

—Frederick Douglass, *Narrative of the Life*

Assertions that the slave narrative begins the African-American literary tradition are repeated so often that they have acquired the force of self-evident truth. Charles Davis makes the argument up front in titling one of his important essays: "The Slave Narrative: First Major Art Form in an Emerging Black Tradition."[1] James Olney echoes Davis, only more strongly, in stating, "the undeniable fact is that the Afro-American literary tradition takes its start, in theme certainly, but also in content and form from the slave narrative."[2] Making an even bolder claim, H. Bruce Franklin argues that the slave

From William L. Andrews, ed., *Critical Essays on Frederick Douglass* (Boston: Twayne Publishers, 1991), 192–214. Copyright 1991 and reprinted with the permission of Twayne Publishers, a division of G. K. Hall & Co., Boston.

I would like to thank William L. Andrews, Janice Knight, Eric Lott, and Richard Yarborough for their helpful comments and suggestions.

[1]Charles Davis, "The Slave Narrative: First Major Art Form in an Emerging Black Tradition," in Henry Louis Gates, Jr., ed., *Black Is the Color of the Cosmos* (New York: Garland Publishing, 1982), 83–119.

[2]James Olney, " 'I was born': Slave Narratives, Their Status as Autobiography and as Literature" in Charles Davis and Henry Louis Gates, Jr. eds., *The Slave's Narrative* (New York: Oxford University Press, 1985), p. 168.

narrative was the "first genre the United States of America contributed to the written literature of the world."[3]

Of the estimated six thousand extant narratives, Frederick Douglass's 1845 *Narrative of the Life of Frederick Douglass, An American Slave, Written by Himself* is considered the first of a first. It is regarded as the prototypical, premier example of the form. It is also viewed as the text that "authorized" most subsequent slave narratives. Such claims of the narrative's priority can only be considered heuristic or factitious, what Paul de Man describes elsewhere as an "instance of rhetorical mystification,"[4] inasmuch as it is not chronologically prior, either to John Saffin's *Adam's Negro's Tryall* (1703), sometimes said to begin the slave narrative genre, or Briton Hammon's *A Narrative of the Uncommon Sufferings . . . of Briton Hammon, A Negro Man* (1760), which is more often considered the beginning.[5] Nevertheless, the *Narrative*'s status of priority persists. John Sekora contends that it is "the first comprehensive, personal history of American slavery."[6] With its publication, says Benjamin Quarles, one of Douglass's biographers, Douglass "became the first colored man who could command an audience that extended beyond local boundaries or racial ties."[7] William Andrews notes that the sales of the *Narrative* made it "the great enabling text of the first century of Afro-American autobiography," the text that created a popular demand for other fugitive slave narratives.[8]

It should be clear, even from these brief and randomly chosen excerpts, that Frederick Douglass and his 1845 *Narrative* have achieved monumental status. As Peter Walker observes, Douglass's presence in American history as "the courageous paterfamilias of a race" has "loomed so large and has been so compelling that he has been drafted into service as a personified social program by such widely divergent ideologues as [the accommodationist] Booker T. Washington and [the Marxist] Philip Foner."[9]

Douglass's function in literary history and interpretation has been similarly

[3]H. Bruce Franklin. "Animal Farm Unbound," *New Letters*, 43 (Spring 1977), p. 27.

[4]Paul de Man, "Genesis and Genealogy," in *Allegories of Reading* (New Haven: Yale University Press, 1979), 102.

[5]In *To Tell a Free Story* (Urbana: University of Illinois Press, 1986), perhaps the definitive study of the first century of Afro-American autobiography, William Andrews sees *Adam Negro's Tryall* as "a precursor of the slave narratives" and Briton Hammon's autobiography as the "first discrete narrative text in which an Afro-American recounts a significant portion of his life" (19, 18). Other students of the field see *The Interesting Narrative of Olaudah Equiano, or Gustavus Vassa, the African* (1789) as the originating text. In a recent article, Joanne M. Braxton argues for yet another beginning, *Belinda, or the Cruelty of Men Whose Faces Were Like the Moon* (1787). See her "Harriet Jacobs' *Incidents in the Life of a Slave Girl*: The Redefinition of the Slave Narrative Genre," *Massachusetts Review*, 27 (Summer 1986), 379–87.

[6]John Sekora, "Comprehending Slavery: Language and Personal History in Douglass's *Narrative* of 1845," *College Language Association Journal*, 29 (December 1985), 169.

[7]Benjamin Quarles. Introduction to *Narrative of the Life* (Cambridge: Harvard University Press, 1968), xix.

[8]Andrews, *To Tell*, 138.

[9]Peter Walker, *Moral Choices: Memory, Desire and Imagination in Nineteenth-Century American Abolition* (Baton Rouge: Louisiana State University Press, 1978), 212–13.

protean. He has been remarkably adaptable, to be more specific, to what Houston Baker has described as the "generational shifts" in the interpretation of Afro-American literature. He has been useful and usable to scholars whose approaches run the gamut from a now-devalued liberal humanism to a currently more valorized poststructuralism. In fact Baker's own shifting treatment of the 1845 *Narrative* is an excellent case in point of Douglass's adaptability to changing critical moments and the vocabularies by which we recognize them.[10] But however adaptable and fluid Douglass's *Narrative* has been to diverse and sometimes mutually antagonistic critical theories and methods, the underlying beliefs in its priority and originary significance remain unchanged. It is this changing sameness that interests me here. Why has the interpretive history, particularly of the last two decades, so privileged and mystified Douglass's narrative as a beginning text?

In an approach to this question, Edward Said's meditation on beginnings is instructive. He argues that "what is first, *is* eminent." Designating an individual as a founder has appeal, Said explains, because "in dealing with a distant past the mind prefers contemplating a strong seminal figure to sifting through reams of explanation." And it is not that such a figure is "simply a hypostasis. Indeed, he must fulfill the requirements of an exacting and . . . inaugural logic in which the creation of *authority* is paramount . . . an original achievement that gains in worth, paradoxically, precisely because it is so often repeated thereafter."[11]

It is easy to find in Said's observations clear and direct implications for a consideration of the 1845 *Narrative* and its originary significance in the African-American narrative tradition. His remarks on the role of texts in the formulation of beginnings are especially appropriate. "Entire periods of history are basically apprehended as functions of a text," Said observes. That is, they are "either made sensible by a text or given identity by a text."[12] Albert Stone's is only one of many treatments of Douglass's *Narrative* to confirm Said's claims. To Stone, this text is "the *first* native American autobiography

---

[10]See Baker's "Revolution and Reform: Walker, Douglass, and the Road to Freedom," in *Long Black Song: Essays in Black American Literature and Culture* (Charlottesville: University Press of Virginia, 1972), in which he contrasts the forms and styles of David Walker's *Appeal* with Douglass's 1845 *Narrative*. He concludes that, while Walker was a revolutionary allied with "the declamatory poets of black America," Douglass was a reformer "allied with the formalists" (79). In "Autobiographical Acts and the Voice of the Southern Slave," in *The Journey Back: Issues in Black Literature and Criticism* (Chicago: University of Chicago Press, 1980), 27–52, Baker offers a different and very interesting reading of the *Narrative*, which employs theories of autobiography to problematize assumptions about the "self," to discuss its constructions in language, and to examine the implications of both for representing slavery and the slave. Most recently, in "Figurations for a New American Literary History," in *Blues, Ideology and Afro-American Literature* (Chicago: University of Chicago Press, 1984), Baker does a proto-Marxist reading of the property relations and the rhetoric and thematics of economics in the *Narrative*.

[11]Edward Said, *Beginnings: Intention and Method* (New York: Columbia University Press, 1985), 32.

[12]Said, *Beginnings*, 198.

to create a black identity in a style and form adequate to the pressures of historical black experience."[13]

The *Narrative* then does double duty: not only does it make slavery intelligible, but the "black experience" as well. And in performing this monumental work, the text thus acts in two directions at once: the here and now and the there and then. It is the *Narrative*'s actions in the here and now that interest me. I am concerned with pursuing the uses to which the present generation of critics and scholars have put the past, specifically this man and his texts and this man as a text. As Douglass himself noted in "Self-Made Men," considered his most famous address, "it is the now that makes the then."[14] I am interested in why the making of Douglass, particularly by this current generation of scholars, has had such widespread explanatory power and appeal, and why it is attached so solidly to the logic of beginning and origin.

These questions assume all the more importance because, as Patricia Parker well notes, "the logic of first and second, and hence of sequence . . . continues to inhabit the discussion of female difference."[15] Some of the most compelling critiques of that logic of beginning, at least as it has operated in Western culture, have come from feminist theorists like Parker who trace it back to the first of the Genesis myths. They have challenged this myth that inscribes Adam's ontological priority as well as his priority in human history and culture, noting that his "firstness" necessitates Eve's "secondariness" as well as her exile from creative or symbolic activity. This myth, associated with the male story, with the name and the Law of the Father, represses the name and the word of the mother. Increasingly literalized, it has been taken as given or fact and operates in both conscious and unconscious beliefs and in cultural structures. In other words, the myth that "Adam was formed first, then Eve" (I Timothy, 2:11–15) has pervaded a variety of cultural texts— sacred and secular—that show the unmistakable trace of Genesis and the sex/ gender economy it has produced in culture.

Perhaps one prerequisite question here is thus whether the force in the critical making of Frederick Douglass and his *Narrative* as founding texts is something yet more basic and powerful, an a priori structure and system of desire that preexists and determines both Douglass's narrative choices and those his critics have made. That structure authorizes and inscribes the relationship between sexual difference and creative activity.

13Albert Stone, "Identity and Art in Frederick Douglass's 'Narrative,' " *College Language Association Journal*, 17 (December 1973), 213.

14Frederick Douglass, "The Trials and Triumphs of Self-Made Men: An Address Delivered in Halifax, England, on 4 January 1860," in John Blassingame, ed., *The Frederick Douglass Papers: Series One* (New Haven: Yale University Press, 1985), 290.

15Patricia Parker, "Coming Second: Woman's Place," in *Literary Fat Ladies: Rhetoric, Gender, Property* (London and New York: Methuen, 1987), 190. For additional feminist critiques of the politics of origins, see Margaret Homans, *Bearing the Word* (Chicago: University of Chicago Press, 1986) and Christine Froula, "Rewriting Genesis: Gender and Culture in Twentieth-Century Texts," *Tulsa Studies in Women's Literature* 7 (Fall 1988), 197–220.

I

This man shall be remembered . . . with lives grown out of his life, the lives
fleshing his dream of the needful, beautiful thing.

—Robert Hayden, "Frederick Douglass"

Students of the 1845 *Narrative* commonly designate the following as its key
sentence: "You have seen how a man was made a slave, you shall see how a
slave was made a man."[16] The clause that follows that pivotal comma—"you
shall see how a slave was made a man"—captures with great prescience the
focus of much contemporary scholarship on slavery. That focus is studiously
on making the slave a man, according to cultural norms of masculinity. This
accounts in part, as I will show below, for why Douglass is so pivotal, so
mythological a figure. I am not out to argue for any distinction between
Douglass "the myth" and Douglass "the man," but rather and simply to view
him as a product of history, a construction of a specific time and place,
developed in response to a variety of social contingencies and individual
desires.

The process and production in literary studies of Douglass as "the first"
have paralleled and perhaps been partly fueled by what revisionist historians
have made of him. We might go even further to argue that "history" has
operated as narrative, in the making of Douglass and his *Narrative*. And so we
face constructions upon constructions. While the mythologization of Douglass
and this text well antedates the 1960s, 1970s and 1980s, these decades are
especially crucial in efforts to understand this process.

These years were characterized by revisionist mythmaking, much of it
prompted by Stanley Elkins's controversial book *Slavery: A Problem in
American Institutional and Intellectual Life* (1959). I need not rehearse in
detail Elkins's now-familiar Sambo thesis emphasizing the effects of black
male emasculation in slavery.[17] Historians, armed with a mountain of supporting data, came forth to refute Elkins's data and his thesis. Among the most
prominent of these revisionists was John Blassingame, whose *The Slave
Community* was rightly celebrated for its attempt to write history from the
perspective of slaves, not planters. Blassingame rejects Elkins's Sambo thesis

---

[16]Frederick Douglass, *Narrative of the Life of Frederick Douglass, An American Slave Written
by Himself* (New York: Signet/New American Library, 1968), 47. Subsequent references are to
this edition and will be indicated in parentheses in the text. I will also make reference to *My
Bondage and My Freedom* (New York: Dover, 1969) and *Life and Times of Frederick Douglass,
Written by Himself* (New York: Pathway Press, 1941).

[17]Perhaps as influential as the Elkins book in sparking revisionist histories of slavery was
Daniel P. Moynihan's federally commissioned *Moynihan Report: The Case for National Action*
(Cambridge: MIT Press, 1965). While Elkins virtually ignored black women in his study,
attributing the failure of black males to achieve "manhood" to a paternalistic slave system that
infantilized them, Moynihan assigns blame to black women for being the predominant heads of
household.

[18]John Blassingame, *The Slave Community* (New York: Oxford University Press, 1979), xi.

as "intimately related to the planters's projections, desires, and biases,"[18] particularly their desire to be relieved of the "anxiety of thinking about slaves as men."[19]

Blassingame sets out to correct the record to show that the slave was not "half-man," "half-child,"[20] as the Elkins thesis tried to show, but a whole man. Blassingame doesn't simply lapse into the reflexive use of the generic "he," but throughout his study assumes the slave to be literally male, an assumption seen especially in his chapter titled "The Slave Family." There he opens with the straightforward observation: "The Southern plantation was unique in the New World because it permitted the development of a monogamous slave family," which was "one of the most important survival mechanisms for the slave." He continues, "the slave faced almost insurmountable odds in his efforts to build a strong stable family . . . his authority was restricted by his master. . . . The master determined when both he and his wife would go to work [and] when or whether his wife cooked his meals." "When the slave lived on the same plantation with his mate he could rarely escape frequent demonstrations of his powerlessness." "Under such a regime," Blassingame adds, "slave fathers often had little or no authority." Despite that, the slave system "recognized the male as the head of the family."[21]

Blassingame is clearly not alone in revising the history of slavery to demonstrate the propensities of slaves toward shaping their lives according to "normative" cultural patterns of marriage and family life. But *The Slave Community* must be seen as a study of the institution that reflects and reproduces the assumptions of a much wider discursive network—scholarly and political—within which the black male is the racial subject.

There have been few challenges to this two-decade-long focus on the personality of the male slave. In her book *Ar'n't I a Woman?* (which might have been more aptly titled, "Can a slave be a woman; can a woman be a slave?"), Deborah White critiques the emphasis on negating Samboism, which characterizes so much recent literature on slavery. She argues that "the male slave's 'masculinity' was restored by putting black women in their proper 'feminine' place."[22] bell hooks offers an even stronger critique of this litera- ture, noting eloquently its underlying assumption that "the most cruel and dehumanizing impact of slavery on the lives of black people was that black men were stripped of their masculinity." hooks continues, "To suggest that black men were dehumanized solely as a result of not being able to be patriarchs implies that the subjugation of black women was essential to the black male's development of a positive self-concept, an ideal that only served to support a sexist social order."[23]

---

[19]Blassingame, *The Slave*, 230.
[20]Blassingame, *The Slave*, xi.
[21]Blassingame, *The Slave*, 172, 152.
[22]Deborah Gray White, *Ar'n't I a Woman* (New York: W. W. Norton, 1985), 22.
[23]bell hooks, *Ain't I a Woman* (Boston: South End Press, 1981), 20–21.

While I would not argue that students of Afro-American literature have consciously joined revisionist historians in their efforts to debunk the Elkins thesis, their work can certainly be said to participate in and reinforce these revisionist histories. And what better way to do this than to replace the Sambo myth of childlike passivity with an example of public derring-do, with the myth of the male slave as militant, masculine, dominant, and triumphant in both private and public spheres?[24]

But the Elkins thesis, and the revisionist histories it engendered, are only part of a larger chain of interlocking events that have worked to mythologize Frederick Douglass. These include the demand for African and African-American Studies courses in universities, the publishers who capitalized on that demand, and the academic scholars who completed the chain. A series of individual slave narratives has appeared, along with anthologies and collections of less-popular narratives. The more popular the narrative, the more frequent the editions, and Douglass's 1845 *Narrative* has headed the list since 1960. Scholarly interest in African-American literature has accelerated correspondingly and, again, the 1845 *Narrative* has been premier. Although in his 1977 essay, "Animal Farm Unbound," H. Bruce Franklin could list in a fairly short paragraph critical articles on the 1845 *Narrative*, scarcely more than a decade later the book had stimulated a small industry of scholarship on its own.[25] Thus Douglass's assumed genius as a literary figure is the work of a diverse and interactive collective that includes publishers, editors, and literary critics who have helped to construct his reputation and to make it primary in Afro-American literature.

A major diachronic study of the production, reception, and circulation history of Douglass's 1845 *Narrative* is urgently needed; but even more urgent is the need for a thoroughgoing analysis of the politics of gender at work in that process. One could argue that the politics of gender have been obscured both by the predominance of nonfeminist interpretations of the *Narrative* and by the text itself. In other words, those who have examined it have tended, with few exceptions, to mimic the work of Douglass himself on the question of the feminine and its relation to the masculine in culture.

For example, in his most recent reading of the 1845 *Narrative*, Houston

[24]Ronald Takaki's interpretation is an example of making Douglass a militant. In "Not Afraid to Die: Frederick Douglass and Violence," in *Violence and the Black Imagination* (New York: Capricorn, 1972), Takaki traces Douglass's rise to a political activist who advocated killing for freedom. In a recent essay, "Race, Violence, and Manhood: The Masculine Ideal in Frederick Douglass's 'The Heroic Slave,'" Richard Yarborough discusses Douglass's obsession with manhood in his novella "The Heroic Slave." There manhood was virtually synonymous with militant slave resistance. In the popular realm, Spike Lee's controversial film *Do the Right Thing* is structured according to this ideology of masculinity, which ranks black leaders (assumed to be male) according to their propensities for advocating violence.

[25]For a bibliographic essay on the various editions of the Douglass narrative as compared to other slave narratives, see Ruth Miller and Peter J. Katopes, "Slave Narratives" and W. Burghardt Turner, "The Polemicists: David Walker, Frederick Douglass, Booker T. Washington, and W. E. B. DuBois," in M. Thomas Inge, Maurice Duke, and Jackson R. Bryer, *Black American Writers: Bibliographical Essays, Vol. 1* (New York: St. Martin's Press, 1978).

Baker assimilates the text to Marxist language and rhetoric, but a more conventional rhetoric of family resounds. Baker's reading foregrounds the disruption of the slave family and offers the terms of its reunion: economic solvency. "The successful negotiation of such economics," says Baker, "is, paradoxically, the *only* course that provides conditions for a reunification of woman and sable man."[26] He continues, "the African who successfully negotiates his way through the dread exchanges of bondage to the type of expressive posture characterizing *The Life's* conclusion is surely a man who has repossessed himself and, thus, achieved the ability to reunite a severed African humanity."[27] A sign of that self-repossession, Baker argues, is Douglass's "certificate of marriage." "As a married man," he concludes, Douglass "understands the necessity for *individual* wage earning."[28] "In the company of his new bride," he goes to a New England factory village where he participates "creatively in the liberation of his people."[29] This reading's implication in an old patriarchal script requires not a glossing, but an insertion and a backward tracking. However important Douglass's wage-earning capacities as a freeman are, one could say that the prior wage, if you will, was Anna Murray's, Douglass's "new bride." A freedwoman, Anna "helped to defray the costs for [Douglass's] runaway scheme by borrowing from her savings and by selling one of her feather beds."[30]

Mary Helen Washington is one of the few critics to insert Anna Murray Douglass into a discussion of the 1845 *Narrative*. She asks, "While our daring Douglass . . . was heroically ascending freedom's arc . . . who . . . was at home taking care of the children?"[31] But such questions are all too rare in discussions of the *Narrative*. Because critical commentary has mainly repeated the text's elision of women, I would like to restore them for the moment, to change the subject of the text from man to woman.

II

I have said that the slave was a man.

—Frederick Douglass,
My Bondage and My Freedom

To attempt to restore the occluded woman in Douglass's *Narrative* is to bring forth gender as a category of analysis. Such a discussion might properly

[26]Houston Baker, *Blues, Ideology, and Afro-American Literature* (Chicago: University of Chicago Press, 1984), 38.
[27]Baker, *Blues*, 38.
[28]Baker, *Blues*, 48.
[29]Baker, *Blues*, 49.
[30]Waldo E. Martin, *The Mind of Frederick Douglass* (Chapel Hill: University of North Carolina Press, 1984), 15.
[31]Mary Helen Washington, "These Self-Invented Women: A Theoretical Framework for a Literary History of Black Women," *Radical Teacher* (1980), 4. In a recent study David Leverenz also notes that "Douglass's whole sense of latter-day self, in both the *Narrative* and its revision,

begin by considering autobiography as genre, particularly inasmuch as gender and genre are etymologically related. As Jacques Derrida, among others, has noted, the question of the literary genre is not a strictly formal or esthetic one. It embraces, in addition, the motif and logic of generation in both natural and symbolic senses, as well as the sexual difference between the feminine and masculine.[32]

In choosing autobiography as a form, Douglass committed himself to what many feminists consider an androcentric genre.[33] In its focus on the public story of a public life, which signifies the achievement of adult male status in Western culture, autobiography reflects and constructs that culture's definitions of masculinity. Douglass's *Narrative* not only partakes of these definitions of masculinity, but is also plotted according to the myth of the self-made man to which these definitions correspond. As Valerie Smith has observed, "by mythologizing rugged individuality, physical strength, and geographical mobility, the [slave] narrative enshrines cultural definitions of masculinity." She continues, "the plot of the standard narrative may thus be seen as not only the journey from slavery to freedom but also the journey from slavehood to manhood" in cultural terms.[34]

In choosing autobiography as a form, Douglass also implicitly and explicitly committed himself to what is perhaps its most salient requirement: that he legitimize himself by naming and claiming a father.[35] Of course, the slave system prevented him from doing either, which may explain why his obsession with learning his origins or his "proper name" was to preoccupy Douglass literally until his dying day.[36] That he believed his master to be his father, engendering a double relation, only confounded this search for origins.

If we read that search symbolically as a secondary expression of the Genesis myth of origins, then Douglass's name changes acquire added signifi-

focuses on manhood; his wife seems an afterthought. He introduces her to his readers as a rather startling appendage to his escape and marries her almost in the same breath." See "Frederick Douglass's Self-Fashioning," in *Manhood and the American Renaissance* (Ithaca: Cornell University Press, 1989), 128.

[32]Jacques Derrida, "The Law of Genre," *Glyph* 7 (Baltimore: Johns Hopkins, 1980). Derrida notes that "in French, the semantic scale of genre is much larger and more expansive than in English and thus always includes within its reach the gender" (221). In his translator's notes to Derrida's essay, Avital Ronnell adds that " 'genre' enjoys a suppleness and freedom of semantic movement that is vigorously constrained in the English. . . . A genderless language, English by definition does not take well to the business of mixing with genres" (232).

[33]See Sidonie Smith, *A Poetics of Women's Autobiography* (Bloomington: Indiana University Press, 1987). See also Domna C. Stanton, ed., *The Female Autograph: Theory and Practice of Autobiography from the Tenth to the Twentieth Century* (Chicago: University of Chicago Press, 1987) and Shari Benstock, ed., *The Private Self: Theory and Practice of Women's Autobiographical Writings* (Chapel Hill: University of North Carolina Press, 1988).

[34]Valerie Smith, *Self-Discovery and Authority* (Cambridge: Harvard University Press, 1987), 34.

[35]See Annette Niemtzow, "The Problematic of Self in Autobiography: The Example of the Slave Narrative," in John Sekora and Darwin Turner, eds., *The Art of Slave Narrative* (Western Illinois University, 1982), 96–109.

[36]See Peter Walker, *Moral Choices*. This search for the white father is a trope at least as powerfully paradigmatic as the more often discussed quest for freedom and literacy.

cance. As noted above, that myth inscribes the name and the Law of the Father, while repressing the name of the mother. It can be argued, then, that in changing the name his mother gave him—Frederick Augustus Washington Bailey—Douglass, as Henry Louis Gates astutely notes, "self-consciously and ironically abandoned a strong matrilineal black heritage of five stable generations."[37] We might argue further that the abandonment of the mother's name can be read as a rejection of the mother's word, to a rejection of the feminine. Although over the course of his three autobiographies, Douglass shifted and refined his representation of his mother, her figuration in the first autobiography is that most commonly accepted by literary critics, when they discuss the mother at all.[38] Generally, critics merely restate as a given Douglass's early descriptions of his separation from her and his emotionless but rhetorically effective account of their short acquaintance: "I do not recollect of ever seeing my mother by the light of day. . . . Very little communication ever took place between us." While critics, in the main, have not been slow to attend to the *Narrative* as rhetorical tour de force, few have delved underneath the surfaces of these descriptions of the mother to uncover their latent grammar.

In striking ways, Douglass's *Narrative* participates in a more basic, a priori narrative that silences and effaces the mother's story.[39] Such a position gains in force if the 1845 *Narrative*, the first of three, is not accepted as the "standard edition" overriding Douglass's accounts of his life in the two subsequent narratives. If the 1845 *Narrative* is not given priority as the first, last, and only word on Douglass, but is considered in relation to the following texts, his problematical relation to his mother emerges with greater and more disturbing clarity. She thus becomes a powerful presence even in her absence.

In *My Bondage and My Freedom*, for example, Douglass writes: "the side of my mother's face is imaged on my memory, and I take few steps in life without feeling her presence; but *the image is mute, and I have no striking words of hers treasured up*" [57, emphasis added]. In *Life and Times*, Douglass repeats earlier accounts of his mother, but adds a reference to his selection of "the head of a figure" from Prichard's *Natural History of Man*, which he believed to be a fair likeness of his mother. Peter Walker offers a complex reading of Douglass's choice of this figure, concluding persuasively that Douglass "found his black mother in the form of a princely man who, as far as the picture showed, may have been white."[40]

[37]Henry Louis Gates, "Frederick Douglass and the Language of the Self," in *Figures in Black: Words, Signs and the "Racial" Self* (New York: Oxford University, 1987), 114.

[38]The historians Dickson Preston, in *Young Frederick Douglass: The Maryland Years* (Baltimore: Johns Hopkins, 1980), and Peter Walker, in *Moral Choices*, discuss the place of the mother in Douglass's autobiographies. Walker describes Douglass's "development of a 'fictive' kinship with his mother" and notes that "the more obvious and striking shift that Douglass made in the course of his autobiographical definition relates to his mother."

[39]For a discussion of this pattern, see Margaret Homans, *Bearing the Word*, and Sidonie Smith, *A Poetics of Women's Autobiography* (Bloomington: Indiana University Press, 1987). See especially chapter 3, "Woman's Story and the Engenderings of Self-Representation."

[40]Walker, *Moral Choices*, 254. Waldo Martin offers an alternative reading of Douglass's choice. While he acknowledges that the selection of this picture "could have suggested . . . the

Douglass's account of his mute mother remembered as a white man captures emphatically the discursive priorities of masculinity and its gendered relation to the feminine. That slavery so destroyed the possibility of a relationship with his mother, Douglass is keen to emphasize. That emphasis works well rhetorically with his general indictment of the institution's destruction of family, which was one of abolitionism's singular strategies. While that destruction was certainly widespread and real, in Douglass's case it was, as Walker has suggested, partly fictive. What, then, other than the generic requirements of the fugitive slave narrative as an abolitionist instrument, explains Douglass's decision to remake his beginnings? This question is less dependent on the first narrative than on the second, and it involves the complex affiliations of femininity and feminism and abolitionism. In other words, *My Bondage and My Freedom* reveals more clearly than the first narrative that Douglass's rewriting of his own origins does more than satisfy the dictates of abolitionism. It also makes intelligible Douglass's and the movement's problematical relation to the feminine.

Douglass is rightly concerned to show that "genealogical trees do not flourish among slaves," that while his mother "had *many children*" "she had NO FAMILY!" [*My Bondage and My Freedom* 48, emphasis in text]. Thus was slavery "an enemy to filial affection" that rendered him a stranger to his siblings, "converted the mother that bore [him] into a myth," and "shrouded [his] father in mystery, and left [him] without an intelligible beginning in the world" (60). And while none would expect anything but such stirring condemnation, I believe that Gregory Jay is right to argue that Douglass's appeal to the "sanctity of the family" is an emotional and moral verity that allied abolitionism "with the powerful conventions of domesticity." In thus using the "family against slavery," Douglass elides, as Harriet Jacobs does not, the fact that "the paternalism and property relations at the heart of the slave system might also play a part in the construction of domestic relations." That Douglass forges this unexamined connection between abolitionism and domesticity at the same moment that the link between slavery and feminism was "being forged by various reform figures, including Douglass himself," is "all the more puzzling and powerful."[41]

But the puzzle is solved in part if we consider that while Douglass rejected the paternalism and property relations buttressing the slave system, he appropriated those buttressing the structure and ideology of the family. Or, as Valerie Smith puts it, "Within his critique of American cultural practices . . . is an affirmation of its definitions of manhood and power" on which traditional domestic arrangements depend.[42]

---

subconscious power of [Douglass's] racial ambivalence," the selection of an ambiguously masculine figure "might have reflected the genderless dimension of his catholic vision of a common humanity transcending sex as well as race." *The Mind of Frederick Douglass*, 5.

[41]Gregory Jay, "American Literature and the New Historicism: The Example of Frederick Douglass," Working Paper #10, Center for Twentieth Century Studies, University of Wisconsin-Milwaukee (Fall 1988): 19.

[42]Valerie Smith, *Self-Discovery*, 20.

Central to Douglass's condemnation is slavery's legal denial of family to slaves, especially its denial to male slaves the rights and privileges of patriarchy, which include ownership of their wives and children. In *My Bondage and My Freedom*, he lists among "the baneful peculiarities of the slave system" the fact that "in law, the slave has no wife, no children, no country, and no home" (429). And he laments that "the name of the child is not expected to be that of its father" (51–52). But however justified he is in condemning slavery for denying the slave the right to wife and children, the absurdity of its male bias should still not go unremarked. The fact that slave women could not take "wives" categorizes them, to borrow from Karen Sanchez-Appler, "not as potential free persons but rather as the sign and condition of another's freedom. The freedom so defined . . . is available to neither child nor woman."[43]

Here and throughout Douglass's autobiographies, his delineation of slavery's "baneful peculiarities" often rests on an implied equation of masculinity with subjectivity and textuality. Throughout, "slave" is conflated with "male." Near the end of *My Bondage* Douglass declares, with performative authority, "I have said the slave was a man" (431). Reflexive and anticipated arguments about the generic he/man, and the nineteenth-century context of the narrative's production, must be deflected here and should not foreclose a discussion of Douglass's tendency to construct the black male as paradigmatic slave. To be sure, that Douglass implicitly and explicitly arrogated subjectivity and primacy to himself is but a part of linguistic convention and a general cultural tendency to privilege maleness. It is also, however, a specific pattern in abolitionist discourse in which women occupied secondary places. The "Ladies Department" of Garrison's *The Liberator*, cordoned off from and coming after the preceding matter, establishes this tendency plainly. Further, as Waldo Martin notes, Douglass lamented that abolitionism, "a grand philanthropic movement," had been "rent asunder by a side issue [women's rights], having nothing, whatever, to do with the great object which the American Anti-Slavery Society was organized to carry forward." According to Martin, though Douglass supported women's rights, he felt feminists "should have postponed their own protests," in his words, "for the slave's sake."[44] However understandable Douglass's position was, especially given the racism in the movement for women's rights, he misses the fact that some slaves were women and that however much their oppressions overlapped with that of male slaves, the particularities of each were such that they could not be merged.

When Douglass's *Narrative* moves from generic descriptions of slave life to focus on the more specific experiences of individuals, it seems, on the surface,

---

[43]Karen Sanchez-Appler, "Bodily Bonds: The Intersecting Rhetorics of Feminism and Abolition," *Representations* 24 (Fall 1988), 48.

[44]Martin, *The Mind of Frederick Douglass*, 151. Martin notes also that "in his hierarchy of social reform priorities, Douglass viewed the abolition of black slavery as primary and the abolition of sexual slavery as secondary" (150).

that he is alert to the differences between the experiences of women and those of men. He chooses to highlight the most familiar mark of their difference in the discourse of slavery: black women's sexual oppression. But while such a move might be considered a radical act of resistance, it soon becomes implicated in the very situation of exploitation that it seeks to expose. Put another way, black women's backs become the parchment on which Douglass narrates his linear progression from bondage to freedom.

III

> For heart of man though mainly right
>   Hides many things from mortal sight
>   Which seldom ever come to light
>   except upon compulsion.
>
>   —Frederick Douglass,
>   "What Am I to You"

Frances Foster is one of the few critics to describe the construction in the popular imagination of the slave woman as sexual victim, a pattern she sees in full evidence in male slave narratives. Foster observes a markedly different pattern in slave narratives written by women. Unlike the male narratives, which portray graphically the sexual abuse of slave women by white men, female narratives "barely mention sexual experiences and never present rape or seduction as the most profound aspect of their existence."[45]

The pattern that Foster describes is abundantly evident in all three of Douglass's autobiographies. One can easily argue that, with perhaps the exception of his mother and grandmother, slave women operate almost totally as physical bodies, as sexual victims, "at the mercy," as he notes in *My Bondage and My Freedom* "of the fathers, sons or brothers of [their] master" (60). Though this is certainly true, slave women were just as often at the mercy of the wives, sisters, and mothers of these men as Harriet Jacobs records in *Incidents in the Life of a Slave Girl*.[46] But in Douglass's account, the sexual villains are white men and the victims black women. Black men are largely impotent onlookers, condemned to watch the abuse. What Douglass watches and then narrates is astonishing—the whippings of slaves, one after another, in almost unbroken succession.

A scant four pages into the text, immediately following his account of his origins, Douglass begins to describe these whippings in graphic detail. He sees Mr. Plummer, the overseer, "cut and slash the women's heads" and

[45]Frances Foster, " 'In Respect to Females . . .': Differences in the Portrayals of Women by Male and Female Narrators," *Black American Literature Forum*, 15 (Summer 1981), 67.
[46]See "The Jealous Mistress," in *Incidents in the Life of a Slave Girl*. Even Douglass himself says as much at another point. He notes that the mistress "is ever disposed to find anything to please her; she is never more pleased than when she sees them under the lash" (23).

"seem to take great pleasure" in it. He remembers being often awakened by the heart-rending shrieks of his aunt as she is beaten. He sees her "tie[d] up to a joist and whip[ped] upon her naked back till she was literally covered with blood. The louder she screamed, the harder he whipped; and where the blood ran fastest, there he whipped longest. He would whip her to make her scream, and whip her to make her hush; and not until overcome by fatigue, would he cease to swing the blood-clotted cowskin" (25).

Though the whippings of women are not the only ones of which Douglass's *Narrative* gives account, they predominate by far in the text's economy as Douglass looks on. There was Mr. Severe, whom "I have seen . . . whip a woman, causing the blood to run half an hour at the time" (29). There was his master, who he had seen "tie up a *lame* young woman, and whip her with a heavy cowskin upon her naked shoulders, causing the warm red blood to drip. I have known him to tie her up early in the morning and whip her before breakfast; leave her, go to his store, return at dinner and whip her again, cutting in the places already made raw with his cruel lash" (68–69). There was Mr. Weeden, who kept the back of a slave woman "literally raw, made so by the lash of this merciless, religious wretch" (87). As the *Narrative* progresses, the beatings proliferate and the women, no longer identified by name, become absolutized as a bloody mass of naked backs.

What has been made of this recital of whippings? William L. Andrews is one of the few critics to comment on the function of whippings in the text. In a very suggestive reading, he argues that Douglass presents the fact of whipping in "deliberately stylized, plainly rhetorical, recognizably artificial ways." There is nothing masked about this presentation. On the contrary, "Douglass's choice of repetition" is his "chief rhetorical effect." It constitutes his "stylistic signature" and expresses his "performing self." In the whipping passages, Andrews adds, "Douglass calls attention to himself as an unabashed artificer, a maker of forms and efforts that recontextualize brute facts according to requirements of self. The freeman requires the freedom to demonstrate the potency of his own inventiveness and the sheer potentiality of language itself for rhetorical manipulation."[47]

However intriguing I find Andrews's reading, I fear that to explain the repetition of whippings solely in rhetorical terms and in the interest of Douglass's self-expression leads to some troubling elisions and rationalizations, perhaps the most troubling elision being the black woman's body. In other words, Douglass's "freedom"—narrative and physical alike—depends on narrating black women's bondage. He achieves his "stylistic signature" by objectifying black women. To be sure, delineating the sexual abuse of black women is a standard convention of the fugitive slave narrative, but the

---

[47]Andrews, *To Tell a Free Story*, 134. Valerie Smith also offers an interesting reading of the whippings. They enable the reader to "visualize the blood that masters draw from their slaves. . . . Passages such as [Douglass's Aunt Hester's beatings] provide vivid symbols of the process of dehumanization that slaves underwent as their lifeblood was literally sapped." *Self-Discovery and Authority*, 21–22.

narration of that abuse seems to function beyond the mere requirements of form. A second look at the first recorded beating, his Aunt Hester's, forces out a different explanation. His choice of words in this account—"spectacle," "exhibition"—is instructive, as is his telling admission that, in viewing the beating, he became both "witness and participant" (25).

Critical commentary has focused almost completely on Douglass as witness to slavery's abuses, overlooking his role as participant, an omission that conceals his complex and troubling relationship to slave women, kin and nonkin alike. In calling for closer attention to the narration of whipping scenes, I do not mean to suggest that Douglass's autobiographies were alone among their contemporaries in their obsession with corporal punishment. As Richard Brodhead has observed, "Corporal punishment has been one of the most perennially vexed of questions in American cultural history," and it had its "historical center of gravity in America in the antebellum decades."[48] Both in antislavery literature and in the literature of the American Gothic, what Brodhead calls the "imagination of the lash" was pervasive. That much antislavery literature had strong sexual undercurrents has been well documented. As many critics have observed, much abolitionist literature went beyond an attack on slavery to condemn the South as a vast libidinal playground.

My aim here, then, is not to argue that Douglass's repeated depiction of whipping scenes is in any way unique to him, but rather to submit those scenes to closer scrutiny for their own sake. In other words, the preponderance of this pattern in antebellum literature should not preclude a detailed examination of its representation in a smaller textual sampling. Neither is my aim to psychoanalyze Douglass, nor to offer an "alternative," more "correct" reading, but rather to reveal that Douglass often has more than one voice, one motivation, and one response to his record of black women's abuse in his *Narrative*.

Freud notes in *Beyond the Pleasure Principle* that "repetition, the re-experiencing of something identical, is clearly in itself a source of pleasure."[49] If, as Douglass observes, the slave master derives pleasure from the repeated act of whipping, could Douglass, as observer, derive a vicarious pleasure from the repeated narration of the act? I would say yes. Douglass's repetition of the sexualized scene of whipping projects him into a voyeuristic relation to the violence against slave women, which he watches, and thus he enters into a symbolic complicity with the sexual crime he witnesses. In other words, the spectator becomes voyeur, reinforcing what many feminist film theorists have persuasively argued: sexualization "resides in the very act of looking."[50] Thus

[48]Richard Brodhead, "Sparing the Rod: Discipline and Fiction in Antebellum America." *Representations* 21 (Winter 1988), 67. See also David Leverenz, *Manhood and the American Renaissance*, for a discussion of beatings in Melville's *Moby Dick* and *White Jacket*, and in *Uncle Tom's Cabin*.

[49]Sigmund Freud, *Beyond the Pleasure Principle*, Volume 18 of *Standard Edition of the Complete Psychological Works of Sigmund Freud* (London: The Hogarth Press, 1955), 36.

"the relationship between viewer and scene is always one of fracture, partial identification, pleasure and distrust."[51]

To be sure, Douglass sounds an urgently and warranted moral note in these passages, but he sounds an erotic one as well that is even more clear if the critical gaze moves from the first autobiography to the second. In a chapter titled "Gradual Initiation into the Mysteries of Slavery," Douglass describes awakening as a child to a slave woman being beaten. The way in which Douglass constructs the scene evokes the familiar male child's initiation into the mysteries of sexuality by peeking through the keyhole of his parents' bedroom:

> My sleeping place was the floor of a little, rough closet, which opened into the kitchen; and through the cracks of its unplaned boards, I could distinctly see and hear what was going on, without being seen by my master. Esther's wrists were firmly tied and the twisted rope was fastened to a strong staple in a heavy wooden joist above, near the fireplace. Here she stood, on a bench, her arms tightly drawn over her breast. Her back and shoulders were bare to the waist. Behind her stood old master, with cowskin in hand, preparing his barbarous work with all manner of harsh, coarse, and tantalizing epithets. The screams of his victim were most piercing. He was cruelly deliberate, and protracted the torture, as one who was delighted with the scene. Again and again he drew the hateful whip through his hand, adjusting it with a view of dealing the most pain-giving blow. Poor Esther had never yet been severely whipped, and her shoulders were plump and tender. Each blow vigorously laid on, brought screams as well as blood. (87–88)[52]

This passage in all its erotic overtones echoes throughout Douglass's autobiographies and goes well beyond pleasure to embrace its frequent symbiotic equivalent: power. It can be said both to imitate and articulate the pornographic scene, which starkly represents and reproduces the cultural and oppositional relation of the masculine to the feminine, the relation between seer and seen, agent and victim, dominant and dominated, powerful and powerless.[53]

Examining the narration of whipping scenes with regard to the sex of the slave reinforces this gendered division and illustrates its consequences. While

---

[50]Jacqueline Rose, *Sexuality in the Field of Vision* (London: Verso, 1986), 112.

[51]Rose, *Sexuality*, 27. See also Laura Mulrey, "Visual Pleasure and Narrative Cinema," *Screen* 16 (Autumn 1975), and Teresa De Laurentis, *Alice Doesn't: Feminism, Semiotics, Cinema* (Bloomington: Indiana University Press, 1984).

[52]Such passages run throughout *My Bondage and My Freedom*. Even in the series of appendices to the text, Douglass keeps his focus riveted on the violation of the slave woman's body. In "Letter to His Old Master" [Thomas Auld], for example, he writes: "When I saw the slave-driver whip a slave-woman, cut the blood out of her neck, and heard her piteous cries, I went away into the corner of the fence, wept and pondered over the mystery." He then asks Auld how he would feel if his daughter were seized and left "unprotected—a degraded victim to the brutal lust of fiendish overseers, who would pollute, blight, and blast the fair soul . . . destroy her virtue, and annihilate in her person all the grace that adorns the character of virtuous womanhood?" (427–28).

[53]See Susanne Kappeler, *The Pornography of Representation* (Minneapolis: University of Minnesota, 1986), 104.

the women are tied up—the classic stance of women in pornography—and
unable to resist, the men are "free," if you like, to struggle. William Demby is
a case in point. After Mr. Gore whips him, Demby runs to the creek and
refuses to obey the overseer's commands to come out. Demby finally asserts
the power over his own body, even though it costs him his life.

But clearly the most celebrated whipping scene of all is Douglass's two-
hour-long fight with Covey, on which the 1845 *Narrative* pivots. Positioned
roughly midway through the text, it constitutes also the midway point between slavery and freedom. This explains in part why the fight is dramatized
and elaborated over several pages, an allotment clearly disproportionate to
other reported episodes. When the fight is over, Douglass boasts that Covey
"had drawn no blood from me, but I had from him" and expresses satisfaction
at "repell[ing] by force the bloody arm of slavery." He concludes, "I had
several fights, but was never whipped" (81–83).

The fight with Covey is the part of the *Narrative* most frequently antholo-
gized, and it is a rare critical text indeed that ignores this scene. I agree with
Donald Gibson that "most commentators on the conflict have . . . interpreted
it as thought it were an arena boxing match." Gibson attributes such a view to
what he terms the "public focus" of Douglass's narrative, "which requires that
the slave defeat the slaveholder."[54] I would add to Gibson's explanation that
this defeat serves to incarnate a critical/political view that equates resistance
to power with physical struggle, a view that fails to see that such struggle
cannot function as the beginning and end of our understanding of power
relations.

The critical valorization of physical struggle and subsequent triumph and
control finds an interesting parallel in discussion of Douglass's narrative
struggles, among the most provocative being that of Robert Stepto in *From
Behind the Veil*. In discussing the relation of Douglass's *Narrative* to the
"authenticating" texts by William Garrison and Wendell Phillips, Stepto
argues that these ancillary texts seem on the surface to be "*at war* with
Douglass's tale for authorial control of the narrative as a whole."[55] While
Stepto grants that there is a tension among all three documents, Douglass's
"tale *dominates* the narrative because it alone authenticates the narrative"
[emphasis added].[56]

In examining the issue of authorial control more generally, Stepto argues:
"When a narrator wrests this kind of preeminent authorial control from the
ancillary voices in the narrative, we may say he controls the presentation of
his personal history, and that his tale is becoming autobiographical."[57] He

[54]Donald Gibson, "Reconciling Public and Private in Frederick Douglass's *Narrative*," *American Literature*, 57 (December 1985), 562.

[55]Robert Stepto, *From Behind the Veil: A Study of Afro-American Narrative* (Urbana· University of Illinois Press, 1979).

[56]Stepto, *From Behind*, 17.

[57]Stepto, *From Behind*, 25.

continues, "Authorial control of a narrative need not always result from an author's defeat of competing voices or usurpation of archetypes or pregeneric myths, but is usually occasioned by such acts. What may distinguish one literary history or tradition from another is not the issue of whether such battles occur, but that of who is competing with whom and over what."[58]

This competition for authorial control in African-American letters, Stepto argues, does not conform to the Bloomian Oedipal paradigm, for "the battle for authorial control has been more of a race ritual than a case of patricide."[59] Stepto is right to note that competition among African Americans is "rarely between artist and artist," but between "artist and authenticator (editor, publisher, guarantor, patron)."[60] Here, of course, Stepto could easily have inserted that these authenticators have generally been white males. Thus the battle for authorial control in Douglass's case was a battle between white and black males.

For Stepto, Douglass's ultimate control rests on his "extraordinary ability to pursue several types of writing with ease and with a degree of simultaneity."[61] But again, the explanation of Douglass's strength depends overmuch on a focus on style emptied of its contents. In other words, what is the "content" of Douglass's "syncretic phrasing," the "introspective analysis," the "participant observations" that make him a master stylist in Stepto's estimation? But, more important, does Douglass's "defeat" of competing white male voices enable him to find a voice distinct from theirs?

Since Douglass's authorial control is the logical outcome of his quest for freedom and literacy, one might approach that question from the angle of the thematics of literacy, of which much has been made by critics. Revealing perhaps more than he knew in the following passage, Douglass describes one of many scenes of stolen knowledge in the *Narrative*. Because his retelling of this episode is all the more suggestive in *My Bondage and My Freedom*, I've selected it instead. "When my mistress left me in charge of the house, I had a grand time; I got Master Tommy's copy books and a pen and ink, and, in the ample spaces between the lines, *I wrote other lines, as nearly like his as possible*" [172, emphasis added].[62]

This hand-to-hand combat between black and white men for physical, then narrative, control over bodies and texts raises the question of who is on whose side? For, in its allegiance to the dialectics of dominance and subordination, Douglass's *Narrative* is, and not surprisingly so, a by-product of Master Tommy's copybook, especially of its gendered division of power relations. The

[58]Stepto, *From Behind*, 45.
[59]Stepto, *From Behind*, 45.
[60]Stepto, *From Behind*, 45.
[61]Stepto, *From Behind*, 20.
[62]Compare this passage with the same scene in the 1845 *Narrative*: "When left thus, I used to spend the time in writing in the spaces left in Master Thomas's copy-book, copying what he had written. I continued to do this until I could write a hand very similar to that of Master Thomas. Thus, after a long, tedious effort of years, I finally succeeded in learning how to write" (58).

representation of women being whipped, in form and function, is only one major instance of this point but the representation of women, in general, shows Master Tommy's imprint.

Abounding in this copybook are conventional ideas of male subjectivity that exclude women from language. The scenes of reading are again cases in point. Throughout the narrative Douglass employs what Lillie Jugurtha aptly terms "eye dialogue." That is, he presents personal exchanges that have the appearance of dialogue without being dialogue. In the following account, Douglass describes the scene in which Mrs. Auld is ordered to cease teaching Frederick to read:

> Mr. Auld found out what was going on, and at once forbade Mrs. Auld to instruct me further, telling her, among other things, that it was unlawful, as well as unsafe, to teach a slave to read. To use his own words . . . he said, "If you give a nigger an inch, he will take an ell. . . . Learning would spoil the best nigger in the world . . . if you teach that nigger (speaking of myself) how to read, there would be no keeping him. It would forever unfit him to be a slave. He would at once become unmanageable, and of no value to his master. As to himself, it would do him no good, but a great deal of harm. It would make him discontented and unhappy." (49)

In glossing this passage, Jugurtha perceptively notices that "there is no second speaker presented here, no Lucretia Auld responding to her husband. . . . One pictures, though one does not hear, a husband and a wife talking. . . . Unobtrusively, perspectives are multiplied. Monologue functions as dialogue."[63] That Sophia Auld was regarded by Douglass early on as a substitute mother figure, links her erasure in the foregoing passage to the erasure of his biological mother in the first part of the 1845 *Narrative* and, by extension, to the erasure of the feminine. In this secular rewriting of the sacred text, Mrs. Auld is exiled from the scene of knowledge, of symbolic activity. As a woman she is not permitted "to teach or to have authority over men; she is to keep silent" (I Timothy 2:11–12).

What critics have learned from and done with Douglass has often constituted a correspondingly mimetic process where the feminine is concerned. In other words, the literary and interpretive history of the *Narrative* has, with few exceptions, repeated with approval its salient assumptions and structural paradigms. This repetition has, in turn, created a potent and persistent critical language that positions and repositions Douglass on top, that puts him in a position of priority. This ordering has not only helped to establish the dominant paradigm of African-American criticism, but it has also done much to establish the dominant view of African-American literary history. In that view, Douglass is, to borrow from James Olney, "the founding father" who "produced a kind of Ur-text of slavery and freedom that, whether individual

---

[63]Lillie Jugurtha, "Point of View in the Afro-American Slave Narratives by Douglass and Pennington," in John Sekora and Darwin Turner, eds., *The Art of Slave Narrative* (Western Illinois University, 1982), 113.

writers were conscious of imitating Douglass or not, would inform the Afro-American literary tradition from his time to the present."[64]

This dynastic model of Douglass and his progeny goes on ordering as if it were intrinsically inevitable and experientially real. According to Arna Bontemps, the *Narrative* contains "the spirit and vitality and the angle of vision responsible for the most effective prose writing by black American writers from William Wells Brown to Charles Chesnutt, from W. E. B. DuBois to Richard Wright, Ralph Ellison, and James Baldwin."[65] This model is being recast, but that recasting often takes the form of an annexation, and, not surprisingly, an annexation again of the feminine. Olney's otherwise brilliant essay is a case in point. His solution to the question of whether he would consider the implications of his literary history for an examination of black women was to attach a coda to the main body of the essay. There he writes,

> Putting aside the male exclusivity in the founding of the American nation and in the shaping of an Afro-American literary tradition (this latter taking the form in my essay of a line from Frederick Douglass, Booker T. Washington, W. E. B. Du Bois, and James Weldon Johnson down to Richard Wright, Malcolm X, Ralph Ellison, and beyond), it is interesting and timely to speculate on another line in Afro-American writing, composed of black women writers, a line that runs parallel to the Douglass-Washington-Wright-Ellison line but that also signifies on and revises that exclusively male tradition.

Here, black women from a postscript or a tailpiece, if you like, lying outside the ambit of Olney's discussion proper, outside the "proper," which is to say, the prior discussion. They constitute a separate (but equal?) tradition. Olney seems to be still within the logic of the primary and the secondary. Further, he begins to construct yet another genealogy, one of critics of African-American sons descending from stalwart fathers in a kind of typological unfolding. Their status as sons who can then be fathers is clear in the utterance of their complete "entitles." Olney notes that "a number of critics of Afro-American literature—Houston Baker, Jr., Henry Louis Gates, Jr., and Robert B. Stepto—to name only three—have demonstrated brilliantly that it is precisely this revisionary playing off against, or signifying on, previous texts that constitutes literary history and, specifically the Afro-American literary tradition."[66]

Olney's drawing of the circle around the literary and critical tradition is an act of male performance, of naming, of setting priorities. This act goes on ordering and reordering our conceptions of African-American literary history and of American literature more generally. In the efforts to revise or recon-

---

[64]Olney, "The Founding Fathers—Frederick Douglass and Booker T. Washington," in Deborah E. McDowell and Arnold Rampersad, eds., *Slavery and the Literary Imagination* (Baltimore: Johns Hopkins 1989), 81.

[65]Arna Bontemps, quoted in Charles Davis and Henry Louis Gates, Jr., eds., *The Slave's Narrative* (New York: Oxford University Press, 1985), xv.

[66]Olney, "The Founding Fathers," 20.

struct the so-called canon of American literature, Douglass's *Narrative* has been easily assimilated and given priority. Olney sees it as operating "both within and against the Franklinesque tradition."[67] Russell Reising sees the *Narrative* as "perhaps *the first* literary, political, and epistemological extension of ideas advanced in Emerson's major early essays."[68] And the editors of the second edition of *The Norton Anthology of American Literature* can be seen to have reinforced Reising's claims in their decision to reprint the 1845 *Narrative* in its entirety. Their preface to the text ends with the assertion that "[Douglass's] life, in fact, has become the heroic paradigm for all oppressed people."[69]

It is this choice of Douglass as "the first," as "representative man," as the part that stands for the whole, that reproduces the omission of women from view, except as afterthoughts different from "the same" (black men). And that omission is not merely an oversight, but given the discursive system that authorizes Douglass as the source and the origin, that omission is a necessity. But if, as Said suggests, " 'beginning' is an eminently renewable subject,"[70] then we can begin again. We can begin to think outside the model that circumscribes an entire literary history into a genetic model and conscripts Douglass in the interest of masculine power and desire. In other words, we might start by putting an end to beginnings, even those that would put woman in the first place.

IV

What we call the beginning is often the end
And to make an end is to make a beginning
The end is where we start from.

> —T. S. Eliot, "Little Gidding"

Because of the contingencies of history, particularly those that have produced "black women writers" as a discipline or discourse object, we might say that the formerly secondary (black women) have become primary. In the opening sentence of his foreword to the excellent and timely Schomburg Library of Nineteenth-Century Black Women Writers, Henry Louis Gates, Jr., proclaims a new beginning: "The birth of the Afro-American literary tradition occurred in 1773, when Phillis Wheatley published a book of poetry."[71] Aptly titling his essay, "In Her Own Write," Gates goes on: "[that]

---

[67]Olney, "The Founding Fathers," 3.

[68]Russell Reising, *The Unusable Past: Theory and the Study of American Literature* (New York: Methuen, 1986), 257.

[69]Ronald Gottesman, *et al.*, eds., *The Norton Anthology of American Literature*, 2nd ed., vol. 1 (New York: W. W. Norton, 1985), 1867.

[70]Said, *Beginnings*, 38.

[71]Henry Louis Gates, Jr., "In Her Own Write," foreword to *The Schomburg Library Series of Nineteenth-Century Black Women Writers* (New York: Oxford University Press, 1988), xi.

the progenitor of the black literary tradition was a woman means, in the most strictly literal sense, that all subsequent black writers have evolved in a matrilinear line of descent" that includes Ann Plato, "the *first* Afro-American to publish a book of essays (1841)," Harriet E. Wilson, "the *first* black person to publish a novel in the United States (1859)," and Anna Julia Cooper, who "*first* analyzed the fallacy of referring to 'the black man' when speaking of black people" [emphases added].[72]

Gates does well to note that "despite this pioneering role of black women in the tradition," "many of their contributions before this century have been all but lost or unrecognized."[73] Seeking to redress this imbalance, he declares that the voices of black women must be uttered and to them we must listen. Indeed, such an appeal should not go and has not gone unheeded, but it need not hinge on a declaration of priority or firstness, a declaration allied to the very discourse and dialectic of dominance and subordination critiqued in the writing of so many black women.

If a genealogical model is to be used to explain the tradition of Afro-American literature and to explore either Douglass's or Wheatley's originary place within it, then such an exploration might begin with a reformulation or refocusing of genealogy as a concept of analysis. Such a reformulation would place greater emphasis on these authors' emergence as discourse objects than on determining either's priority in the tradition. Pursuing the former, we might ask, what has made Frederick Douglass so sacred a text with such overpowering influence and cultural authority? At whose expense and for whose gain has he been so made? What current situation enables his displacement by Phillis Wheatley, to some the now-reinstated "representative" black writer? In other words, the process of cultural production involved in making Douglass and Wheatley, or, for that matter, any "first" or "prior" figure, and the uses to which that production has been put, is the most urgent, "genealogical" task.

Happily, such work has already begun. Though it still operates within the logic of first and second, one forthcoming essay by Henry Louis Gates is an example. Gates examines the abolitionist press and traces the process by which Frederick Douglass "as a standard bearer of Negro creativity and cultivation was marked by the simultaneous eclipse of the previously favored exemplar, Phillis Wheatley."[74] After the publication of Douglass's 1845 *Narrative*, Wheatley disappeared almost completely from the abolitionist press, a disappearance not unrelated to the cultural identification of "manliness" with exemplariness.[75] Such an examination helps to redirect the conceptual metho-

---

[72]Gates, "In Her Own," xiii.

[73]Gates, "In Her Own," xi.

[74]Henry Louis Gates, Jr., "From Wheatley to Douglass: The Politics of Displacement," in Eric Sundquist, ed., *Frederick Douglass: New Literary and Historical Essays* (Cambridge: Cambridge University Press, 1991), 47–65.

[75]Also in the Sundquist volume is an essay by Richard Yarborough, titled "Race, Violence, and Manhood: The Masculine Ideal in Frederick Douglass's 'The Heroic Slave.'" 166–188. Yarborough subtly examines the connection that Douglass attempts to establish between manhood and violent resistance in Douglass's novel.

dologies and categories applied to the Afro-American literary tradition, particularly in discussions of the slave narrative. While the genre has been mainly examined taxonomically, that is, with a focus on its discrete, formal characteristics, a reconfigured genealogical model would examine the historical and cultural function of the slave narrative, both in the moment of its emergence and in contemporary scholarly discourse.

The cultural function of the slave narrative as genre and its relations to the inscription of gendered ideologies of masculinity and femininity represents a reordering of priorities in Afro-American literary study. With that shift we can begin to change the sequence and possibly set a new course for arrangements of gender and genre alike. Then, we will be able to rewrite the last lines of that familiar doxology: as it was in the beginning is now and ever shall be, world without end, Amen, Amen.

"Hear My Voice,
Ye Careless Daughters"

Narratives of Slave and Free Women
before Emancipation

Hazel V. Carby

A survey of the general terrain of images and stereotypes produced by antebellum sexual ideologies is a necessary but only preliminary contribution to understanding how the ideology of true womanhood influenced and, to a large extent, determined the shape of the public voice of black women writers. What remains to be considered is how an ideology that excluded black women from the category "women" affected the ways in which they wrote and addressed an audience. The relevance of this question extends beyond the writing of slave narratives, and I will first examine texts written by free black women living in the North before turning to a slave narrative, Harriet Jacobs's *Incidents in the Life of a Slave Girl.*

In 1850, Nancy Prince published in Boston her *Life and Travels.* A free woman, Nancy Prince declared that her object in writing was not "a vain desire to appear before the public"; on the contrary, her book was the product of her labor by which she hoped to sustain herself. In other words, Prince regarded her writing as her work. The publication of her *Life and Travels* was the occasion for an assertion of Prince's intention to retain and maintain her independence:

> The Almighty God our heavenly father has designed that we eat our bread by the sweat of our brow; that all-wise and holy Being has designed and requires of us that we be diligent, using the means, that with his blessing we may not be burdensome, believing we shall be directed and go through.[1]

But this statement was double-edged: it was at once an assertion of her present condition and a comment on her history which was retold in the main body of the text. Prince's assertion appealed to the values of the "Protestant

[1]Nancy Prince, *A Narrative of the Life and Travels of Mrs. Nancy Prince. Written by Herself* (Boston: by the author, 1850), preface. Page numbers will be given parenthetically in the text.

ethic," while the opening pages of her text were an apt demonstration of economic racial discrimination; however hard the young Nancy and her family labored in the North, the fruits of that society were not granted to them. At fourteen years old, Nancy replaced a sick friend in service and "thought herself fortunate" to be with a religious family, as she herself had received religious instruction and had been taught "right from wrong" by her grand-father. Prince recounted the details of her arduous duties and cruel treatment and then interrogated the hypocritical religion of her employers:

> Hard labor and unkindness were too much for me; in three months, my health and strength were gone. I often looked at my employers, and thought to myself, is this your religion? I did not wonder that the girl who had lived there previous to myself, went home to die. They had family prayers, morning and evening. Oh! yes, they were sanctimonious! I was a poor stranger, but fourteen years of age, imposed upon by these good people. (11–12)

After seven years of "anxiety and toil," Prince married and went to live in Russia, where her husband was employed and where there was "no prejudice against color" (20–23). Prince established her international perspective in a section which detailed life in Russia and then condemned the racism which permeated the United States, North and South. In a direct address to her audience, which Prince considered to be primarily a Northern readership, she described how, upon her return to her own country, "the weight of prejudice . . . again oppressed [her]," even while she retained her belief in ultimate justice:

> God has in all ages of the world punished every nation and people for their sins. The sins of my beloved country are not hid from his notice; his all-seeing eye sees and knows the secrets of all hearts; the angels that kept not their first estate but left their own habitations, he hath reserved in everlasting chains unto the great day. (43)

By extending the logic of religious conviction, Prince revealed the hypocrisy at the heart of American society. Her thinly veiled threat of revenge gained additional power from her earlier, obviously sympathetic response to those she had witnessed rebelling against the injustices of Russian society.

The dignity and power of Prince's narrative was gained from her position at once inside and outside the society she wished to condemn. Her narrative voice was given strength through her presentation of herself as a true practitioner of Christian principles who was able to comment on the hypocriti-cal attitudes and forms of behavior that she saw practiced throughout the country. Prince used her knowledge of other societies to compare and contrast with her own. Somewhat ironically, she commented that she "may not see as clearly as some" because of the weight of oppression, but, of course, this rhetorical device revealed exactly how appropriate a witness and how effective a narrator of racist practices she was (42). Prince made clear her double position inside U.S. society as a citizen and outside it as an outcast because of her color; her final narrative position, however, was above "this world's tumultuous noise," at the side of the ultimate judge (89).

In her narrative, one action in particular used, but also questioned, a fundamental attribute of true womanhood: the possession of sexual purity. Having discovered that her eldest sister had been "deluded away" into a brothel and become a prostitute, Prince responded: "[t]o have heard of her death, would not have been so painful to me, as we loved each other very much" (12). This statement was in accord with conventional expectations of the importance of sexual purity; death was easier to accept than loss of virtue. However, Prince did not continue to follow the conventional pattern of regarding her sister as "lost" forever but searched for, found, and rescued her. Far from seizing the narrative opportunity to condemn her sister, Prince claimed her "soul as precious" and revealed the contradiction of a sexual ideology that led her sister to feel she was neither "fit to live, nor fit to die." Returning her sister to the bosom of a family Prince declared not shame but a sense of "victory" (13–16). As author, Prince used the structure of spiritual autobiography not to conform to a conventional representation of experience but to begin to question the limits of those conventions as they contradicted aspects of her own experience. *A Narrative of the Life and Travels of Mrs. Nancy Prince. Written by Herself* is an early example of a black woman who attempted to use a conventional narrative form, spiritual autobiography, in unconventional ways.[2] Princes's adoption of a public voice assumed and asserted the authority of her experience.

The conviction that writing was work was attested to by another free black woman, Harriet Wilson, in her narrative *Our Nig; or, Sketches from the Life of a Free Black* (1859).[3] A comparison of Wilson's motives for writing with those of Prince is fruitful. Wilson stated in her preface:

> In offering to the public the following pages, the writer confesses her inability to minister to the refined and cultivated, the pleasure supplied by abler pens. It is not for such these crude narrations appear. Deserted by kindred, disabled by failing health, I am forced to some experiment which shall aid me in maintaining myself and my child without extinguishing this feeble life.

Prince established that her book was the product of her labor, and Wilson appealed to her audience to buy her narrative as a product of her labor so that she and her son could survive. But, unlike Prince, Wilson sought her patronage not from a white Northern audience but from her "colored brethren."

---

[2]See the recent edition of *The Life and Religious Experience of Jarena Lee; Memoirs of the Life, Religious Experience, Ministerial Travels and Labors of Mrs. Zilpha Elaw; and A Brand Plucked from the Fire: An Autobiographical Sketch by Mrs. Julia A. J. Foote*, in William L. Andrews, ed., *Sisters of the Spirit: Three Black Women's Autobiographies of the Nineteenth Century* (Bloomington: Indiana University Press, 1986).

[3]Harriet E. Wilson, *Our Nig; or, Sketches from the Life of a Free Black, in a Two-Story White House, North. Showing That Slavery's Shadows Fall Even There*, introduction by Henry Louis Gates, Jr. (Boston: by the author, 1859; reprint New York: Random House, 1983). References are to the 1983 edition; page numbers will be given parenthetically in the text.

Wilson attempted to gain authority for her public voice through a narrative that shared its experience with a black community which she addressed as if it were autonomous from the white community in which it was situated.

In his introduction to Wilson's text, Henry Louis Gates, Jr., calls it the first novel by a black writer because of its use of the plot conventions of sentimental novels (xiii). But the use of these particular conventions can be found not only in the novel but also in many slave narratives. I would argue that *Our Nig* can be most usefully regarded as an allegory of a slave narrative, a "slave" narrative set in the "free" North. The first indication of the possibility of an allegorical reading occurs in the subtitle, "Sketches from the Life of a Free Black, in a Two-Story White House, North. Showing That Slavery's Shadows Fall Even There." Wilson used her voice as a black woman addressing a black audience to condemn racism in the North and criticize abolitionists. This placed Wilson in a position similar to that of Prince, both inside and outside the society subject to critique. Whereas Prince gained narrative dignity and power from her experience of other countries, her outcast status, and her "true" religious principles, Wilson's narrative authority derived from an assertion of independence from the patronage of the white community. Her narrative was written apart from any links to the abolitionist movement, and her direct appeal to the black community marginalized a white readership.

The "two-story white house" can be interpreted initially as the equivalent of the Southern plantation, in which the protagonist, Frado, was held in virtual slavery. Scenes of punishment and brutality, whippings, and beatings were evoked, as in a conventional slave narrative, to document the relentless suffering and persecution to which the slave was subject. The Northern house, like its Southern counterpart, was the sovereign territory of a tyrant, ruled by a mistress whom Wilson described as being "imbued with *southern principles*" (preface). Mrs. Bellmont, the white mistress, was described as having power over the whole family—husband, sons, daughters, and Frado— and was symbolic of the power of the South. The domestic realm, within which Wilson represented Mrs. Bellmont as the ultimate power, was the terrain of struggle over the treatment of Frado in which debates about the position and future of blacks in the United States are re-created. Sensitivity and compassion were to be found in some members of the family, including Mr. Bellmont and one of his sons, but their protests were ignored; the power of the mistress, like the power of the South, was never effectively challenged. The actions of Mrs. Bellmont determine and structure the overall pattern of her slave's life in the house; a house which increasingly resembles the nation, as the resolve of Mrs. Bellmont's opponents to improve Frado's conditions disintegrated at the slightest possibility of conflict. Mr. Bellmont was portrayed as preferring to leave the house to the tyrannical rages of his wife, hiding until the recurring ruptures receded and Frado had again been punished. In a close resemblance to the position of many abolitionists, Mr. Bellmont and his son offered sympathy and loud protestations but were unwilling to assert the moral superiority of their position by fighting the mistress, the South, and imposing an alternative social order. Both men merely dressed Frado's wounds and turned their backs when battles were renewed. The two-story house was an allegory for the divided nation in which the object of controversy and subject of oppression was *Our Nig*. Like Prince, Wilson gained her narrative authority from adapting literary conventions to more adequately conform to a narrative representation and re-creation of black experience. It is important to identify the source of many of these conventions in the sentimental novel and also to recognize that Wilson's particular use of sentimental conventions derives from the sentimental novel via slave narratives to produce a unique allegorical form. That *Our Nig* did not conform to the parameters of contemporary domestic fiction can be attributed to this cultural blend.

The issue of conformity to conventions has been linked to questions concerning the authenticity of slave narratives by historians, particularly in the case of Harriet Jacobs's narrative, *Incidents in the Life of a Slave Girl* (1861).[4] Arguing, convincingly, that historians need to recognize both the "uniqueness" and the "representativeness" of the slave narrative, John Blassingame, in *The Slave Community*, concluded that Jacobs's narrative is inauthentic because it does not conform to the guidelines of representativeness.[5] Blassingame questioned the narrative's orderly framework and the use of providential encounters and continued:

> the story is too melodramatic: miscegenation and cruelty, outraged virtue, unrequited love, and planter licentiousness appear on practically every page. The virtuous Harriet sympathizes with her wretched mistress who has to look on all of the mulattoes fathered by her husband, she refuses to bow to the lascivious demands of her master, bears two children for another white man, and then runs away and hides in a garret in her grandmother's cabin for seven years until she is able to escape to New York. . . . In the end, all live happily ever after.[6]

With regard to internal evidence and the question of the authority of the public voice, the critique that Blassingame offers focuses heavily, though perhaps unconsciously, on the protagonist, Linda Brent, as conventional heroine.

In comparing slave narratives to each other, historians and literary critics have relied on a set of unquestioned assumptions that interrelate the quest for freedom and literacy with the establishment of manhood in the gaining of the published, and therefore public, voice. The great strength of these autobiog-

---

[4]Harriet Jacobs, [Linda Brent], *Incidents in the Life of a Slave Girl, Written by Herself*, L. Maria Child, ed. (Boston: for the author, 1861). A paperback edition with an introduction by Walter Teller was published in New York by Harcourt Brace Jovanovich in 1973; the pages cited in parentheses are in this edition.

[5]John Blassingame, "Critical Essay on Sources," *The Slave Community: Plantation Life in the Antebellum South*, 2nd ed. (New York: Oxford University Press, 1979), pp. 367–82.

[6]Ibid., p. 373.

raphies, Blassingame states, is that, unlike other important sources, they embody the slaves' own perception of their experiences. Yet it is taken for granted that this experience, which is both unique and representative, is also male:

> If historians seek to provide some understanding of the past experiences of slaves, then the autobiography must be their point of departure; in the autobiography, more clearly than in any other source, we learn what went on in the minds of *black men*. It gives us a window to the "inside half" of the slave's life which never appears in the commentaries of "outsiders." Autobiographers are generally so preoccupied with conflict, those things blocking their hopes and dreams, that their works give a freshness and vitality to history which is often missing in other sources.[7]

The criteria for judgment that Blassingame advances here leave no room for a consideration of the specificity and uniqueness of the black female experience. An analogy can be made between Blassingame's criticism of *Incidents* as melodrama and the frequency with which issues of miscegenation, unrequited love, outraged virtue, and planter licentiousness are found foregrounded in diaries by Southern white women, while absent or in the background of the records of their planter husbands. Identifying such a difference should lead us to question and consider the significance of these issues in the lives of women as opposed to men, not to the conclusion that the diaries by women are not credible because they deviate from the conventions of male-authored texts. Any assumption of the representativeness of patriarchal experience does not allow for, or even regard as necessary, a gender-specific form of analysis. Indeed, the criteria chosen by Blassingame as the basis for his dismissal of the narrative credibility of Jacobs's narrative are, ideologically, the indicators of a uniquely female perspective.

Jean Fagan Yellin, a literary historian, critic, and biographer of Jacobs, has (from external evidence) established the authenticity of Jacobs's narrative.[8] Jacobs wrote under the pseudonym Linda Brent. *Incidents in the Life of a Slave Girl* was first published in Boston in 1861, under the editorship of Lydia Maria Child, and a year later it appeared in a British edition.[9] In the discussion that follows, the author will be referred to as Jacobs, but, to

---

7Ibid., p. 367 (emphasis added).

8This evidence has focused on the discovery of a collection of Jacobs's letters to Amy Post held in the Post family papers at the University of Rochester library. See Dorothy Sterling, ed., *We Are Your Sisters: Black Women in the Nineteenth Century* (New York: W. W. Norton, 1984); and Jean Yellin, "Written by Herself: Harriet Jacobs' Slave Narrative," *American Literature* 53 (November 1981): 479–86; [Yellin], "Texts and Contexts of Harriet Jacobs' *Incidents in the Life of a Slave Girl: Written by Herself*," in Charles T. Davis and Henry Louis Gates, Jr., eds., *The Slave's Narrative* (New York: Oxford University Press, 1985), pp. 262–82; and her introduction to a new annotated edition of *Incidents in the Life of a Slave Girl* (Cambridge: Harvard University Press, 1987). Yellin has also verified details of Jacobs's life in Edenton, North Carolina, and is preparing to write her biography.

9Harriet Jacobs, [Linda Brent], *The Deeper Wrong: Or, Incidents in the Life of a Slave Girl, Written by Herself*, L. Maria Child, ed. (London: W. Tweedie, 1862).

preserve narrative continuity, the pseudonym Linda Brent will be used in the analysis of the text and protagonist.

Incidents in the Life of a Slave Girl is the most sophisticated, sustained narrative dissection of the conventions of true womanhood by a black author before emancipation. It will be the object of the following analysis to demonstrate that Jacobs used the material circumstances of her life to critique conventional standards of female behavior and to question their relevance and applicability to the experience of black women. Prior to a close examination of the text itself, it is necessary to document briefly the conditions under which Jacobs wrote her autobiography and gained her public voice.

At the time of writing, Jacobs worked as a domestic servant for and lived with Nathaniel P. Willis and his second wife, the Mr. and Mrs. Bruce of the text. Unlike either his first or second wife, Nathaniel Willis was proslavery. Against Jacobs's wishes but to protect her from the fugitive slave law, the second Mrs. Willis persuaded her husband that Jacobs should be purchased from her owners and manumitted by the family. Because of her suspicions of Nathaniel Willis, Jacobs did not want him to be aware that she was writing of her life in slavery; the need for secrecy and the demands of her domestic duties as nurse to the Willis children forced Jacobs to write at night.[10] Jacobs recognized that the conditions under which she lived and wrote were very different from those under which other female authors were able to write and under which her audience, "the women of the North," lived. In her preface, Linda Brent stated:

> Since I have been at the North, it has been necessary for me to work diligently for my own support, and the education of my children. This has not left me much leisure to make up for the loss of early opportunities to improve myself; and it has compelled me to write these pages at irregular intervals, whenever I could snatch an hour from Household duties. (xiii)

Unlike her white female audience or contemporary authors, Jacobs had neither the advantages of formal education nor contemplative leisure. She contrasted both her past life as a slave and her present condition, in which the selling of her labor was a prime necessity, with the social circumstances of her readership. Jacobs thus established the context within which we should understand her choice of epigram, from Isaiah (32:2): "Rise up, ye women that are at ease! Hear my voice, Ye careless daughters! Give ear unto my speech" (iv). Jacobs had achieved her freedom from slavery, but she was still bound to labor for the existence of herself and her children.

The closing pages of *Incidents* contrasted the "happy endings" of the conventional domestic novel with the present condition of the narrator, Linda Brent:

> Reader, my story ends with freedom; not in the usual way with marriage. . . . We are as free from the power of slaveholders as are the white people of the north; and

[10]For Jacobs on Willis, see Yellin, "Texts and Contexts," pp. 265, 279n.

though that, according to my ideas, is not saying a great deal, it is a vast improvement in *my* condition. (207)

Contrary to Blassingame's interpretation, *Incidents* does not conform to the conventional happy ending of the sentimental novel. Linda Brent, in the closing pages of her narrative, was still bound to a white mistress.

Jacobs's position as a domestic servant contrasted with the lives of the white women who surrounded and befriended her. Mrs. Willis, though she was instrumental in gaining her manumission, had the power to buy her and remained her employer, her mistress. Jacobs's letters to Amy Post, although to a friend, revealed her consciousness of their different positions in relation to conventional moral codes. Desiring a female friend who would write some prefatory remarks to her narrative, Jacobs consulted Post, but the occasion led her to indicate that the inclusion of her sexual history in her narrative made her "shrink from asking the sacrifice from one so good and pure as yourself."[11] It was as if Jacobs feared that her own history would contaminate the reputation of her white friend. Lydia Maria Child, who became Jacobs's editor, and Harriet Beecher Stowe, with whom Jacobs had an unfortunate brush, were both described by her as "satellite[s] of so great magnitude."[12] This hierarchy in Jacobs's relations with white women was magnified through the lens of conventional ideas of true womanhood when they appeared in print together, for Jacobs's sexuality was compromised in the very decision to print her story and gain her public voice. As she wrote to Post, after Post had agreed to endorse her story, "Woman can whisper her cruel wrongs into the ear of a very dear friend much easier than she can record them for the world to read."[13] Jacobs had children but no husband and no home of her own. In order to be able to represent herself in conventional terms as a "true" woman, Jacobs should have had a husband to give meaning to her existence as a woman. [A]ny power or influence a woman could exercise was limited to the boundaries of the home. Linda Brent, in the concluding chapter of her narrative, recognized that this particular definition of a woman's sphere did not exist for her, and this factor ensured her dependence on a mistress. She stated, "I do not sit with my children in a home of my own. I still long for a hearthstone of my own, however humble. I wish it for my children's sake far more than my own" (207).

The ideological definition of the womanhood and motherhood of Linda Brent (and Jacobs) remained ambivalent as Linda Brent (and Jacobs) were excluded from the domain of the home, the sphere within which womanhood and motherhood were defined. Without a "woman's sphere," both were rendered meaningless. Nevertheless, the narrative of Linda Brent's life stands as an exposition of her womanhood and motherhood contradicting and trans-

---

11Jacobs to Post, May 18 and June 18 (1857?), cited in Yellin, "Written by Herself," pp. 485–86.
12Jacobs to Post, October 8 (1860?), in ibid., p. 483.
13Jacobs to Post, June 21 (1857?), cited in Yellin, "Texts and Contexts," p. 269.

forming an ideology that could not take account of her experience. The structure of Jacobs's narrative embodied the process through which the meaning of Linda Brent's and Jacobs's motherhood and womanhood were revealed. Jacobs, as author, confronted an ideology that denied her very existence as a black woman and as a mother, and, therefore, she had to formulate a set of meanings that implicitly and fundamentally questioned the basis of true womanhood. *Incidents* demystified a convention that appeared as the obvious, commonsense rules of behavior and revealed the concept of true womanhood to be an ideology, not a lived set of social relations as she exposed its inherent contradictions and inapplicability to her life.[14]

Jacobs rejected a patronizing offer by Harriet Beecher Stowe to incorporate her life story into the writing of *The Key to Uncle Tom's Cabin*. This incorporation would have meant that her history would have been circumscribed by the bounds of convention, and Jacobs responded that "it needed no romance." The suggestion that Stowe might write, and control, the story of Jacobs's life raised issues far greater than those which concerned the artistic and aesthetic merit of her narrative; Jacobs "felt denigrated as a mother, betrayed as a woman, and threatened as a writer by Stowe's action."[15] Jacobs knew that to gain her own public voice, as a writer, implicated her very existence as a mother and a woman; the three could not be separated. She also knew from experience, as did Prince and Wilson, that the white people of the North were not completely free from the power of the slaveholders, or from their racism. To be bound to the conventions of true womanhood was to be bound to a racist, ideological system.

Many slave authors changed the names of people and places in their narratives to protect those still subject to slavery. However, Jacobs's need for secrecy in the act of writing and her fear of scorn if discovered meant that her pseudonym, Linda Brent, functioned as a mechanism of self-protection. The creation of Linda Brent as a fictional narrator allowed Jacobs to manipulate a series of conventions that were not only literary in their effects but which also threatened the meaning of Jacobs's social existence. The construction of the history of Linda Brent was the terrain through which Jacobs had to journey in order to reconstruct the meaning of her own life as woman and mother. The journey provided an alternative path to the cult of true womanhood and challenged the readers of *Incidents* to interrogate the social and ideological structures in which they were implicated and to examine their own racism. Jacobs denied that she wrote to "excite sympathy" for her own "sufferings" but claimed that she wanted to "arouse the women of the North to a realizing

---

[14]I am grateful to Jean Yellin for reading an earlier draft of this chapter and helping me clarify my ideas. Yellin argues that "Jacobs' narrator dramatizes the failure of her efforts to adhere to the sexual patterns she had been taught to endorse . . . and tentatively reaches toward an alternative moral code" ("Texts and Contexts," pp. 270–71). I am arguing that this alternative is the development of a discourse of black womanhood and that, far from being tentative, this movement away from the ideology of true womanhood is assertive.

[15]Yellin, "Written by Herself," p. 482.

sense of the condition of two millions of women at the South, still in bondage, suffering what I suffered, and most of them far worse" (xiv). Jacobs established that hers was the voice of a representative black female slave, and in a contemporary interpretation this appeal is defined as being an appeal to the sisterhood of all women:

> Seen from this angle of vision, Jacobs' book—reaching across the gulf separating black women from white, slave from free, poor from rich, reaching across the chasm separating "bad" women from "good"—represents an attempt to establish an American sisterhood and to activate that sisterhood in the public arena.[16]

However, these bonds of sisterhood are not easily or superficially evoked. "Sisterhood" between white and black women was realized rarely in the text of *Incidents*. Jacobs's appeal was to a potential rather than an actual bonding between white and black women. The use of the word *incidents* in the title of her narrative directs the reader to be aware of a consciously chosen selection of events in Jacobs's life.[17] Many of the relationships portrayed between Linda Brent and white women involve cruelty and betrayal and place white female readers in the position of having to realize their implication in the oppression of black women, prior to any actual realization of the bonds of "sisterhood."

The narrative was framed by Linda Brent's relationships to white mistresses. The relationship to Mrs. Willis with which the narrative concluded has already been discussed. The opening chapter, "Childhood," described Linda's early disillusion with a mistress whom she loved and trusted. Linda's early childhood was happy, and only on the death of her mother did Linda learn that she was a slave. *Sister* and *sisterhood* were made ambiguous terms for relationships which had dubious consequences for black women. Early in the text Linda referred to her mother and her mother's mistress as "foster sisters" because they were both fed at the breast of Linda's grandmother. This intimate "sisterhood" as babes was interrupted by the intervention of the starkly contrasting hierarchy of their social relationship. Linda's grandmother, the readers were told, had to wean her own daughter at three months old in order to provide sufficient food for her mistress's daughter. Although they played together as children, Linda's mother's slave status was reasserted when she had to become "a most faithful servant" to her "foster sister." At the side of the deathbed of Linda's mother, her mistress promised her that "her children [would] never suffer for anything" in the future. Linda described her subsequent childhood with this mistress as "happy," without "toilsome or disagreeable duties." A diligent slave, Linda felt "proud to labor for her as much as my young years would permit," and she maintained a heart "as free from care as that of any free born white child" (4–5).

16Yellin, "Texts and Contexts," p. 276.
17See the discussion of incidents in relation to plot in Nina Baym, *Novels, Readers and Reviewers: Responses to Fiction in Antebellum America* (Ithaca: Cornell University Press, 1984), pp. 75–79.

Unlike Kate Drumgoold in *A Slave Girl's Story,* [Brooklyn, N.Y., 1898], Linda Brent did not attempt to replace this mistress as surrogate mother. The phrase carefully chosen by Jacobs was "almost like a mother." The juxtaposition of the concepts of a carefree childhood with laboring registered an experience alien to that of the readership. This gentle disturbance to middle-class ideas of childhood moved toward a climactic shock at the death of the mistress, when Linda was bequeathed to the daughter of her mistress's sister. Linda and her community of friends had been convinced that she would be freed, but, with bitterness, Linda recalled the years of faithful servitude of her mother and her mistress's promise to her mother. In a passage that used a narrative strategy similar to that used by Prince in her *Life and Travels,* Jacobs's narrator indicted the behavior of her mistress according to conventional moral codes. Linda Brent reasserted the religious doctrine espoused by her mistress to condemn her action and reveal the hypocrisy of her beliefs:

> My mistress had taught me the precepts of God's word: "Thou shalt love thy neighbor as thyself." "Whatsoever ye would that men should do unto you, do ye even so unto them." But I was her slave, and I suppose she did not recognize me as her neighbor. (6)

The disparity between "almost a mother" and the lack of recognition as "neighbor" highlighted the intensity of Jacobs's sense of betrayal. Having taught her slave to read and spell, this mistress had contributed to the ability of Jacobs to tell her tale, but the story Jacobs told condemned the mistress, for it was her "act of injustice," that initiated the suffering in Linda Brent's life.

Because of the hierarchical nature of their social, as opposed to emotional, relationships, white mistresses in the text were placed in positions of power and influence over the course of the lives of slave women, an influence that was still being exerted at the close of the narrative after Linda's emancipation. Linda did not recount the actions of her mistress as if they were only an individual instance of betrayal but placed them within a history of acts of betrayal toward three generations of women in her family: herself, her mother, and her grandmother. Each served as faithful servant, each trusted to the honor of her mistress, and each was betrayed. The reconstruction of these acts through time and over generations was an attempt to assert their representative status within a historical perspective of dishonesty and hypocrisy.

The polarization between the lives of white sisters and black sisters was a recurring motif. The material differences in their lives that determined their futures and overwhelmed either biological relation or emotional attachment were continually stressed in the text. Linda Brent told the reader:

> I once saw two beautiful children playing together. One was a fair white child; the other was her slave, and also her sister. When I saw them embracing each other, and heard their joyous laughter, I turned sadly away from the lovely sight. I foresaw the inevitable blight that would fall on the little slave's heart. I knew how

soon her laughter would be changed to sighs. The fair child grew up to be a still fairer woman. From childhood to womanhood her pathway was blooming with flowers. . . . How had those years dealt with her slave sister, the little playmate of her childhood? She was also very beautiful; but the flowers and sunshine of love were not for her. She drank the cup of sin, and shame, and misery, whereof her persecuted race are compelled to drink. (28–29)

Any feminist history that seeks to establish the sisterhood of white and black women as allies in the struggle against the oppression of all women must also reveal the complexity of the social and economic differences between women. Feminist historiography and literary criticism also need to define the ways in which racist practices are gender-specific and sexual exploitation racialized. The dialectical nature of this process is reconstructed in the "incidents" that Jacobs reconstructed between the slave woman and her mistress.

Linda Brent described her second mistress, Mrs. Flint, in ways that utilized the conventions of an antebellum ideal of womanhood while exposing them as contradictory:

Mrs. Flint, like many southern women, was totally deficient in energy. She had not strength to superintend her household affairs; but her nerves were so strong, that she could sit in her easy chair and see a woman whipped, till the blood trickled from every stroke of the lash. (10)

Mrs. Flint forced Linda Brent to walk barefoot through the snow because the "creaking" of her new shoes "grated harshly on her refined nerves" (17). In these and other passages the conventional figure of the plantation mistress is ironically undermined. The qualities of delicacy of constitution and heightened sensitivity, attributes of the Southern lady, appear as a corrupt and superficial veneer that covers an underlying strength and power in cruelty and brutality.

Linda Brent realized that because of Dr. Flint's overt sexual advances and intentions, she represented an actual as well as potential threat to the dignity and pride of Mrs. Flint. Jacobs demonstrated the slave's capacity to analyze the grief and pain of her mistress; the slave, however, waited in vain for a reciprocal display of kindness or sympathy. The sisterhood of the two abused women could not be established, for Mrs. Flint, who "pitied herself as a martyr . . . was incapable of feeling for the condition of shame and misery in which her unfortunate, helpless slave was placed" (32).

In an attempt to appeal directly to the compassion of her white Northern readers, Jacobs contrasted the material conditions of black female slaves with their own lives:

O, you happy free women, contrast *your* New Year's day with that of the poor bond-woman! With you it is a pleasant season, and the light of the day is blessed. . . . Children bring their little offerings, and raise their rosy lips for a caress. They are your own, and no hand but that of death can take them from you. But to the slave mother New Year's day comes laden with peculiar sorrows. She sits on a cold cabin floor, watching the children who may all be torn from her the next morning; and often does she wish that she and they might die before the day dawns. (14)

Linda Brent was a demonstration of the consequences for motherhood of the social and economic relations of the institution of slavery. Jacobs recognized that plantation mistresses were subject to forms of patriarchal abuse and exploitation, but because they gave birth to the heirs of property they were also awarded a degree of patriarchal protection. Slave women gave birth to the capital of the South and were therefore, in Linda Brent's words, "considered of no value, unless they continually increase their owner's stock" (49). Upon this hierarchical differential in power relations an ideology was built which ensured that two opposing concepts of motherhood and womanhood were maintained. As Linda Brent argued, "that which commands admiration in the white woman only hastens the degradation of the female slave"(27). If a slave woman attempted to preserve her sexual autonomy, the economic system of slavery was threatened: "[I]t [was] deemed a crime in her to wish to be virtuous" (29).

The barriers to the establishment of the bonding of sisterhood were built in the space between the different economic, political, and social positions that black women and white women occupied in the social formation of slavery. Their hierarchical relationship was determined through a racial, not gendered, categorization. The ideology of true womanhood was as racialized a concept in relation to white women as it was in its exclusion of black womanhood. Ultimately, it was this racial factor that defined the source of power of white women over their slaves, for, in a position of dependence on the patriarchal system herself, the white mistress identified her interests with the maintenance of the status quo. Linda Brent concluded:

No matter whether the slave girl be as black as ebony or as fair as her mistress. In either case, there is no shadow of law to protect her from insult, from violence, or even from death; all these are inflicted by fiends who bear the shape of men. The mistress, who ought to protect the helpless victim, has no other feelings towards her but those of jealousy and rage. (26–27)

Jacobs thus identified that mistresses confirmed their own social position at the expense of denying the humanity of their slaves particularly when they were insecure in their own relation to patriarchal power: "I knew that the young wives of slaveholders often thought their authority and importance would be best established and maintained by cruelty" (94).

The Northern women who formed Jacobs's audience were implicated in the preservation of this oppression in two ways. In a passage that directly addressed the reader, Linda Brent accused Northerners of allowing themselves to be used as "bloodhounds" to hunt fugitives and return them to slavery (34–35). More subtly, Linda Brent also illustrated how Northerners were not immune to the effects of the slave system or to the influence of being able to wield a racist power when she described how, "when northerners go to the south to reside, they prove very apt scholars. They soon imbibe the sentiments and disposition of their neighbors, and generally go beyond their teachers. Of the two, they are proverbially the hardest masters" (44). *Incidents* also documented the numerous acts of racist oppression that Linda Brent had to suffer while in the Northern states. A major motive for her escape from the South was her determination to protect her daughter, Ellen, from the sexual exploitation she herself had experienced. However, Ellen was subject to sexual harassment in the household in which she lived and worked as a servant in New York, which made Linda Brent question the nature and extent of her freedom in the "free" states of the North. Described as being in a position of "servitude to the Anglo-Saxon race," Linda Brent urged the whole black community to defy the racism of Northerners, so that "eventually we shall cease to be trampled underfoot by our oppressors" (180–82).

This spirit of defiance characterized Jacobs's representations of all Linda Brent's encounters with her master. Conventional feminine qualities of submission and passivity were replaced by an active resistance. Although Flint had "power and law on his side," she "had a determined will," and "there was might in each." Her strength and resourcefulness to resist were not adopted from a reservoir of masculine attributes but were shown to have their source in her "woman's pride, and a mother's love for [her] children" (87). Thus, Jacobs developed an alternative set of definitions of womanhood and motherhood in the text which remained in tension with the cult of true womanhood.

The slave became the object of the jealousy and spite of her mistress; Jacobs wrote that Mrs. Flint even vented her anger on Linda Brent's grandmother for offering Linda and her children protective shelter: "She would not even speak to her in the street. This wounded my grandmother's feelings, for she could not retain ill will against the woman who she had nourished with her milk when a babe" (91). In an effective adaptation of convention it was Linda Brent's grandmother who was portrayed as a woman of genuine sensitivity. The two women were polarized: the grandmother exuded a "natural" warmth, but Mrs. Flint, as Jacobs's choice of name emphasized, displayed an unnatural, cold, and hard heart. For the grandmother, the act of nurturing gave rise to sustained feelings of intimacy; Mrs. Flint's rejection of this mothering relationship implied that she was an unnatural woman. Linda Brent stated that she was "indebted" to her grandmother for all her comforts, "spiritual or temporal" (9). It was the grandmother's labor that fed and clothed her when Mrs. Flint neglected her slave's material needs, and it was the grandmother who stood as the source of a strong moral code in the midst of an immoral system. In a considerable number of ways, Jacobs's figure of the grandmother embodied aspects of a *true* womanhood; she was represented as being pure and pious, a fountainhead of physical and spiritual sustenance for Linda, her whole family, and the wider black community. However, the quality of conventional womanhood that the grandmother did not possess was submissiveness, and Linda Brent was portrayed as having inherited her spirit. Her love for her grandmother was seen to be tempered by fear; she had been brought up to regard her with a respect that bordered on awe, and at the moment when Linda Brent needed the advice of another woman most desperately she feared to confide in her grandmother, who she knew would condemn her. Out of the moment of her most intense isolation Jacobs made her narrator forge her own rules of behavior and conduct of which even her grandmother would disapprove.

Dr. Flint was characterized by Jacobs as the epitome of corrupt white male power. He was a figure that was carefully dissected to reveal a lack of the conventional qualities of a gentleman. His lack of honor was established early in the text when he defrauded Linda Brent's grandmother. Presented as a representative slaveholder, Dr. Flint embodied the evil licentiousness that was the ultimate threat to virtue and purity. He whispered foul suggestions into Linda's ears when she was still an innocent girl and used his power to deny her the experience of romance, preventing her from marrying her first, true love. In the chapter entitled "The Lover," a free-born black carpenter was described as possessing the qualities that were absent in Dr. Flint. Honor was posed against dishonor, respect for Linda's virtue against disrespect and insult. The lover Jacobs described as both "intelligent and religious," while Dr. Flint appeared as an animal watching a young girl as his prey. The "base proposals of a white man" were contrasted with the "honorable addresses of a respectable colored man" (40–41). But, despite the fact that Dr. Flint was the embodiment of the corruption of the slave system, as his prey Linda Brent was not corrupted by him, and her struggle was an aggressive refusal to be sexually used and compromised or to succumb to the will of the master.

Instead, hoping to gain a degree of protection from Dr. Flint, Linda Brent decided to become the lover of a white "gentleman," a Mr. Sands. She thought that in his fury Dr. Flint would sell her to her newly acquired lover and that it would be easier in the future to obtain her freedom from her lover than from her master. Linda's reasoning was shown to be motivated by consideration not only for her own welfare but also for improving the chances of survival for any children she might bear. From her experience she knew that Dr. Flint sold his offspring from slave women and hoped that if her children were fathered by Sands he could buy them and secure their future.

The struggle of Linda Brent to retain some control over her sexuality climaxed in a confession of her loss of virtue. It was at this point in the narrative that Jacobs most directly confronted conventional morality. In order to retain narrative authority and to preserve a public voice acceptable to an antebellum readership, Jacobs carefully negotiated the tension between satisfying moral expectations and challenging an ideology that would condemn her as immoral. Jacobs's confession was at once both conventional and unconventional in form and tone. The narrator declared in a direct address to her readers that the remembrance of this period in her "unhappy life" filled her with "sorrow and shame" and made no reference to sexual satisfaction, love, or passion, as such feelings were not meant to be experienced or encouraged outside of marriage and were rarely figured to exist within it.[18] Yet Jacobs refused to follow convention in significant ways. In contrast to the expected pattern of a confessional passage, which called for the unconditional acceptance of the judgment of readers, Linda Brent's act of sexual defiance was described as one of "deliberate calculation": the slave actively chose one fate as opposed to another. Jacobs attempted to deflect any judgmental response of moral condemnation through consistent narrative reminders to the reader that the material conditions of a slave woman's life were different from theirs. Readers were the "happy women" who had been "free to choose the objects of [their] affection." Jacobs, through Linda Brent, claimed the same right in her attempt to assert some control over the conditions of her existence: "It seems less degrading to give one's self, than to submit to compulsion. There is something akin to freedom in having a lover who has no control over you, except that which he gains by kindness and attachment" (55). Jacobs argued that the practice of conventional principles of morality was rendered impossible by the condition of the slave. Her own decision to take a lover was not described as immoral or amoral but as outside conventional ethical boundaries. In a key passage for understanding the extent to which Jacobs challenged ideologies of female sexuality, Linda Brent reflected, "in looking back, calmly, on the events of my life, I feel that the slave woman ought not to be judged by the same standard as others"(56). Within the series of "incidents" that Jacobs represented, this decision was pivotal to the structure of the text and to the development of an alternative discourse of womanhood. Previous events focused on the disruption to a normative journey through childhood, girlhood, and romantic youth; following incidents established the unconventional definitions of womanhood and motherhood that Jacobs, herself, tried to determine.

Linda Brent's decision as a slave, to survive through an act that resulted in her loss of virtue, placed her outside the parameters of the conventional heroine. Barbara Welter has described how heroines who were guilty of a loss of purity, in novels or magazines, were destined for death or madness.[19] According to the doctrine of true womanhood, death itself was preferable to a loss of innocence; Linda Brent not only survived in her "impure" state, but she also used her "illicit" liaison as an attempt to secure a future for herself

[18]Nina Baym's observations on morality in novels and reviews of novels are enlightening in any consideration of the extent to which writers could challenge convention. See *Novels, Readers and Reviewers*, pp. 173–89, where she makes the argument that female sexuality was consistently policed by reviewers: "Two basic Victorian assumptions about female character—that women do not experience sexual desire and that they are naturally suited to monogamous marriage where they are the servants of their husbands, their children, and society at large—are here exposed as cultural constrictions whose maintenance requires constant surveillance, even to the supervision of novel reading" (183).

[19]Barbara Welter, *Dimity Convictions: The American Woman in the Nineteenth Century* (Columbus: Ohio University Press, 1976), p. 23.

and her children. Jacobs's narrative was unique in its subversion of a major narrative code of sentimental fiction: death, as preferable to loss of purity, was replaced by "Death is better than slavery" (63). *Incidents* entered the field of women's literature and history transforming and transcending the central paradigm of death versus virtue. The consequences of the loss of innocence, Linda Brent's (and Jacobs's) children, rather than being presented as the fruits of her shame, were her links to life and the motivating force of an additional determination to be free.

Linda Brent's second child was a girl, and the birth caused her to reflect on her daughter's possible future as a slave: "When they told me my new-born babe was a girl, my heart was heavier than it had ever been before. Slavery is terrible for men; but it is far more terrible for women. Superadded to the burden common to all, *they* have wrongs, and sufferings, and mortifications peculiarly their own" (79). The narrative that Jacobs wrote was assertively gender-specific and resonated against the dominant forms of the male slave narrative. But the sexual exploitation that Linda Brent confronted and feared for her daughter was, at the same moment, racially specific, disrupting conventional expectations of the attributes of a heroine. Death became the price that Linda Brent was prepared to pay to free her daughter from slavery: "I knew the doom that awaited my fair baby in slavery, and I determined to save her from it, or perish in the attempt." The slave mother made this vow by the graves of her parents, in the "burying-ground of the slaves," where "the prisoners rest together; they hear not the voice of the oppressor; the servant is free from his master" (92). Jacobs added the voice of her narrator to a history of slave rebels but at the same time completed a unique act. The transition from death as preferable to slavery to the stark polarity of freedom or death was made at this narrative moment. "As I passed the wreck of the old meeting house, where, before Nat Turner's time, the slaves had been allowed to meet for worship, I seemed to hear my father's voice come from it, bidding me not to tarry till I reached freedom or the grave" (93). Freedom replaced and transcended purity. Linda Brent's loss of innocence was a gain; she realized the necessity of struggling for the freedom of her children even more than for herself. Thus, the slave woman's motherhood was situated by Jacobs as the source of courage and determination.[20]

In order to save her children, Linda Brent apparently had to desert them. To precipitate a crisis and persuade Dr. Flint that he should sell the children to their father, Sands, Linda escaped and hid. The children were sold and returned to their great-grandmother's house to live, where, unknown to them, their mother was in hiding. However, Linda Brent's hopes for emancipation for her children were shattered when her daughter, Ellen, was "given" as a

---

[20]Jacobs intended that this note of rebellion be repeated in her final chapter which was about John Brown, but at the suggestion of Lydia Maria Child the chapter was dropped. Had it been retained, it would have strengthened this interpretation of the importance of the linking of freedom and death.

waiting maid to Sands's relatives in New York. After years in hiding, Linda escaped to New York and found employment. Her daughter was neglected, inadequately fed and clothed, and when Benjamin, her son, was finally sent north to join her, Linda realized that in order to protect her children she must own herself, freeing them all from the series of white people's broken promises that had framed her life.

Having obtained Ellen's freedom, Linda Brent confided her sexual history to her daughter as the one person whose forgiveness she desired. As opposed to the earlier confession, which was directly addressed to readers, Jacobs portrays Linda as in need of the unmediated judgment of Ellen. Ellen refused to condemn her mother and told her that she had been aware of her sexual relations with Sands, rejected her father as meaning nothing to her, and reserved her love for Linda. The motherhood that Jacobs defined and shaped in her narrative was vindicated through her own daughter, excluding the need for any approval from the readership. Jacobs bound the meaning and interpretation of her womanhood and motherhood to the internal structure of the text, making external validation unnecessary and unwarranted. Judgment was to be passed on the institution of slavery, not on deviations from conventions of true womanhood.

Jacobs gained her public voice and access to a sympathetic audience through the production of a slave narrative, a cultural form of expression supported and encouraged by the abolitionist movement. She primarily addressed the white Northern women whom she urged to advocate the abolition of the system of slavery. However, Jacobs's narrative problematized assumptions that dominated abolitionist literature in general and male slave narratives in particular, assumptions that linked slave women to illicit sexuality. Jacobs's attempt to develop a framework in which to discuss the social, political, and economic consequences of black womanhood prefigured the concerns of black women intellectuals after emancipation. For these intellectuals the progress of the race would be intimately tied to and measured by the progress of the black woman.

Black women writers would continue to adopt and adapt dominant literary conventions and to challenge racist sexual ideologies. Like Prince, Wilson, and Jacobs, they would explore a variety of narrative forms in the attempt to establish a public presence and continue to find ways to invent black heroines who could transcend their negative comparison to the figure of the white heroine. The consequences of being a slave woman did not end with the abolition of slavery as an institution but haunted the texts of black women throughout the nineteenth century and into the twentieth. . . .

The Representation of Slavery and the Rise of Afro-American Literary Realism, 1865–1920

William L. Andrews

The most famous metaphor of slavery in the history of Afro-American literature appears in the climax of the *Narrative of the Life of Frederick Douglass, an American Slave,* in which Douglass reconstructs the significance of his struggle with the slave-breaker, Edward Covey, on a hot August morning in 1834. Triumph over Covey, known as "the snake" among his slaves, became Douglass's "glorious resurrection, from the tomb of slavery, to the heaven of freedom."[1] A little more than a half century after Douglass's *Narrative* was published, the most infamous metaphor of slavery in the history of black American literature appeared in the first chapter of Booker T. Washington's *Up from Slavery.* When we "look facts in the face," Washington states, "we must acknowledge that, notwithstanding the cruelty and moral wrong of slavery, the ten million Negroes inhabiting this country, who themselves or whose ancestors went through the school of American slavery, are in a stronger and more hopeful condition, materially, intellectually, morally, and religiously, than is true of an equal number of black people in any other portion of the globe."[2] The disparities between these two metaphors are striking. The antebellum writer says slavery was like a tomb, in which he languished in what Orlando Patterson would call "social death" and from which he was resurrected only by rebellious effort.[3] The postbellum writer, on the other hand, compares slavery to a school, in which he and his fellows received, rather than lost, social purpose and from which they graduated not by violence but by sanctioned behavior like industry and dutifulness. I do not

From Deborah E. McDowell and Arnold Rampersad, eds., *Slavery and the Literary Imagination* (Baltimore: The Johns Hopkins University Press, 1989), 62–80. Reprinted with permission of William L. Andrews.

[1]*Narrative of the Life of Frederick Douglass, an American Slave, Written by Himself,* edited and with an introduction by Houston A. Baker, Jr. (New York: Viking Penguin, 1982), 113.

[2]*The Autobiographical Writings,* vol. 1 of *The Booker T. Washington Papers,* ed. Louis R. Harlan and John W. Blassingame (Urbana: University of Illinois Press, 1972), 222–23. Subsequent quotations from *Up from Slavery* are from this edition, cited parenthetically in text and notes.

[3]Orlando Patterson, *Slavery and Social Death* (Cambridge: Harvard University Press, 1982), 38–45.

call attention to this difference between Douglass and Washington in order to question the reliability of one or the other as historian of slavery. The metaphorical shift between the two most influential slave narratives in American literature urges a more important inquiry, I believe, into the dynamics of Afro-American literary, rather than sociopolitical, history.

Throughout the nineteenth century and well into the twentieth, autobiographies of former slaves dominated the Afro-American narrative tradition. Approximately sixty-five American slave narratives were published in book or pamphlet form before 1865. Between the Civil War and the onset of the depression, at least fifty more ex-slaves saw their autobiographies in print, to a large extent eclipsing in their own time the influence, if not the memory, of their antebellum predecessors. Yet with the exception of criticism on *Up from Slavery*, there has been little investigation into what I shall call the postbellum slave narrative, nor has there been any serious study of the large number of black autobiographies in the late nineteenth and early twentieth centuries that were written in the shadow of the postbellum slave narrative, especially Washington's.[4] It is imperative to read the slave narrative tradition wholly, however, if we wish to reckon with the significance of the crucial shift in the metaphor of slavery that highlights the Douglass and Washington texts. If we read the Afro-American autobiographical tradition from 1765 to 1920 in toto, we can see that major parameters of this tradition—such as the representation of slavery—underwent revision, not only according to the differing perspectives of individual writers but also in relation to the changing social and political priorities of successive generations of freedmen and freedwomen.

The slave narrative took on its classic form and tone between 1840 and 1860, when the romantic movement in American literature was in its most influential phase. Transcendentalists like Theodore Parker welcomed antebellum slave narratives (and Douglass's in particular) into the highest echelon of American literature, insisting that "all the original romance of Americans is in them, not in the white man's novel."[5] Douglass's celebration of selfhood in his 1845 *Narrative* might easily be read as a black contribution to the literature of romantic individualism and anti-institutionalism. Ten years later Douglass's second autobiography, *My Bondage and My Freedom*, deconstructs his 1845 self-portrait with typical romantic irony. The idea of heroic slaves like Douglass resurrecting themselves from graves of the spirit by forceful resistance to authority undoubtedly appealed to an era fascinated by the romantic agon, the life-and-death contest of the spirit of revision against all that represses it.[6] But after the Civil War, few ex-slave autobiographers recounted

---

[4]For a brief, introductory look at the subject, see my "Forgotten Voices of Afro-American Autobiography, 1865–1930," *A/B: Auto/Biography Studies* 2 (Fall 1986): 21–27.

[5]Theodore Parker, "The American Scholar," in *The American Scholar*, ed. George Willis Cooke, vol. 8 of *Centenary Edition of Theodore Parker's Writings* (Boston: American Unitarian Association, 1907), 37.

[6]For further discussion of the relationship of mid-nineteenth-century black American literature to romanticism, see William L. Andrews, "The 1850s: The First Afro-American Literary Renais-

their lives in the manner of Douglass. The stunningly different treatments of bondage and selfhood in *Up from Slavery*, for instance, signal a new wave of revisionism in postbellum Afro-American literature, instanced in the reaction of later slave autobiographers to what they perceived as romanticized interpretations of the pre-emancipation past, whether by black or white writers. By the turn of the century, slave narrators viewed slavery and its significance to the advancement of black people in an increasingly pragmatic perspective, delineated most effectively in *Up from Slavery*. This immensely influential slave narrative articulates a quasi-literary realism whose rhetoric, conventions, and cultural import need to be examined if we are to reckon adequately with the effort on the part of turn-of-the-century black novelists to make fiction address matters of fact.

The antebellum slave narrative was the product of fugitive bondmen who rejected the authority of their masters and their socialization as slaves and broke away, often violently, from slavery. Since the slave's right to rebel was a hotly debated issue in the 1840s and 1850s, the classic antebellum slave narrative highlights the brutalizing horrors of slavery in order to justify forcible resistance and escape as the only way a black could preserve his or her humanity. Through an emphasis on slavery as deprivation—buttressed by extensive evidence of a lack of adequate food, clothing, and shelter; the denial of basic familial rights; the enforced ignorance of most religious or moral precepts; and so on—the antebellum narrative pictures the South's "peculiar institution" as a wholesale assault on everything precious to humankind. Under slavery, civilization reverts to a Hobbesian state of nature; if left to its own devices slavery will pervert master and mistress into monsters of cupidity and power-madness and reduce their servant to a nearly helpless object of exploitation and cruelty. Ultimately this objectifying power of slavery is what the antebellum slave narrative protests against most eloquently by demonstrating the evolution of a liberating subjectivity in the slave's life, up to and including the act of writing autobiography itself.

Antebellum slave narrators like Douglass and Henry Bibb[7] trace their salvation back to an intuition of individual uniqueness and a sense of special destiny which they claim has inspired them since their early youth. "The fire of liberty," Bibb states, "seemed to be a part of my nature; it was first revealed to me by the inevitable laws of nature's God."[8] The slave's outward struggle for physical freedom emanates from an inner conflict played out in the arena of his consciousness, where the fire of his Promethean self contends with the

sance," in William L. Andrews, ed., *Literary Romanticism in America* (Baton Rouge: Louisiana State University Press, 1981), 38–60.

[7]The overwhelming majority of slave narratives, both before and after the Civil War, were written or dictated by men. Of the approximately 115 slave narratives separately published in the United States and Great Britain between 1760 and 1930, only thirteen were dictated or written by black women. For this reason my examples of typical slave narrators are male.

[8]*Narrative of the Life and Adventures of Henry Bibb* (New York: By the Author, 1849), 17.

"mental and spiritual darkness" (in James Pennington's typical image)[9] of slavery. Ironically, however, the enlightenment provided by the Promethean fire within only reveals the tremendous gulf between the slave's subjective view of himself as a unique essence and slavery's objectified view of him as a thing. As a result of such revelations, the slave's world takes on an absolute, binary character.[10] The only way he can assert his existence as a subject is by rebelling against the system that renders him an object. In the act of rebellion, the slave realizes himself, gives order to the chaos of his condition, and claims what we might call an existential authenticity and freedom while still in bondage.

What the slave rebel seeks in his flight to the North, however, is much more than an existential alternative to the non-being of slavery. The quest is for an ideal of freedom, a condition in which one may liberate the essential self within through expressive action and the power of the word. Few fugitive slaves say that their goal, when they fled the South, was to make a name for themselves as speakers and/or writers in the North. Still, the most memorable antebellum slave narrators treat their arrival on the abolitionist lecture platform or their acceptance of the antislavery pen as the fulfillment of their destiny. Literacy is considered the ultimate form of power in the antebellum slave narrative, for at least two reasons. First, language is assumed to signify the subject and hence to ratify the slave narrator's humanity as well as his authority. Second, white bigotry and fear presumably cannot withstand the onslaught of the truth feelingly represented in the simple personal history of a former slave. This romantic trust in the power of language did not go unchallenged in the antebellum black autobiography, as I have argued in my book *To Tell a Free Story*.[11] Still, given the paucity of alternative weapons for blacks in the antislavery struggle, the idea that the word could make them free remained an article of faith in Afro-American literature of the antebellum era.

The abolition of involuntary servitude in 1865 forced the slave narrator in the postwar era to reevaluate the purpose of his or her prospective literary enterprise. Since ex-slaves no longer needed to denounce slavery to white America, the story of their past no longer carried the same social or moral import. Upon the demise of Reconstruction, however, and the rise of reactionary racism in the New South, many ex-slaves felt a renewed sense of purpose as firsthand commentators on the South before and after the war. The author

[9]James W. C. Pennington, *The Fugitive Blacksmith*, in *Great Slave Narratives*, ed. Arna Bontemps (Boston: Beacon Press, 1968), 237.

[10]The slave's binary view of the world was not his or her creation alone, however. The "we-they" distinction that allowed whites to view and treat slaves as utterly other preceded and to a large extent compelled the diametrical image of the world in the slave's eyes. See Winthrop D. Jordan, *White over Black: American Attitudes toward the Negro, 1550–1812* (Baltimore: Penguin Books, 1969), 94–97.

[11]See especially the chapter entitled "The Uses of Marginality, 1850–1865" in my *To Tell a Free Story: The First Century of Afro-American Autobiography, 1760–1865* (Urbana: University of Illinois Press, 1986), 167–204.

of the new slave narrative, however, was no longer the rebel-fugitive whose ascent to freedom in the North had been celebrated in romantic fashion in the antebellum era. The large majority of postbellum ex-slave autobiographers— three out of every four, to be more exact—take pride in having endured slavery without having lost their sense of worth or purpose and without having given in to the despair that the antebellum narrator pictures as the lot of so many who languished in slavery.[12] Acknowledging that rare "moral courage" was required to engineer a successful escape from slavery, the typical postbellum narrator insists that slaves who never took such a step could still claim a dignity and heroism of their own. "There were thousands of high-toned and high-spirited slaves," Henry Clay Bruce recalls in his 1895 narrative, "who had as much self-respect as their masters, and who were industrious, reliable and truthful. . . . These slaves knew their own helpless condition" and understood that "they had no rights under the laws of the land." Yet "they did not give up in abject servility, but held up their heads and proceeded to do the next best thing under the circumstances, which was, to so live and act as to win the confidence of their masters, which could only be done by faithful service and an upright life." When these "reliables," as Bruce terms them, were "freed by the war, the traits which they had exhibited for generations to such good effect, were brought into greater activity, and have been largely instrumental in making the record of which we feel so proud to-day."[13]

These remarks from Bruce's autobiography, *The New Man*, exemplify the pragmatism of the postbellum slave narrative in several respects. Bruce implicitly rejects the existential thesis of the antebellum narrative, namely, that because slavery was inimical to a slave's intellectual, moral, and spiritual development, rebellion was necessary to the slave's assertion and preservation of selfhood. Bruce argues that slaves could and did achieve "self-respect" without rebelling or running away to the North. Instead of the "either-or"

---

[12]The means of emancipation among the postbellum narrators were many. A few postbellum slave narratives recount the rebellion and flight of fugitives well before the Civil War. See, for example, Mattie J. Jackson, *The Story of Mattie J. Jackson*, ed. L. S. Thompson (Lawrence, Mass.: L. S. Thompson, 1866) or *Autobiography of James L. Smith* (Norwich, Conn.: By the Author, 1881). A few other narrators preferred to purchase their freedom rather than run away. See Elizabeth Keckley, *Behind the Scenes: Thirty Years a Slave and Four Years in the White House* (New York: G. W. Carleton, 1868) or Elisha Green, *Life of the Rev. Elisha W. Green* (Maysville, Ky.: Republican Printing, 1888). Some narrators recall having bided their time in slavery until the upheavals of war had so weakened their masters' control that slipping away to the Union army was relatively safe. See Allen Parker, *Recollections of Slavery Times* (Worcester, Mass.: Charles W. Burbank, 1895) or Louis Hughes, *Thirty Years a Slave* (Milwaukee: By the Author, 1896). Still others waited until formal emancipation came with the collapse of the Confederacy. See Jacob Stroyer, *My Life in the South* (Salem, Mass.: Newcomb & Gauss, 1898), Rev. I. E. Lowery, *Life on the Old Plantation in Ante-bellum Days* (Columbia, S.C.: State Company, 1911), or Monroe F. Jamison, *Autobiography and Work of Bishop M.F. Jamison, D.D.* (Nashville: By the Author, 1912).

[13]Henry Clay Bruce, *The New Man: Twenty-nine Years a Slave, Twenty-nine Years a Free Man* (York, Pa.: P. Anstadt & Sons, 1895), 38–39.

conditions of the antebellum narrator—either self-affirming rebellion or self-abnegating acceptance of chattelism—Bruce, like most postbellum narrators, stresses that slaves could and did choose "the next best thing" according to relative, rather than absolute, standards of value. There is ample evidence of forcible, as well as passive, resistance to mean-spirited masters in slave narratives like Bruce's, a testimony to the fact that slaves in the postbellum narrative treasure their dignity as much as their counterparts in the antebellum narrative. But in the postbellum narrative, the measure of a slave's dignity is much more pragmatic than existential, more public than private, and more tangible and considerably less ideal than it is in the most famous antebellum narratives. Thus, while Douglass's fight with Covey epitomizes the antebellum ideal of "manhood," a typical postbellum slave narrator like George Henry sets out to prove "that though black I was a man in every sense of the word" by recalling his superlative achievements as a hostler, a ship's captain, even as overseer, in slavery.[14] In the postbellum narrative, a slave does not have to fight back to claim a free man's sense of empowering honor; diligence in his duties and pride in a task well done say as much or more about a black man's respectability as running away, especially if that black man is also a family man.[15] Ultimately, men like Bruce and Henry appeal to the pragmatic test of history to vindicate their sense of honor. The success stories that these "new men" chronicle in their post-emancipation years are designed to demonstrate that the course they followed as slaves prepared them well to seize opportunity in freedom and turn it to honorable account, both socially and economically.

The pragmatism of the postbellum slave narrator stems primarily from his willingness to interpret and evaluate slavery according to its practical consequences in the real world of human action. While the antebellum narrative did not ignore the practical effects of slavery on blacks and whites in the South, it rested its antislavery case on religious and ethical absolutes like Bibb's "inevitable laws of nature's God," or what William Craft called "the sacred rights of the weak."[16] The postbellum narrator rarely appeals to such ideals or to the righteous indignation that let his antebellum predecessor condemn slavery so categorically. Instead he asks his reader to judge slavery simply and dispassionately on the basis of what Booker T. Washington liked to call "facts," by which the Tuskegean meant something other than empirical

[14]George Henry, *Life of George Henry* (Providence, R.I.: By the Author, 1894), 23.

[15]Orlando Patterson points out that because slavery was understood as a state of dishonor, the denial of power or value to a slave followed logically. When a slave narrator like Douglass speaks of rebellion restoring his sense of "manhood," he is actually alluding to his crucial desire for honor, on which every free man's sense of individual power and social value depends. See *Slavery and Social Death*, 10–13. In the postbellum slave narrative, the same acute sense of the importance of acquiring honor in an inherently dishonorable condition is prevalent, but the mode of achieving it is usually not Douglass's, often because of extenuating circumstances such as marriage or family ties.

[16]See William Craft, *Running a Thousand Miles for Freedom*, in *Great Slave Narratives*, ed. Arna Bontemps (Boston: Beacon Press, 1969), 272.

data. In *Up from Slavery,* as in many other postbellum slave narratives, a factual evaluation of slavery exploits what William James would later call the "practical cash-value" of the word, its significance in the present day.[17] What slavery was in the past is not so important as what slavery means, or (more importantly) can be construed to mean, in the present. A factual view of slavery, for Washington, is concerned less with a static concept of historical truth, frozen in the past, than with the need for rhetorical power in the ever-evolving present. To the postbellum slave narrator, particularly Washington, slavery needed to be reviewed and reempowered as a concept capable of effecting change, of making a difference ultimately in what white people thought of black people as freedmen, not slaves. The facts of slavery in the postbellum narrative, therefore, are not so much what happened *then*—bad though it was—as what *makes* things, good things, happen now.

Looking the facts of the present (more than the past) in the face, Washington could justifiably call slavery a school in which black Americans had learned much about the necessity of hard work, perseverance, and self-help as survival skills in their difficult passage in the antebellum South. The fact of turn-of-the-century American "scientific" racism, which stereotyped "the Negro" as degraded, ignorant, incompetent, and servile, demanded that slavery be re-presented anew, not as a condition of deprivation and degradation, but as a period of training and testing, from which the slave graduated with high honors and even higher ambitions. Given the changed sociopolitical circumstances, it is not surprising to find the postbellum slave narrator treating slavery more as an economic proving ground than an existential battleground for southern black people. The slave past, if effectively represented, could provide the freedman and freedwoman with credentials that the new industrial-capitalist order might respect. By the turn of the century, blacks were realizing their need for a usable American past on which they could build.[18] They could also see that southern whites needed to be reminded of who had built the Old South and who could help to build a New South as well.[19] The agenda of the postbellum slave narrative thus emphasizes un-

---

[17]William James, "What Pragmatism Means," in *American Thought: Civil War to World War I,* ed. Perry Miller (New York: Holt, Rinehart, and Winston, 1954), 169.

[18]Much of the despair registered in the slave narratives of the late antebellum era stems from their writers' conviction that American history was not progressive because slavery held the process of American social and political evolution in thrall. In search of historical precedent for their message, most antebellum slave narrators buttressed their narratives in mythical history as recorded in the Bible, which showed how God had delivered the people of Israel from their bondage. Only after emancipation did the slave narrative incorporate a historical consciousness that chronicles progressive change at work in contemporary America. In the late nineteenth century, as black sociopolitical prospects declined, the postbellum slave narrator often turned for consolation back to the slave past, partly to remind himself and his readers of how far the race had really come, and partly to recover something valuable and sustaining to his present struggles.

[19]Washington's Atlanta Compromise address evokes the sentimental image of the slave "whose fidelity and love you have tested in days when to have proved treacherous meant the ruin of your firesides" not simply to pander to white stereotypes but to exploit them in an argument that pictures the freedmen and freedwomen as builders, not destroyers, of the South in the past and

abashedly the tangible contribution that blacks made to the South, in and after slavery, in order to rehabilitate the image of the freedman, not the idea of slavery, in the eyes of business America.

Although in some ways a typical postbellum slave narrative, *Up from Slavery* stands out today, as always, because of its articulation of an accommodationist strategy that, though by no means original, Washington managed to identify as his own.[20] What we would call accommodationism, however, is what the Tuskegean would have termed realism. What are the sources of real power in the real world? asks the writer of *Up from Slavery*. In the antebellum slave narrative, as I have already noted, the answer is almost unanimous. Knowledge is power, and the fundamental source of knowledge is literacy, the ability to open one's mind to the words of others and to liberate other minds with a text of one's own. As an ex-slave and an educator, Washington pays lip service to the importance of reading in his own life and in the training of his people. But in his preferred persona as pragmatic student of power, he demotes men of the word and elevates men of action to the putative leadership of his people. The irony of the preeminent black speaker and writer of his day identifying himself as a man of real acts, not mere words, should not prevent us from recognizing the literary significance of Washington's antiliterary thesis. *Up from Slavery* is, in its own quiet and indirect—should I say sly?—way, a manifesto of a quasi-literary realism that attempts to restrict the traditional sovereignty of the black wordsmith by chaining the signifier to a preexistent signified and thus making the word merely reflective, rather than constitutive, of reality.

Washington's realism entails a radical distinction between deeds and words. "The actual sight of a first-class house that a Negro has built is ten times more potent than pages of discussion about a house that he ought to build, or perhaps could build" (p. 297). Action, Washington insists, produces things; discussion, by contrast, produces only more discussion. "Instead of studying books so constantly, how I wish that our schools and colleges might learn to study men and things!" (p. 243). The men Washington studies are, of course, white men of action and substance, like Andrew Carnegie, Collis P. Huntington, and William McKinley. In stark contrast with them are black men of words—in particular, southern politicians, preachers, and educators. These men, Washington argues, have too often made speaking and writing a refuge from doing, from working productively for the good of the race. As he surveys the recent history of his people, he finds that politicians stirred up in the

---

the future (p. 332). Washington was by no means unique among postbellum slave narrators in stressing the constructive role of slaves in building the Old South and making possible the aristocratic tradition of which the New South liked to boast. See, for instance, John Quincy Adams, *Narrative of the Life of John Quincy Adams, When in Slavery, and Now as a Freeman* (Harrisburg, Pa.: By the Author, 1872), 46–47.

[20]See August Meier, *Negro Thought in America: 1880–1915* (Ann Arbor: University of Michigan Press, 1963), 85–99.

people only an "artificial" desire to hold public office; preachers inspired in literate black men only a self-serving "call to preach"; teachers merely pandered to "the craze for Greek and Latin learning" (p. 256) among pathetically ignorant blacks. Instead of doing tangible good, all this preaching and teaching and speech-making created in the minds of rural southern blacks a pernicious notion, namely, that an alternative resource of power existed to what Washington called the "real, solid foundation" (p. 260) of black advancement, the agrarian life. Even Washington had to acknowledge that the black community had traditionally revered the man of the word as "a very superior human being, something bordering almost on the supernatural" (p. 256) in the case of those who understood the mystery of foreign languages. Such men seemed not to require "the solid and never deceptive foundation of Mother Nature" (p. 261), that is, a grounding in the life of "the soil," to exercise power and excite envy among southern blacks.[21] Washington's fear was that the example of Afro-American men of the word would encourage young blacks to believe that the route to black power was not hand-to-mouth, from act to word, but rather just the reverse, from performing word to reforming act. Washington pays inadvertent tribute to these black masters of the speech-act by noting that they "live by their wits" instead of by their hands and that the white South regards them with a perplexed and uneasy suspicion.

Few can read *Up from Slavery* today without recognizing that Washington also lived by his wits and in a consummate manner. A former political stump speaker and student of the ministry, Washington clearly understood the power of the word in the mouth of an artful and ambitious black man. "I never planned to give any large part of my life to speaking in public," he blandly remarks, adding, "I have always had more of an ambition to *do* things than merely to talk *about* doing them" (p. 320). Yet no black man could have built Tuskegee Institute without knowing that action proceeds from speech and that speech is itself a most potent form of action. Washington acknowledges that he authorized the erection of Porter Hall, the first building on the Tuskegee campus, before he had the money to pay for it. He relied on his charm and good name in the community to secure loans to complete the edifice. He had no capital at all when he conceived of putting up a second building, but, as he offhandedly comments, "We decided to give the needed building a name" (p. 309) anyway. Naming the building Alabama Hall proved, of course, a shrewd political maneuver that helped to ensure the continuation of the state funding on which Washington depended so much in the early years. This speech-act alone, so reminiscent of the talismanic power of naming in the slave narrative tradition, belies Washington's insistence that words merely publicize deeds. Thus, even though he claims that he always "had a desire to do something to make the world better, and *then* be able to speak to the world about that

---

[21]"I remember that the first colored man whom I saw who knew something about foreign languages impressed me at that time as being a man of all others to be envied" (p. 256).

thing" (p. 249; emphasis mine), Washington had the wit to see that speaking makes doing possible and that reality is contingent on language, not the other way around.

Nevertheless, in an effort to subvert the "almost supernatural" status of the man of words in the black community, the author of *Up from Slavery* presents himself as a naturalist, arguing that only from a rootedness in "nature" does he derive the "strength for the many duties and hard places that await me" (p. 356) in the real world. Washington is not talking about communing with Nature in some romantic fashion. His need is more immediate and tangible: "I like, as often as possible, to touch nature, not something that is artificial or an imitation, but the real thing" (p. 355). Hence it is no surprise to find Washington depreciating belles-lettres and enthusing over newspapers as "a constant source of delight and recreation." Obviously, fiction, poetry, and drama are artificial and merely imitative of "the real thing." Only one kind of storytelling can satisfy Washington's appetite for realism, namely, "biography," for which he claims "the greatest fondness." Why he should prefer biography to all other kinds of reading is plain enough: "I like to be sure that I am reading about a real man or a real thing" (p. 355). But the way Washington prefaces his predictable desire for the "real thing"—"I like to be *sure*"— suggests that he knows that readers of biography do not always get what they expect or want, nor does biography always assure its readers of their ability to distinguish between the real and the artificial. Maybe this is one reason why Washington is at such pains in writing his own biography to portray himself as a plain and simple man of facts, "the real thing" among autobiographers, a man who represents himself as no more than what he is. Washington *knows* the prejudice in his white audience against black men of words as truth-tellers; this is a major reason why he claims he is a man of acts and facts.[22] By repeatedly declaring his "great faith in the power and influence of facts" and his conviction that one can touch the real thing in biography, Washington acts to shore up the foundation of *Up from Slavery*, which we can see is not so much grounded in real things as in linguistic demonstrations of realism.

Capitalizing on the postbellum slave narrator's pragmatic revision of the facts of slavery, *Up from Slavery* promulgates a concept of realism which challenges the traditional status of the sign in the Afro-American narrative tradition. By claiming a radical distinction between action and speech and by disclaiming language as anything more than a referential medium, Washington denies the performative dimension of representation. The consummate rhetorician, he tries to pass for a realist, we might say, since this lets him keep his agenda masked behind a semblance of nonrhetorical *vraisemblance*. If Washington could define the terms by which realism would be judged in Afro-

---

[22]White suspicion of the veracity of slave narrators is almost as old as the slave narrative itself, which is one reason why there are so many authenticating documents in *Up from Slavery*. See Robert B. Stepto, *From Behind the Veil* (Urbana: University of Illinois Press, 1979), 3–31.

American writing, then he could consign literary representation to a *reactive* status in Afro-American culture, thereby robbing it of the expressive power that the word had held in the black community since the antebellum era. The rise of Tuskegee realism then, foregrounded by the postbellum slave narrative and reinforced by numerous autobiographies of Washington's protégés, imitators, and admirers, discounts the hard-won victory of antebellum narratives like *My Bondage and My Freedom* and *Incidents in the Life of a Slave Girl*, texts that liberated black narrative from an alienating and objectifying focus on the sign as a referent to an object—slavery—rather than a subject—the questing consciousness of the former slave. Tuskegee realism, ever respectful of Washington's much-heralded "gospel of the toothbrush," sanitizes the mouth of the speaking subject until it attains that acme of "unselfishness" which is, in Washington's eyes, the hallmark of every successful man of action.

Neither the rise of pragmatism in the slave narrative nor the articulation of Tuskegee realism in *Up from Slavery* exerted a profound impact on the idealism of the protest fiction that dominated much late nineteenth- and early twentieth-century black belletristic prose in America. Protest romances from Frances Ellen Watkins Harper's *Iola Leroy* (1892) to Du Bois's *The Quest of the Silver Fleece* (1911) answer the call that Pauline Hopkins delivered in the preface to her novel *Contending Forces* (1900): "We must ourselves develop the men and women who will faithfully portray the inmost thoughts and feelings of the Negro with all the fire and romance which lie dormant in our history."[23] The problem with devoting the novel to romances of racial uplift, however, was that this could easily play into the hands of Tuskegee realism. Washington would have been happy to see the novel in its place, as a defensive, (merely) inspirational reaction to unjust realities.[24] The way to combat Tuskegee realism was not to justify romance, however well intentioned. Black wordsmiths needed to decertify—literally, to make *uncertain*— the "real, solid foundation" on which Tuskegee realism claimed its hegemony. This is what happens in two prominent fictive texts of this period, Charles W. Chesnutt's *The Conjure Woman* (1899) and James Weldon Johnson's *The Autobiography of an Ex-Colored Man* (1912).

As fictive autobiographies, both of these books exploit the anxiety that Washington expressed about biography as a representation of "a real man or a real thing." *The Conjure Woman* purports to be a collection of dictated slave narratives transcribed by a white entrepreneur from Ohio. However, by mediating his intention through Uncle Julius McAdoo's narratives and the conflicting interpretations of them offered by the Ohioan and his wife, Chesnutt made it hard for many readers to tell what the man behind all these

---

[23]Pauline Hopkins, *Contending Forces* (1900; reprint, Carbondale: Southern Illinois Press, 1978), 14.

[24]Hazel Carby points out that when Washington saw a novelist like Hopkins as a threat, he took forceful action—by buying the organ, *The Colored American Magazine*, in which her novels were first serialized.

masks really meant. Reviewers who did not know that Chesnutt was an Afro-American (neither Chesnutt nor his publishers mentioned this fact when *The Conjure Woman* came out) extrapolated from the text an implied author who, though a Northerner, had thoroughly immersed himself in the local color of the South and had written to entertain his white readership with the quaint customs and folklore of the southern Negro. Comparatively few reviewers perceived a "dark side" and tragic note in Chesnutt's representation of the slavery past.[25] The disparity between the two implied authors attributed to *The Conjure Woman* demonstrated that the real is not a constant but a function of words like "Negro" and "white" which are themselves but traces of racial *différance* in the cultural text of the racist American reading community.

Even more destabilizing of black biographical reality is Johnson's *Autobiography of an Ex-Colored Man*. Published anonymously, the novel was designed by its author to be taken as a real, not a fictive, work. Most reviewers, as well as a large part of the black reading community,[26] were taken in by the *vraisemblance* of the novel, which, if one were to analyze it in detail, reads almost like a catalog of the stock in trade of nineteenth-century realism. What distinguishes the ex-colored man as a persona is not his storytelling but his leisurely digressions from the facts of his life into the realm of social and cultural commentary. His breadth of experience, his criticism of whites and blacks alike, and his almost Olympian detachment from racial loyalties give him an objectivity toward the whole race question that sounds almost Tuskegean. Moreover, Washington would surely have concurred with the ex-colored man's regretful judgment of his having passed for white as a selfish and socially unproductive act. An even more obvious invocation of the Tuskegee line comes at the end of the novel, when Washington himself makes a cameo appearance representing all the "earnestness and faith" of a progressive race, as contrasted with the self-protective cynicism of the ex-colored man.

What do these apparent endorsements of Tuskegee realism mean, however, if the narrator who makes them is not a "real man"? Does the fictiveness of the narrator invalidate the authority of what he says? Does fictive language have less—or perhaps more—performative potential than natural language?[27] Did Johnson invent a fictive character like the ex-colored man out of a belief that such a vehicle could actually represent certain facts more fully and freely than an actual man? If so, is this a testimonial to the strength of the Afro-American novel or the weakness of Afro-American autobiography? However

[25]I base these generalizations on the critical response to *The Conjure Woman* which I found on my perusal of the scrapbooks of contemporary press clippings and reviews of that book housed in the Chesnutt Collection of the Fisk University Library, Nashville, Tennessee.

[26]In his autobiography, Johnson recalls a dinner party at which he met a man who obliquely confessed to having authored *The Autobiography of an Ex-Colored Man!* See *Along This Way* (1933; reprint, New York: Viking, 1968), 238–39.

[27]I use the terms "fictive" and "natural" as Barbara Herrnstein Smith uses them in *On the Margins of Discourse* (Chicago: University of Chicago Press, 1978), 15, 21–25.

we answer these questions posed by the problematic "author-function" of *The Autobiography of an Ex-Colored Man,* we can see clearly enough that the novel does not leave unscathed many of the assumptions about realism—how to recognize it, how to read it—that Washington held dear.[28] If Johnson wrote the ex-colored man's story with no other purpose than to unveil the cultural conventions that predisposed his readership to believe an "autobiography" by a doubly phony white man over a novel authored by a real black man, namely, Johnson himself, his effort must be considered a signal success in the history of Afro-American autobiography, as well as fiction.

The pragmatic reassessment of slavery and the rise of Afro-American realism illustrate a process of revisionism at work in black narrative of the late nineteenth century that exempted virtually nothing in the past from being remade anew. Whatever black reality *was* historically, whatever one generation of black narrators said it was, their successors refused to be bound by it. First pragmatic slave narrators, then the Tuskegee realists, and then novelists like Chesnutt and Johnson insisted on their right to reappropriate the signifying potential of black reality and, through what we might call deconstructive acts, prepare the discursive ground once again for a new assay of the basis on which a usable truth could be constructed. From the perspective of the New Negroes of the Harlem Renaissance, Johnson had only begun to probe the deeper resources of subjective consciousness in *The Autobiography of an Ex-Colored Man*; Chesnutt had only glimpsed the import of black folk culture in the magical realism of *The Conjure Woman*. Nevertheless, in their revisionistic attitude toward prevailing notions of the real, and in their emphasis on reality as a function of consciousness mediated through language, these were enabling texts. They not only pointed new directions for the Harlem Renaissance; they bore witness to the postbellum slave narrators' determination to keep the past alive and meaningful to the present. In short, the work of Chesnutt and Johnson helped preserve Afro-American realism as a literary tradition, a bridge between the antebellum and modern eras, that makes Tuskegee available for the Invisible Man to reinvent and enables the transposing of the "apparently incoherent" slave songs of Douglass's *Narrative* into the *Song of Solomon*.

28I use the term "author-function" as Michel Foucault defines it in "What Is an Author?" in Josué V. Harari, ed., *Textual Strategies* (Ithaca: Cornell University Press, 1979), 141–60.

Crusader for Justice: Ida B. Wells

Joanne M. Braxton

Who shall say that such a work accomplished by one woman exiled and maligned by that community among whom she had so long and so valiantly labored, bending every effort to the upbuilding of the manhood and womanhood of all races, shall not place her in the front rank of philanthropists, not only of the womanhood of this race, but among those laborers of all ages and all climes?

—G. B. Mossell (1894)

. . . Like *The Education of Henry Adams* (1907) or *The Autobiography of W. E. B. Du Bois* (1968), Ida B. Wells's *Crusade for Justice* represents a posthumously published autobiography by a well-known public figure. Wells employs the medium of the historical memoir, a subgenre of autobiography dominated almost entirely by men, to create her lasting version of the self.

"The memoir," James Cox asserts, "is a category of autobiography that needs attention," part of the "lost ground" of American literature. "There is a distinct tiresomeness about the ease with which literary critics assure themselves that 'mere' fact has nothing to do with the art of autobiography. The truth or falsity of autobiography is thereby subordinated to the creativity, the design, 'the inner' truth of the narrative." Cox observes, moreover, that "autobiographies devoted to the emotional consciousness of the writer have been much more subject to investigation than the memoir, particularly the memoir of a well-known public figure."[1] Thus, Wells's *Crusade for Justice*, as the memoir of a well-known public figure who is also a black woman, constitutes part of the "lost ground" of Afro-American literary tradition. It does much to establish continuity within black female autobiographical tradition, for this text has distinct characteristics common to both nineteenth- and twentieth-century autobiographies by black American women. The title *Crusade for Justice* refers primarily to Wells's recollections of her public life, but it also borrows from the confessional mode of autobiography to allow Wells the latitude to discuss her experience of marriage and family as it influenced her

From Joanne M. Braxton, *Black Women Writing Autobiography* (Philadelphia: Temple University Press, 1989), 102–38. © 1989 Temple University. Reprinted by permission of Temple University Press.

[1]James Cox, "Recovering Literature's Lost Ground through Autobiography," in *Autobiography: Essays Theoretical and Critical*, ed. James Olney (Princeton: Princeton University Press, 1980), 124–125.

work and public life. Therefore, the "confessional" aspect is more fully developed in *Crusade* than in most historical memoirs.

In at least one respect, Wells departs from the traditional autobiographical stance of an older person looking back and settling accounts;[2] she is not a wise and paternal elder, some "articulate hero" looking back at the end of a quest fulfilled. In *Crusade*, the outraged mother of the slave narrative emerges in the personal myth of a "fiery reformer, feminist, and race leader."[3] Speaking as the outraged mother who carries her nursing son on an antilynching speaking tour, Wells's autobiographical posture is that of a protector of black manhood and a nurturer and defender of black womanhood. Marked by unpredictable shifts in narrative movement similar to those found in earlier autobiographies by black American women, *Crusade* emphasizes the public sphere more in the first half of the narrative, and home and family life more in the second, with a perceptible break at Chapter 30, "A Divided Duty." Although Stephen Butterfield argues that *Crusade* represents "the slave narrative in its purest and truest light," this autobiography is organized according to more sophisticated principles than the slave narrative, and the sensibility is a broadened one.[4] Although Wells deemphasizes her personal life in order to focus on her public career and achievements, *Crusade for Justice* qualifies as what James Olney calls a "duplex" autobiography in that Wells gives the reader enough of a view of her domestic sphere to round out what she presents of herself as a public person.

The structure of *Crusade for Justice*, like that of many autobiographies, is chronological rather than thematic or topical. Organized into forty-six short chapters, the memoir has the same "disconnected" quality of many women's narratives.[5] Although it begins with Wells's recounting of her painful adolescence, the autobiographical "I" shifts to the viewpoint of the mature young woman fighting against lynching, then to that of an older woman wise in many ways, looking back on her life, ordering her experience in the re-creation of the self.

Part of its intrinsic cultural value is that *Crusade for Justice* presents prime source material for speculation on the role of race and sex in the development of Wells's psychosocial identity and her autobiographical point of view. In his *Life History and the Historical Moment*, Erik Erikson defines the autobiographer's psychosocial identity primarily in relation to "the personal coherence of the individual and the group." Erikson postulates that "one must first ask oneself under what circumstances the memoirs were written, what their

[2]See Patricia Meyers Spacks, "Stages of Self: Notes on Autobiography," in Albert E. Stone, ed., *The American Autobiography*, Englewood Cliffs, N.J.: Prentice-Hall, 1981. 44–45.

[3]Alfreda M. Duster, Introduction, *Crusade for Justice: The Autobiography of Ida B. Wells* (Chicago: University of Chicago Press, 1970), xiii–xiv.

[4]Stephen Butterfield, *Black Autobiography* (Amherst: University of Massachusetts Press, 1974), 200.

[5]See Estelle C. Jelinek, ed., Introduction, *Women's Autobiography* (Bloomington: Indiana University Press, 1980), 1–20.

intended purpose was, and what form *they assumed*. Only then can one proceed to judge the less conscious motivations, which may have led the autobiographer to emphasize selectively some experiences and omit other equally decisive ones . . . to correct what might spoil the kind of immortality he has chosen for himself."[6] Certainly such questions must be asked of Wells's autobiography, which was written toward the end of her career and her life, when she might have been susceptible to such "less conscious motivations." And if Erikson had read *Crusade for Justice*, he might have criticized it as one of those "autobiographies . . . written at certain late stages of life for the purpose of recreating oneself in the image of one's method."[7]

Wells began her autobiography in 1928; she died in 1934, leaving her work in midsentence. According to Alfreda M. Duster, her youngest child and editor of the posthumously published autobiography:

> Ida B. Wells really wrote her own autobiography beginning in 1928. Our home had a large dining room with a huge dining table that could be expanded by putting "leaves" where the halves were pulled apart. That table was extended to its fullest length and was covered with papers, notes, books, etc.
>
> She spent most of her days there, except when she was attending meetings, giving lectures, or answering requests for help from people in trouble, which were many.
>
> She wrote the preface and the first three chapters by hand, writing and re-writing, then she secured the services of my brother's secretary, Miss Sinclair, for the rest of the chapters or re-typed at the next session.[8]

Although the editors at the University of Chicago Press supplied the book and chapter titles (since Wells did not), the manuscript was otherwise printed "just as she wrote it," partly because the editor was aware that as Wells's daughter, anything she wrote would be suspect. Thus the text may be regarded as essentially Wells's own, although the published work represents an impressive feat of mother-daughter bonding and personal and political commitment spanning two generations. *Crusade for Justice* is a family and community document as well as the celebration of an individual triumph. . . .

Presumably, . . . Duster had some voice in the selection of the title and subtitle, which were not supplied by the autobiographer. The title, *Crusade for Justice*, signals the central concerns and forecasts the dominant metaphors and "necessary fictions" of the text; it also suggests a holy war, a figure of thought that runs throughout Wells's narrative. The subtitle, *The Autobiography of Ida B. Wells*, indicates the intention to minimize the autobiographer's personal life in order to portray her participation in a vast historical drama; *Crusade for Justice* is clearly presented as the story not only of Ida B. Wells but also of her times.

[6]Erik Erikson, *Life History and the Historical Moment* (New York: Norton, 1975), 135.
[7]Ibid., 125.
[8]Alfreda M. Duster, letter to Joanne M. Braxton, January 30, 1983.

Duster's introduction occupies a crucial position, following the foreword by John Hope Franklin and preceding Wells's own preface. Unlike the authenticating subtexts of nineteenth-century slave narratives, which seem to challenge or undermine the narrator's authorial control, the Duster introduction engages in a kind of literary call and response with Wells's preface and the larger text, resulting in a remarkable resonance between *Crusade for Justice* and its authenticating subtexts. Duster begins her introduction by quoting Norman B. Wood's *The White Side of a Black Subject:*

> God has raised up a modern Deborah in the person of Miss Ida B. Wells, whose voice has been heard throughout England and the United States . . . pleading as only she can plead for justice and fair treatment for her people. . . . we believe God delivered her from being lynched at Memphis, that by her portrayal of the burnings at Paris, Texas, Texarkana, Arkansas and elsewhere she might light a flame of righteous indignation, in England and America which by God's grace, will never be extinguished until a Negro's life is as safe in Mississippi and Tennessee as in Massachusetts or Rhode Island.[9]

Duster asserts that Wood's "was not an unusual description" of Wells, "who was described over and over again as militant, courageous, determined, impassioned, and aggressive."[10] In the remainder of the first paragraph, Duster authenticates her mother's slave birth, her uncommon parentage and upbringing, and much of the factual content of the early chapters of *Crusade*.

But Duster does more than attest to the truth value of her mother's narrative; by quoting a white author who likens her mother to Deborah, a prophetess and judge among the Hebrews of the Old Testament, she participates in the myth-making process. Like the Old Testament heroine, who "arose a mother in Israel" to lead an army against the enemies of her people, Ida B. Wells led the crusade against lynching, full of outrage and indignation, going where men feared to tread. Thus Duster's rhetorical strategy works partly because she directs the reader's attention away from herself as authenticator, and because she contributes to the development of Wells's myth. Near the end of her introduction, Duster forecasts and softens the "strained analogy" that opens her mother's preface, as she supports Wells's personal identification with Joan of Arc:

> In the preface to her autobiography she mentions that a young lady compared her to Joan of Arc. The analogy is, at best, strained, but the odds against [Wells] were in many ways greater. True enough, Joan was a peasant girl in a time when peasants and girls had nothing to say to the ruling class in France. But Ida B. Wells was a black woman born into slavery who began carrying the torch against lynching in the very South bent upon the degradation of the blacks.[11]

---

[9]Duster, *Crusade*, xiii. See also Norman B. Wood, *The White Side of a Black Subject* (Chicago: American Publishing House, 1897), 381–382.

[10]Duster, *Crusade*, xiv.

[11]Ibid., xxxi.

The torch of righteous indignation carried in the crusade against the barbaric practice of lynching becomes one of the central metaphors of Wells's text.

Wells's own preface affirms the "holy war" motif as she begins with the reference to Joan of Arc in an indirect advancement of a statement of her autobiographical purpose and intention:

> A young woman recently asked me to tell her of my connection with the lynching agitation which was started in 1892. She said she was at a YWCA vesper service when the subject for discussion was Joan of Arc, and each person was asked to tell of someone they knew who had traits of character resembling this French heroine and martyr. She was the only colored girl present, and not wishing to lag behind the others, she named me. She was then asked to tell why she thought I deserved such mention. She said, "Mrs. Barnett, I couldn't tell why I thought so.[12]

Wells's identification with Joan of Arc recalls the preface to Sojourner Truth's *Narrative* where Truth evokes the same image; thus Wells revises and recasts Truth's chosen historical metaphor. Wells underscores her historical intention as she builds her personal myth of self:

> When she told me she was twenty-five years old, I realized that one reason she did not know was because the happenings about which she inquired took place before she was born. It is therefore for the young who have so little of our history recorded that I am for the first time in my life writing about myself. I am all the more constrained to do this because there is such a lack of authentic race history of Reconstruction times written by a Negro himself. (*Crusade*, 3–4)

Moreover, Wells's preface advances a historical association with Frederick Douglass, an association often reinforced in the text. Wells writes:

> We have Frederick Douglass's history of slavery as he knew and experienced it. But of the storm and stress immediately after the Civil War, of the Ku Klux Klan, of ballot stuffing, wholesale murders of Negroes who tried to exercise their new-found rights as free men and citizens, the carpetbag invasion about which the South published much that is false, and the Negroes' political life in that era—our race has little of its own that is definite or authentic. (*Crusade*, 4)

The autobiographer's goal is clearly one of definition, documentation, and authentication; her story is intended not only as her own but as the story of her people and her times. She presents her life as a representative and symbolic one.

Wells's documentary mode is signaled by the form of the "linear narrative," which is heavily influenced by journalism and reportage, and authenticated by quotes from newspapers, letters, and "other verifiable, external records." Yet another clue concerns the autobiographer's "attention to chronology and causes," and her brooding historical consciousness, which seems to pervade

---

[12]Ida B. Wells, *Crusade*, xiii–xiv. Hereafter cited in the text as *Crusade*, followed by page number.

every word.[13] In *Crusade for Justice*, Wells attempts to compensate for a public image frequently maligned in the white press. Like the fugitive slaves, Wells feels compelled to tell her story from her own point of view. She wants to set the record straight.

The development of Wells's consciousness resembles the growth of Harriet "Linda Brent" Jacobs's as it unfolds in a series of autobiographical turning points, which might also be viewed as autobiographical "cover memories." A cover memory, according to Erik Erikson, is "a roughly factual event that has come to symbolize in condensed form a complex of ideas, affects and memories . . . living on in adulthood" as an "account to be settled."[14] The narrative movement of *Crusade for Justice* proceeds from one cover memory to the next; thus, "settling accounts" becomes an important figure of thought and a locus of thematic meaning in the text.

As in many other autobiographies by black women, childhood receives scant treatment; Wells treats her childhood in fewer than fifteen pages. While these memories seem dim, what Wells recalls from childhood prefigures a motif of central importance in the later text: the division between public and private duty. Born into slavery, Wells's "earliest recollections" are of reading the newspaper to her father and "an admiring group of his friends." Of her father, she writes, "He was interested in politics and I heard the words of the Ku Klux Klan long before I knew what they meant. I dimly knew that it meant something fearful, by the way my mother walked the floor at night when my father was at a political meeting." Wells portrays her mother as a "deeply religious woman" who "won the prize for regular attendance at Sunday school" and taught her children "the work of the home" as well as the virtue of literacy as a tool of liberation. "She was not forty when she died, but she had borne eight children and brought us up with a strict discipline that many mothers who had had educational advantages have not exceeded. She used to tell us how she had been beaten by slave owners and the hard times she had as a slave" (*Crusade*, 9). Jim and Lizzie Wells provide for Ida a direct contact with an oppressive slave past. Jim reinforces the connection of freedom, literacy, and struggle, while Lizzie triumphs as nurturer, protector, and defender of her family.

The young Ida B. Wells does not understand the implications of everything that she sees and experiences. The narration in the early pages of the autobiography by the mature Ida B. Wells profits from the child's point of view; although incidents narrated seem randomly chosen, Wells endows each "cover memory" with symbolic significance. The feminist critic Patricia Spacks argues that attitudes of many women autobiographers toward adolescence differ from those of men in that women tend to remember adolescence with a kind of "nostalgic pleasure," but that black women writing autobiography do

[13]Albert E. Stone, *Autobiographical Occasions and Original Acts* (Philadelphia: University of Pennsylvania Press, 1982), 29.

[14]Erikson, *Life History*, 161.

not fit this model: They typically have tragically short childhoods. The black woman autobiographer typically substitutes a concern for survival for the flirtations and diversions of traditional "white" adolescence.[15]

The death of Wells's parents during a yellow fever epidemic propels the teenage girl into a world of adult reality. Reborn into a world of "Hard Beginnings," Wells is suddenly charged with the responsibilities of an adult. In presenting this experience, the autobiographer employs both the inquiring mind of the historian and the selectivity of the artist. Wells's narration of her conversation with the conductor of the train that took her home develops the myth of the stalwart "Christian soldier," who serves family and community under the most adverse circumstances. She finds ample opportunities for heroism in her everyday life and possesses the courage necessary to fulfill a heroic role:

> It was a freight train. No passenger trains were running or needed. And the caboose in which I rode was draped in black for two previous conductors who had fallen victim to this dreaded disease. The conductor who told me this was sure that I had made a mistake to go home. I asked him why he was running the train when he knew he was likely to get the fever as had those others for whom the car was draped. He shrugged his shoulders and said that somebody had to do it. "That is exactly why I am going home. I am the oldest of seven living children. There's nobody but me to look after them now. Don't you think I should do my duty, too?" (*Crusade*, 12)

In choosing these images and metaphors, Wells, like many other twentieth-century autobiographers, accentuates her adolescent performance. She also conforms to this pattern by diminishing the importance of the actions of her siblings in this crisis. "There were six of us left, and I the oldest, was only fourteen years old. After being a happy, light-hearted schoolgirl, I suddenly found myself at the head of a family" (*Crusade*, 12). Wells's recognition that she will have to rely on personal resources parallels that of Harriet Jacobs. Like the fugitive slaves, Wells achieves self-reliance by facing hardship. Reflecting the values of the slave narrative, Ida struggles to keep her family together, even after well-meaning friends and neighbors offer to take the children in:

> I said that it would make my mother and father turn over in their graves to know their children had been scattered like that and that we owned the house and if the Masons would help find work, I would take care of them. Of course they scoffed at the idea of a butterfly fourteen-year-old schoolgirl trying to do what it had taken the combined effort of mother and father to do. . . .
> I took the examination for a country schoolteacher and had my dress lengthened, and I got a school six miles out in the country. (*Crusade*, 16)

In striving for self-sufficiency, the young woman unconsciously oversteps the

---

[15]See Spacks, "Stages of Self," 48.

boundaries of community-sanctioned propriety. The death of Wells's parents and her efforts to keep the family together precipitate an adolescent identity crisis, for Ida rebels against her perceived lack of power and an unwritten code of social etiquette designed to protect young black women from the sexual advances of white men.

For example, after Wells's father had died, the family physician, a friendly white man, had locked up $300 of Jim Wells's money for safekeeping, and sent for Ida, the oldest child. When Ida returned to Holly Springs, the doctor made arrangements to have the money transferred to her. This conscientious act of decency leads to a confrontation:

> But someone said that I had been downtown inquiring for Dr. Gray shortly after I had come from the country. They heard him tell my sister he would get the money, meaning my father's money, and bring it to us that night. It was easy for that type of mind to deduce and spread that already, as young as I was, I had been heard asking white men for money and that was the reason I wanted to live there by myself with the children.
>
> As I look back at it now I can perhaps understand the type of mind which drew such conclusions. And no one suggested that I was laying myself open to gossiping tongues. (*Crusade*, 17)

This negative interaction impresses the young Ida B. Wells with an awareness of her sexual identity as well as her social powerlessness. Here Wells's ingrained concept of duty to family conflicts with the conventional notions of ideal womanhood espoused by her community. By demanding to be allowed to stand as the head of her family, Wells had unintentionally violated the racial and sexual etiquette of her community, which dictated that respectable young black women, white men, and money did not mix. Generally, the community did what it could do to discourage its women from having anything to do with white men; this conservative behavior served to minimize the potential for violence to some degree. Reinforcing the "hometraining" she had received from gentler hands, this incident helped both to form and to transform Ida's identity.

Outraged at the unjust accusation, Wells becomes even more set in her ways. In relating this experience in the pages of her autobiography, Wells introduces the idea of identity formation through conflict, a motif that can be linked to the literary strategy of settling accounts, as the autobiographer moves from one psychological turning point to the next.

The early narrative treatment of another incident, which occurred in 1884, clearly demonstrates the growth of what Erikson might view as a "pattern of analogous events . . . that combine to suggest a plausible direction."[16] Here a defiant Wells confronts the Chesapeake and Ohio Railroad with regard to its "color policy":

---

[16]Erikson, *Life History*, 141.

But ever since the repeal of the Civil Rights Bill by the United States Supreme
Court . . . there had been efforts all over the South to draw the color line on the
railroads.

When the train started and the conductor came along to collect tickets, he took
my ticket, then handed it back to me and told me that he could not take my ticket
there. I thought that if he didn't want the ticket that I wouldn't bother about it and
so went on reading. In a little while when he finished taking tickets, he came back
and told me that I would have to go into another car. I refused, saying that the
forward car was a smoker, and as I was in the ladies car, I proposed to stay. He tried
to drag me out of the seat, but the moment he caught hold of my arm I fastened my
teeth into the back of his hand.

I had braced my feet against the seat in front and was holding to the back, and
as he already had been badly bitten, he didn't try it again by himself. He went
forward and got the baggageman and another man to help him and of course they
succeeded in dragging me out. (*Crusade*, 18–19)

This "cover memory" contributes to a pattern in the development of Wells's
consciousness. The outraged young schoolteacher with her teeth in the back
of the conductor's hand is one of the selves of the autobiographer. In *Crusade
for Justice* Wells performs on a historical stage, seeking a larger audience than
that of the white "ladies and gentlemen" in the train car. She authenticates
her narrative elaborately, quoting one of her many subtexts, a headline from
the *Memphis Commercial Appeal* that read: "Darky Damsel Obtains a Verdict
for Damages against the Chesapeake and Ohio Railroad—What it Cost to Put
a Colored School Teacher in a Smoking Car—Verdict for $500." Eventually,
the railroad appealed the case to the state supreme court, which reversed the
findings of the lower court, and ordered Wells to pay court costs. Even so,
Wells's strategic inclusion of this incident in her "authenticating narrative"
strengthened her posture as a crusader for justice.

Never enthusiastic about teaching, Wells found the profession too confin-
ing; she felt stifled and isolated. In the chapter titled "Iola," she writes: "The
confinement and monotony began to grow distasteful. The correspondence I
had built up in newspaper work gave me an outlet through which to express
the real 'me' " (*Crusade*, 31). Journalism propels Wells out of teaching, as her
outrage flares into another, more public conflict with community leaders. As a
writer and editor for the *Memphis Free Speech*, Wells writes an editorial that
attacks the morals of Memphis teachers. This sparks a dispute that embar-
rasses her employers on the Memphis School Board and contributes to the
suicide of a black female teacher who had allegedly been involved in an affair
with a white lawyer employed by the same board. Wells's public revelations
were not news to the rest of the community, but she had disrupted a delicate
balance of race relations by revealing a situation about which community
leaders had agreed to keep quiet.

Losing her job as a result of the controversy, Wells becomes totally
involved in publishing. As an investigative reporter, she continues to define
her identity through the adversary relationship. Publishing provides Wells
with a wider audience and greater opportunities for identity-defining experi-

ences. Thus, early in *Crusade*, Wells reveals her established pattern of forming her identity through public conflict.

In 1892, the lynching of three black Memphis citizens stirs Wells's moral indignation, and her reaction places her in a position of national prominence. Wells's autobiographical response to the "Lynching at the Curve" proves Robert Stepto's assertion that "personal history may be created through immersion in an elaborately authenticated historical event." By re-creating this historical event as an "act of language," Wells elevates it to the equivalent of metaphor in what Stepto calls "rhetorical usefulness."[17] As an event, the "Lynching at the Curve" lives on in Wells's autobiographical consciousness as a "supreme account to be settled."

> One day some colored and white boys quarreled over a game of marbles and the colored boys got the better of the fight which followed. The father of the white boys whipped the victorious colored boy, whose father and friends pitched in to avenge the grown man's flogging of a colored boy. The colored men won the fight, whereupon the white father and grocery keeper swore out a warrant for the arrest of the colored victors.
>
> Sunday morning's paper came out with lurid headlines telling how officers of the law had been wounded while in the discharge of their duties, hunting up criminals whom they had been told were harbored in the People's Grocery Company, this being "a low dive in which drinking and gambling were carried on: a resort of thieves and thugs." So ran the description in the leading white journals of Memphis of this successful effort of decent black men to carry on a legitimate business. (*Crusade*, 48–49)

Wells used this case as a prime example of the economic motivation behind some lynchings. According to Wells's analysis, the quarrel over the game of marbles was designed to involve black men in a dispute that would cost them their business.

The "Tennessee Rifles," a black militia group, guarded the jail where the black men were held as long as they felt the [wounded] white "officers" were in danger of dying. When they left their post, after deciding that tensions were easing, a group of white men crept into the jail at night, carried the black prisoners a mile outside the city, and "horribly shot them to death" (*Crusade*, 50). The lynching had a profound effect on Wells. Although she was in Natchez when the incident occurred, she knew all three men personally. That week, in the newspaper *Free Speech*, Wells carried words of advice for Memphis blacks:

> The city of Memphis has demonstrated that neither character nor standing avails the Negro if he dares to protect himself against the white man or become his rival. There is nothing we can do about the lynching now, as we are out-numbered and without arms. There is therefore only one thing left that we can do; save our money

---

[17]Robert Stepto, *From Behind the Veil: A Study of Afro-American Narrative* (Urbana: University of Illinois Press, 1979), 26.

and leave a town which will neither protect our lives and property, nor give us fair trial in the courts, but takes us out and murders us in cold blood when accused by white persons. (*Crusade,* 52)

This editorial, which Wells excerpted in her autobiography, precipitated a series of events that led to the smashing of Wells's press and her forced exile. Following Wells's advice, blacks disposed of their property and left Memphis, bringing business to a virtual standstill. . . . The article that led to the final destruction of Wells's press pointed to the root cause of many lynchings. Some few months after the lynching at "the curve," Wells wrote the following in a May 1892 editorial in *Free Speech*:

Eight Negroes lynched since the last issue of the *Free Speech*. Three were charged with killing white men and five with raping white women. If Southern white men are not careful . . . a conclusion will be reached which will be very dangerous to the moral reputation of their women.

In response to this editorial, a white rival paper, the *Memphis Commercial Appeal,* called on "chivalrous" white men to avenge this insult to the honor of white womanhood. As a result, the type and furnishings of Wells's *Free Press* were demolished, and a note was left behind saying that anyone attempting to publish the paper again would be killed. Wells received the information while attending a series of conferences in the Northeast. She had lost her paper, and been threatened and exiled from her home, for telling the truth as she saw it.

This experience, perhaps more than any other, contributed to Ida B. Wells's self-image; it reinforced her sense of self as a black woman who did her Christian duty by decrying the evils of lynching and the moral decay at its root. According to Erikson, "Leadership is prominently characterized by the choice of the proper place, the exact moment, and the specific issues that help" to make a point "momentously."[18] Wells liberated her power to effect change and became a woman of action in response to a given historical moment and a specific issue, lynching. In psychosocial terms, her lifelong struggle against lynching became what Erikson would have called a defense against "identity confusion."

As an investigative reporter, Wells published several booklets on lynching. The first of these, *Southern Horrors, Lynch Law in All Its Phases,* originally appeared as an article in the June 25, 1892, issue of T. Thomas Fortune's *New York Age,* the paper on which Wells worked after her forced departure from Memphis. In *Southern Horrors,* Wells established the falseness of the rape charge as an alleged cause of lynching and exposed many of these "rapes" as mere cover-ups for interracial love affairs between black men and white women. She also pointed to a deeper irony:

The miscegenation laws of the South only operate against the legitimate union of the races; they leave the white man free to seduce all the colored girls he can, but

[18]Erikson, *Life History,* 55.

it is death to the colored man who yields to the force and advances of a similar attraction in white women. White men lynch the offending Afro-American, not because he is a despoiler of virtue, but because he succumbs to the smiles of white women.[19]

Decrying the sexual double standard at the root of America's race war, Wells recognized the issue as one embedded in cultural and sexual stereotypes of black men, as well as conventional (and often false) notions of white womanhood. Although lynching proved an effective sanction against sex between black men and white women, white men were rarely punished for their sexual exploitation of black women. Such interracial liaisons degraded not only black women but white women, who perceived the features of a husband or a brother in a young mulatto face.

It was during this early part of her public career that the "Sage of Anacostia" became interested in Wells's work:

> Frederick Douglass came from his home in Washington to tell me what a revelation of existing conditions this article had been to him. He had been troubled by the increasing number of lynchings, and had begun to believe that there was an increasing lasciviousness on the part of Negroes. He wrote a strong preface to the pamphlet which I afterward published embodying these facts. This was the beginning of a friendship with the "Sage of Anacostia" which lasted until the day of his death, three years later. I have never ceased to be thankful for this contact with him. (*Crusade*, 72–73)

Despite Wells's assertion and Douglass's authentication of her life and work, there is no known evidence to suggest that he ever believed "there was an increasing lasciviousness on the part of Negroes." The above passage illustrates a certain self-serving behavior that is characteristic of Wells's autobiographical persona, a form of posing that, when manifested in life, did not endear her to the leadership that moved forward to fill the void left by Douglass's passing. Even though the Wells assertion may be true, a more modest estimation of her contribution to Douglass's ideas would have been more persuasive to the cautious reader.

Douglass's preface to *Southern Horrors*, written at Wells's request, emerges as yet another key subtext in the interpretation of Wells's authenticating strategy. On October 17, 1892, Wells queried Douglass on stationery from the *New York Age*. "Dear Mr. Douglass," she wrote, "I take the liberty of addressing you to ask if you will be so kind as to put in writing the encomiums you were pleased to lavish on my article on Lynch Law published in the June 25 issue of the Age."[20] Wells wrote that she was "revising the matter for a pamphlet" and asked for a letter she could use as an introduction;

[19]Ida B. Wells, *Southern Horrors, Lynch Law in All Its Phases* (New York: Arno Press, 1969; originally published 1892), 2.

[20]Ida B. Wells, letter to Frederick Douglass, October 17, 1892. Frederick Douglass Collection, Library of Congress, Washington, D.C.

the pamphlet later appeared as *Southern Horrors.* In 1895, Wells recycled Douglass's letter as an introduction to *A Red Record: Tabulated Statistics and Alleged Causes of Lynching in the United States, 1892–1893–1894.*

Douglass's letter authenticated Wells's "moral sensibility" and the bravery of her response to the "persistent infliction of outrage and crime against colored people." He also affirmed the significance of Wells's investigative reporting when he wrote, "There has been no word equal to it in convincing power. I have spoken, but my word is feeble in comparison. You give us what you know and testify from actual knowledge. You have dealt with the fact, and cool, painstaking fidelity and left those naked and uncontradicted facts to speak for themselves."[21] In the view of many veterans of the antislavery movement, the struggle against lynching was a continuation of the fight for a freedom that would never be secure until blacks were able to exercise full civil rights without fear of reprisal. A spirit of black resistance metamorphosed into a budding nationalist consciousness, uniquely Afro-American in character. A contemporary of Booker T. Washington, W. E. B. Du Bois, Frances E. W. Harper, Anna Julia Cooper, and Mary Church Terrell, Ida B. Wells contributed to the development of this black political awareness. In this endeavor, race, not sex, served as Wells's point of departure, for she knew that black women were oppressed primarily because they were black and not because they were women. . . .

Although the *New York Age* was on an exchange list with many white periodicals, Wells maintained that none of them commented on her investigative reporting. Initially, it seems, very little attention was paid to Wells in the white press; her support came from the black community. In 1892, the black women of Brooklyn and New York City gave Wells a testimonial that called immediate national attention to her antilynching activities. This event marked the beginning of Wells's public speaking career. Nowhere is Wells more modest in her autobiography than she appears in the chapter entitled "The Homesick Exile," as she looks back on her first public speech:

> When the committee told me that I had to speak I was frightened. I had been a writer, both as a correspondent and editor for several years. I had some little reputation as an essayist from schoolgirl days. . . . But this was the first time I had ever been called on to deliver an honest-to-goodness address.
>
> After every detail of that horrible lynching affair was imprinted on my memory, I had to commit it all to paper, and so got up to read my story on that memorable occasion. As I described the cause of trouble at home my mind went back to the scenes of the struggle, to the thought of the friends who were scattered throughout the country, a feeling of loneliness and homesickness for the days and the friends that were gone came over me and I felt the tears coming. (*Crusade,* 79)

Wells dates this 1892 testimonial as the beginning of the black women's club

---

[21]Frederick Douglass, letter to Ida B. Wells, October 25, 1892. Frederick Douglass Collection, Library of Congress.

movement, thus asserting a founding role. She describes her early work in establishing clubs in New York, Boston, Providence, Newport, and New Haven. Following addresses by Wells in these cities, black women met to organize clubs such as the Women's Era Club of Boston and the Twentieth Century Club of New Haven. Wells's involvement in the black women's club movement should not be diminished, for it involved the active fusion of powerful influences: black feminism and black nationalism. The result of this fusion was the development of a race-centered, self-conscious womanhood in the form of the black women's club movement. Whereas the white woman's movement reflected her commitment to temperance and suffrage, the black woman's movement was born in the outrage of the slave mother and the struggle against lynching. Racial oppression, not sexism, was the primary issue. For an Ida B. Wells or a Frances E. W. Harper, a blow at lynching was a blow at racism and at the brutally enforced sexual double standard that pervaded the South. It was a defense of the entire race. . . .

During the year 1892, Wells began to receive what she interpreted as the "loyal endorsement and support" of the black press, but she was disappointed that the white press remained virtually untouched by her campaign. Through Peter Still, the black former Underground Railroad agent, she met Catherine Impey, editor of the *Anti-Caste* of Somerset, England, who was visiting with Quaker relatives in Philadelphia. Their meeting, Wells writes, "resulted in an invitation to England and the beginning of a worldwide campaign against lynching" (*Crusade*, 82). As Wells relates in her autobiography, she was visiting in the Washington home of Frederick Douglass when the invitation to go to England arrived. Her metaphor for this opportunity reaffirms her relationship to the narrative tradition of the fugitive slaves:

> It seemed like an open door in a stone wall. For nearly a year I had been in the North, hoping to spread the truth and get moral support for a demand that those accused of crimes be given a fair trial and punished by law instead of by mob. Only in one city—Boston—had I been given a meager hearing, and the press was dumb. I refer, of course, to the white press, since it was the medium through which I hoped to reach the white people of the country, who alone could mold public sentiment. (*Crusade*, 86)

Wells made two trips to England, one in 1893 and one in 1894, on both occasions seeking a larger, more receptive audience. She lectured throughout England and Scotland, and during the 1894 trip she served as overseas correspondent for the *Inter-Ocean* newspaper. Her lectures were well attended, and she generally received good coverage in the English press. Thus Wells internationalized her movement. . . .

. . . Wells knew that one way to get American papers to comment on lynching was to arouse public opinion abroad. Black abolitionists and former slaves had provided early models for this strategy. Wells simply followed the route of fugitive slaves, who used English public opinion to bring about an end to the cruelty and brutality of slavery. In fact, she was even received as the "honored guest" of Ellen Richards, the woman who had previously purchased the freedom of Frederick Douglass and William Wells Brown.[22]

In her public speeches and lectures in England, Wells continued to attack the racial and sexual myths believed by many Americans who condoned lynching, and she articulated the roots of the American race war. Additionally, she pointed out that women as well as men were lynched, often for violating the unspoken code of racial etiquette:

> It is true they had read of lynchings and while they thought them dreadful had accepted the general belief that it was for terrible crimes perpetrated by Negro men upon white women. I read the account of that poor woman who was boxed up in a barrel and rolled down a hill in Texas, and asked if that lynching could be excused on the same ground. (*Crusade*, 154)

Through this and similar examples, Wells demonstrated the cruelty and brutality of lynching and defeated the "threadbare notion" that whites lynch blacks because they rape white women. Moreover, Wells attested, some white women were "willing victims":

> I found that white men who had created a race of mulattoes by raping and consorting with Negro women were still doing so whenever they could; these same white men lynched, burned, and tortured Negro men for doing the same thing with white women; even when the white women were willing victims. (*Crusade*, 71)

It took courage for Wells to publish these radical statements, for here she attacked the heart of southern racial mythology. Wells's attitude toward interracial sexual relationships was determined by her belief that these relationships could not exist on a basis of social parity with same-race relationships. Rightly or wrongly, she viewed black men who accepted sexual favors from white women as "weak." Relationships between black women and white men she viewed as one-way exploitation.

In Europe, Wells continued her established pattern of seeking and defining her identity through public conflict. . . . In a chapter titled "A Regrettable Interview," Wells treats the controversy that disrupted her second trip to Europe. Because she continued to assail the indifference of the WCTU and other "Christian and moral influences" in the United States toward lynching, Wells became very unpopular with some of Frances Willard's [Frances Willard, organizer and leader of the Women's Christian Temperance Union] English friends. When Wells reprinted an interview from the *New York Voice* in which Willard condoned lynching in the influential British magazine *Fraternity*, Lady Henry Somerset countered with a new interview with Willard intended to cast doubt on Wells and her mission. In this interview, Willard, for the first time, expressed a cautious stand against lynching.

---

[22]Gertrude B. Mossell, *The Work of the Afro-American Woman* (New York: Oxford University Press, 1988; originally published 1894), 38.

Still showing her concern for setting the record straight, Wells documents this chapter with quotes from both the Somerset interview and her editorial response to it, which appeared the next day in the same publication, the *Westminster Gazette.* Wells's editorial represents a written equivalent of Harriet "Linda Brent" Jacobs's "sass":

> Sir:
>
> The interview published in your columns today hardly merits a reply, because of the indifference to suffering manifested. Two ladies are represented sitting under a tree at Reigate, and, after some preliminary remarks on the terrible subject of lynching, Miss Willard laughingly replies by cracking a joke. And the concluding sentence of her interview shows the object is not to determine best how they may help the Negro who is being hanged, shot and burned, but "to guard Miss Willard's reputation."
>
> With me, it is not myself nor my reputation, but the life of my people which is at stake, and I affirm that this is the first time to my knowledge that Miss Willard has said one single word in denouncing lynching or demand for law. The year 1890, the one in which her interview in *The Voice* appears, had a larger lynching record than any previous year, and the number and territory of lynching have increased, to say nothing of the number of human beings burned alive.

Here Wells asserts her relation to the unifying symbol of her autobiography and her life, and to a personal myth of self that reflects the outraged mother defending the life of her people. This is accomplished through the "crusade" motif that provides the central metaphor for Wells's experience in the same way that "education" serves for Henry Adams. The extensive use of quotes in the chapter on Wells's experiences in England serve as part of the text's "historicizing paraphernalia." The quotes authenticate both the text and the author's image of self, as they signal the historical intention in Well's autobiographical impulse. Unfortunately they also contribute to the eclectic quality and choppiness of form that characterize the text as a whole, especially the fourteen chapters on Well's experiences as an antilynching lecturer abroad.

White newspapers in the United States, receiving marked copies of the articles from the British press, attempted to defame the crusader, providing another account to be settled. Wells's old enemy, the *Memphis Commercial Appeal*, referred to her as a "Negro Adventuress." Defending her autobiographical stance in the chapter "You Can't Change the Record," Wells quotes an article from the June 13, 1894, *Liverpool Daily Post* that showed British reaction to the article published in the *Memphis Daily Commercial:* "If we were to convey an idea of the things said we should not only infringe upon the libel law, but have every reason to believe that we would do a gross and grotesque injustice." In the "Ungentlemanly and Unchristian" chapter, Wells writes about how she met the editor of the *St. Louis Republic* while speaking against lynching in that city in 1894: "He remarked that he had been to great pains in sending persons throughout the south where I had lived in an effort to get something that he could publish against me. 'Well,' he answered, 'you were over there giving us hail columbia, and if I could have found anything to your discredit I would have been free to use it on the ground that all is fair in war' " (*Crusade*, 234). The effect of these attacks, the autobiographer argues, was to increase public interest in her cause: "The *Brooklyn Daily Eagle* said that it would pay Memphis to send for me and pay me a salary to keep silent; that as long as I was living in Memphis and publishing only a 'one horse' newspaper few people outside my district knew about me" (*Crusade*, 221).

"With help from her detractors," writes the cultural historian Paula Giddings, "Wells' British tour was a personal triumph, and in the end had a great impact on the antilynching campaign. . . . English opinion had also broken the silence of many prominent American leaders. No longer could they afford to ignore 'the talented schoolmarm,' and such influential people as Richard Gilder, editor of *Century* magazine, Samuel Gompers, the labor leader, and yes, Frances Willard eventually lent their names in support of the campaign."[23] In some sense, Wells seems to have understood and appreciated the dynamics of confrontation and identity formation as it functioned in her life and work, as well as the importance of choosing the proper time, public place, and issue for speaking out and assuming leadership. Never before had a black woman so publicly articulated the roots of the immediate oppression of her people or mounted an international campaign against the horror that oppression implied. Ironically, Wells's exile from Memphis gave her the opportunity to have an impact of greater magnitude. Yet this impact would be felt in Memphis as much as elsewhere. Giddings argues that the decrease in lynchings in 1893 and each year thereafter "can be directly attributed to the efforts of Ida B. Wells" and that "the effect of Wells' campaign was aptly demonstrated" in her "home city" of Memphis. "Memphis exported more cotton than any other city in the world, and Wells' assertions had been especially damaging to its image. So, as a direct result of her efforts, the city fathers were pressed to take an official stand against lynching—and for the next twenty years there was not another incident of vigilante violence there."[24]

After her first trip to England in 1893, Ida B. Wells returned to Chicago and a position on the *Chicago Conservator*. On June 27, 1895, she married Ferdinand L. Barnett, one of the founders of the *Conservator*. Wells's courtship coincides with a noticeable gap in her narrative; yet this is not surprising when one considers that *Crusade for Justice* is primarily a story of Wells's public life. She says only that Barnett proposed before she went to England the second time and that, when she returned, they married. Some of the details of their courtship are available from Alfreda Duster, who reports that her parents met "in the work." After the death of his first wife, Barnett, the father of two small sons, was often asked if he would marry again: "He wasn't interested in just anybody, he was looking for a certain type of woman who

---

[23]Paula Giddings, *When and Where I Enter: The Impact of Black Women on Race and Sex in America* (New York: Morrow, 1984), 92.
[24]Ibid.

would mean something to his life and career. And evidently Mama fit that pattern. He pursued and married her."[25]

When Wells "came back the second time, she went across the country, trying to organize anti-lynching leagues . . . and while she was touring the country, her itinerary was known and wherever she stopped there would be a letter from my father. And so they had a long distance correspondence courtship and I understand—I never saw one—but I understand my father could write a beautiful love letter."[26] According to her daughter, Wells was delighted to have found a man who believed in, and would agitate for, the same principles. At the time of their marriage, Wells began using the hyphenated surname Wells-Barnett. She was then thirty years old. "So far as her perception was concerned," says Duster, "she was continuing her work. She was continuing in journalism because she took over the editorship of the *Conservator* within a week after they married. She wrote and she didn't want to lose the identity of Ida B. Wells."[27]

A perceptible change in Wells's autobiographical focus and the direction of her narrative occurs in the chapter entitled "A Divided Duty." Thereafter, the text concentrates more on local affairs and on Wells's private life, the "rounding-out possibility" of the domestic sphere. Wells's treatment of the early years of her marriage explores the tension between the roles of public crusader and private woman—a theme introduced early in the autobiography and further developed in the written re-creation of her first speaking engagement in New York. Having returned from Europe and married Barnett, Wells purchased the *Conservator* from her husband "and others who owned it," embarking on "A Divided Duty": "I decided to continue my work as a journalist, for this was my first, and might be said, my only love (*Crusade,* 242). Immediately following her marriage, Wells "took charge of the *Conservator* office." "My duties as editor, as president of the Ida B. Wells Woman's Club, and speaker in many white women's clubs in and around Chicago kept me pretty busy. But I was not too busy to give birth to a male child the following 25 March 1896" (*Crusade,* 244–245).

Ida Wells-Barnett remained active. She named her first-born Charles Aked Barnett, after the Reverend C. F. Aked of Liverpool, one of her English antilynching allies. Shortly after the child's birth, she undertook an antilynching speaking tour: "And so I started out with a six month old nursing baby and made trips to Decatur, Quincy, Springfield, Bloomington, and many other towns. I honestly believe that I am the only woman in the United States who ever travelled with a nursing baby to make political speeches" (*Crusade,* 244). Perhaps one of the greatest moments of her life came at the founding meeting

---

[25]Interview conducted by Marcia Greenlee with Alfreda M. Duster on March 8–9, 1978, for the Black Women's Oral History Project at the Schlesinger Library, Radcliffe Collection, Harvard University, 62. Quotes are used with the written permission of Alfreda Duster, August 6, 1981.

[26]Ibid., 11.

[27]Ibid., 16.

of the National Association of Colored Women (NACW). Present were Rosetta Sprague, daughter of Frederick Douglass, Ellen Craft, daughter and name-sake of another famous slave narrator, Frances Ellen Watkins Harper, and "General" Harriet Tubman, the "Moses" who had led hundreds of fugitive slaves to freedom. Harriet Tubman, "the grand old woman" of the convention and the oldest member in attendance, "arrived to a standing ovation." Charles Aked Barnett, the youngest in attendance, was named "Baby of the Associa-tion." Thus, with the founding of the NACW, a symbolic torch was passed to a new generation, proclaiming both the emergence of "Black women into the forefront of the struggle for Black and women's rights" and the launching of "the modern civil rights movement."[28]

The latter portion of *Crusade for Justice* alternates between the activities of the political organizer and the life of hearth and home. The following anecdote symbolizes Wells's life of "divided duty" and demonstrates the complex practical problems facing a public figure who is also a mother:

> When the time came for me to speak I rose and went forward. The baby, who was wide awake, looked around, and failing to see me but hearing my voice, raised his voice in angry protest. Almost unconsciously I turned to go to him, whereupon the chairman, who instantly realized the trouble, put someone else in the chair, went back to the back of the platform, and took the baby out into the hall where he could not hear my voice and kept him there until I had finished my task. (*Crusade,* 245)

Ida Wells-Barnett soon discovers the demands of motherhood: "I found that motherhood was a profession by itself, just like schoolteaching and lecturing, and that once one is launched on such a career, she owed it to herself to become as expert as possible in the practice of her profession" (*Crusade,* 255). Even though she writes that she had not "entered into the bonds of holy matrimony with the same longing for children that so many other women have," she believes that the creator has given woman "a wonderful place in the scheme of things" and revels in "having made this discovery" for herself. She writes that she is happy to have rejected birth-control information on her wedding night (*Crusade,* 241).

On the birth of her second son, Herman K. Barnett, in 1897, Wells-Barnett resigned the editorship of the *Conservator* and gave up the presidency of the Ida B. Wells Woman's Club in order to give full attention to raising her children. For the next fifteen years, motherhood was her primary occupation. Wells's autobiographical reticence about her private experiences in marriage reinforces the public nature of her narrative, as well as its authenticating structure. Apparently, many in the antilynching movement felt that Wells had "deserted the cause" by taking up her new "profession of motherhood." In "Divided Duty," Wells narrates an encounter with Susan B. Anthony:

[28]Giddings, *When and Where I Enter,* 94.

She said, "I know of no one in all this country better fitted to do the work you had in hand than yourself. Since you have gotten married, agitation seems practically to have ceased. Besides, you have a divided duty. You are here trying to help in the formation of this league and your eleven-month-old baby needs your attention at home. You are distracted over the thought that maybe he is not being looked after as he would be if you were there, and that makes for a divided duty."

Although it was a well-merited rebuke from her point of view, I could not tell Miss Anthony that it was because I had been unable, like herself, to get the support which was necessary to carry on my work that I had become discouraged in the effort to carry on alone. (*Crusade*, 255)

So "carry on alone" becomes a central motif of the autobiography. When Wells married Barnett, she felt her own people censured her for having "abandoned the struggle." From her point of view, "they were more outspoken because of the loss to the cause than they had been in holding up my hands when I was trying to carry a banner" (*Crusade*, 241). The passage cited above reflects a tone of conciliation affected by Wells's autobiographical persona from time to time. By telling the reader that some feminist leaders criticized her for diverting her energy away from her active public role into the private maternal sphere, and by registering her disappointment in not receiving more support from the black community for her crusade, Wells wins our sympathy for her difficult role of "carrying on alone." Through the use of the earlier quotation attributed to Susan B. Anthony, Wells suggests that the overall success or failure of the antilynching campaign depended, at this time, largely on her individual effort. There is considerable validity to her claim. In the estimation of the historian August Meier, "Later on, after World War I, the NAACP entered upon the anti-lynching campaign, but at the turn of the century opposition to this vicious practice was essentially one and the same with the activities of Ida Wells-Barnett."[29] Dedicated to both motherhood and activism, Wells refused to sacrifice either the public or the private role, but motherhood increased the enormity and complexity of her task.

In a later chapter, "Illinois Lynchings," Wells relates her reluctance to continue the antilynching work after the birth of her children. In addition to the charge that she has "deserted the cause," she also has been "accused by some of our men of jumping ahead of them and doing work without giving them a chance" (*Crusade*, 311). For these and other reasons, she writes, she has become less willing to do the hard and "thankless" work of investigating lynchings. But she *did* go, with the encouragement and blessing of her husband and family. Wells's "duty" absolves the "true woman" of the need to be politically quiescent:

I thought of that passage of Scripture which tells of wisdom from the mouth of babes and sucklings. I thought if my child wanted me to go I ought not to fall by the wayside. . . .

[29]August Meier, Introduction to *On Lynchings*, by Ida B. Wells-Barnett (New York: Arno Press, 1969), i.

Next morning all four of my children accompanied my husband and me to the station and saw me start on the journey. (*Crusade*, 311–312)

As a result of her efforts, Wells contends, the governor issued a statement that outlawed lynching in Illinois. And he refused to reinstate the Cairo sheriff who had cooperated with the mob that took the life of "Frog" James. Wells writes: "That was in 1909, and from that day until the present there has been no lynching in the state. Every sheriff, whenever there seem to be any signs of the kind, immediately telegraphs the governor for troops" (*Crusade*, 346). Of course, many lynchings went unreported. Despite the lack of a clear causal relationship between the actions of Wells-Barnett and those of the governor, her investigation did exercise a significant influence on public opinion.

In her role as wife and mother, Ida B. Wells fulfills the dream of Harriet "Linda Brent" Jacobs—the dream of having a legitimate relationship with a man who will cherish and protect her. Ferdinand L. Barnett offered Wells this security, as well as a degree of financial independence and unlimited "moral" support for her mission. In the pages of her autobiography, Wells diminishes her personal importance to emphasize the importance of "the work," the crusade of the outraged mother. On the other hand, she highlights the relationships she shared with her dependent children, for they help illustrate her life of "divided duty." With the support of her dynamic mate, Wells-Barnett was able both to raise a family and to carry on her struggle against lynching. Barnett pushed her ahead, and in the folk idiom of Zora Neale Hurston, he propped her up on "every leanin' side."

A look at the interview with Alfreda Duster on record at the Black Women's Oral History Project at Harvard University yields some of the personal information missing from the text. To the young Alfreda, Ida B. Wells-Barnett was "just mother," a homemaker active in civic life. Duster remembers that her father did most of the cooking and that it was her job to have the potatoes cooked and ready for dinner when her father came home; she also remembers that her mother took an active part in the educational life of her children, often visiting teachers at school.[30] Like her own dear parents, Wells-Barnett stimulated in her children a love of reading and an appreciation for the importance of a good education. The archetypal outraged mother, Wells-Barnett was both protective and strict with her children. When her daughters were young, she established a rule that they must play in plain sight of the front door at all times. Discovered out of view, in a friend's house, young Alfreda received a spanking.[31]

Wells never grew quiescent. Despite the responsibilities of motherhood, she remained active in the struggle against lynching, the women's club movement, and the formation of the NAACP. Even when she had given up her work at the *Conservator* and the presidency of the Ida B. Wells Club, she

[30]Duster—Greenlee interview, 4.
[31]Ibid.

remained active in the city where she founded the Negro Fellowship League and the Alpha Suffrage Association. She was also a charter member of the National Negro Committee, a forerunner of the NAACP. In her work with the Alpha Suffrage Association in Chicago in 1914, Wells organized black women to canvass their neighborhoods and report their progress:

> The women at first were very much disappointed.
> They said that the men jeered at them and told them that they ought to be home taking care of the babies. Others insisted that the women were trying to take the place of men and wear the trousers. I urged each one of the workers to go back and tell the women that we wanted them to register so that they could help put a colored man in the city council. (*Crusade,* 346)

Black men's reluctance to support female suffrage was understandable in the light of the racist attitudes of some white suffrage leaders and segregation within the suffrage movement. In fact, some southern white women hoped suffrage would offer "a means to the end of securing white supremacy."[32] But Wells continued to attack racism within the movement as she organized the black community. In the end, her appeal to the black men of Chicago was successful.

Overall, Wells's work with the Alpha Suffrage Association would seem to indicate that black men who were reluctant to support women politically overcame that reluctance when presented with sound arguments about black women's suffrage. Many black men agreed with the analysis of W. E. B. Du Bois: "Votes for women means votes for Black women." The consensus of masculine opinion, in the words of Paula Giddings, was that "political empowerment of the race required the participation of Black women."[33] Thus Wells advanced the cause of the race through advancing the cause of black women and challenging publicly, at every opportunity, the racism of white suffragists. But always, even in this endeavor on behalf of women, the interests of the race came first.

If Du Bois was correct when he asserted that the Afro-American is a kind of seventh son gifted with double consciousness of himself as a black and an American, then Wells acquired a triple consciousness of herself—as an American, a black, and a woman. For Wells, existence was a phenomenon in which belief and action could not be separated. She believed, and therefore she acted, attaining an escape from the South that liberated her for an even greater potential. Her autobiography reflects a model of "antislavery" expression. Because lynching was one of the tools by which whites hoped to reduce blacks to their previous condition of servitude, antilynching agitation was truly antislavery agitation in the hearts and minds of its supporters. Despite the enormity of her task, Wells forged a legitimate black feminism through the synthesis of black nationalism and the suffrage movement, providing a useful

[32]Giddings, *When and Where I Enter,* 126.
[33]Ibid., 121.

model with race, not sex, as a point of departure. Her work established not only the ideological basis for later antilynching work by the NAACP but also for similar work done by the Association of Southern Women for the Prevention of Lynching, a white group headed by the Texas feminist Jessie Daniel Ames. This Wells accomplished either because of, or in spite of, her racial and sexual identity.

In *Crusade for Justice: The Autobiography of Ida B. Wells*, the intelligence and sensibility of the narrator far exceed that of the unlettered slave. Here an aging author "confront[s] and connect[s] nineteenth and twentieth century experience" by placing herself at the center of a "repossessed past."[34] Yet this twentieth-century autobiography possesses distinct formal attributes that help to identify its place in a tradition of black women writing autobiography. Wells's autobiographical consciousness alternates between the confession and the historical memoir, allowing the autobiographer the necessary latitude to discuss both her public and her private duty. This Wells required in order to demonstrate her development, not only as a political activist, but as a wife and mother. Throughout the autobiography, the concept of extended family reaches out to others in "the work." In this way, *Crusade for Justice*, Wells's historical memoir, looks forward to the modern political autobiographies of Anne Moody, Shirley Chisholm, and Angela Davis. It represents an important link between the old and the new, part of the "lost ground" of Afro-American literary tradition.

34Stone, *Autobiographical Occasions*, 29.

Autoethnography: The An-Archic Style of *Dust Tracks on a Road*

Françoise Lionnet

The words do not count. . . . The tune is the unity of the thing.

—Zora Neale Hurston, 1942

The greatness of a man is to be found not in his acts but in his style.

—Frantz Fanon, 1952

"Black women have written numerous autobiographies, among which *Dust Tracks on a Road* takes the prize for inscrutability": this is the statement with which Michele Wallace concludes her recent evaluation of Zora Neale Hurston's work, and of the interest that revisionist critics of different stripes have taken in Hurston's corpus during the past decade.[1] Hurston's contributions as novelist, anthropologist, and folklorist are now widely recognized. Provocative questions remain, however, about the 1942 autobiography, which does not fit into any of the usual expectations about the genre. This is not terribly surprising in view of the fact that Hurston was not one to conform to any established narrative "models."

In fact, to glance at the table of contents of *Dust Tracks* is to notice that it presents itself as a set of interactive thematic *topoi* superimposed on a loosely chronological framework. The seemingly linear progression from "My Birthplace" to "Looking Things Over" is more deceptive in that regard than truly indicative of a narrator's psychological development, quest for recognition, or journey from innocence to experience as traditionally represented in confessional autobiographies. The chapter titled "Seeing the World as It Is," with which Hurston originally meant to conclude the book,[2] is a philosophical essay on power, politics, and human relations on a planetary scale. It is the radical testament of a writer who rejects *ressentiment* and, refusing to align herself

[1]Michele Wallace, "Who Dat Say Who Dat When I Say Who Dat? Zora Neale Hurston Then and Now," *Voice Literary Supplement* 16 (April 1988), pp. 18–21.

[2]See Robert Hemenway's comments in Appendix to *Dust Tracks on a Road*, ed. Hemenway, 2d ed. (Urbana: University of Illinois Press, 1984), p. 288. All references will be included in the text and flagged *DT* when necessary.

with any "party," explains that it is because she does "not have much of a herd instinct" (344–45). Rather than recounting the events of her life, Hurston is more interested in showing us who she is—or, to be more precise, how she has become what she is—an individual who ostensibly values her independence more than any kind of political commitment to a cause, especially the cause of "Race Solidarity," as she puts it (327). Hers is a controversial and genealogical enterprise that has been much criticized, charged with accommodationism (xxxviii) and with disappointing the expectations of "frankness" and "truthfulness" which are all too often unquestioningly linked to this genre of self-writing.[3] Openly critical of *Dust Tracks* in his Introduction to the second edition, her biographer, Robert Hemenway, puts it thus: "Style . . . becomes a kind of camouflage, an escape from articulating the paradoxes of her personality" (xxxviii and see xxxiv–xxxv, for example).

An-Archy and Community

In light of the skepticism with which contemporary literary theory has taught us to view any effort of self-representation in language, I would like to propose a different approach to the issue of Hurston's presumed insincerity and untrustworthiness.[4] It may perhaps be more useful to reconsider *Dust Tracks on a Road* not as autobiography but rather as self-portrait, in the sense redefined by Michel Beaujour—"des textes qui se tiennent par eux-mêmes, plutôt que la mimesis d'actions passées"[5]—and to try to elaborate a conceptual framework that would not conflict with Hurston's own avowed methodology as essayist and anthropologist. Indeed, what I would like to suggest here is that *Dust Tracks* amounts to autoethnography, that is, the defining of one's subjective ethnicity as mediated through language, history, and ethnographical analysis; in short, that the book amounts to a kind of "figural anthropology" of the self.[6]

---

[3]By *genealogical* I mean the reconstruction of the self through interpretations that integrate as many aspects of the past as are deemed *significant* by the agent of the narrative discourse. It is clear that Hurston considers cultural forms more significant than specific events. Thus, the self she fashions through language is not a fixed essence, partaking of an immutable and originary racial substance. Rather, it is a *process* of active self-discovery through self-invention by means of the folk narratives of ethnic interest. For a recent thorough and definitive analysis of these Nietzschean questions, see Alexander Nehamas, *Nietzsche: Life as Literature* (Cambridge: Harvard University Press, 1986). David Hoy has done an excellent and useful review of this book: see "Different Stories" in *London Review of Books*, Jan. 8, 1987, pp. 15–17. In the Afro-American context, genealogical revisionism is of course a common theme of literature. See Kimberly W. Benston, " 'I Yam What I Yam': Naming and Unnaming in Afro-American Literature," *Black American Literature Forum* 16 (Spring 1982); as well as Jahnheinz Jahn, *Muntu: An Outline of the New African Culture* (New York: Grove Press, 1961), p. 125.

[4]For an overview of contemporary theories of autobiography, see Paul John Eakin, *Fictions in Autobiography: Studies in the Art of Self-Invention* (Princeton: Princeton University Press, 1985), chap. 4 in particular.

[5]Michel Beaujour, *Miroirs d'encre* (Paris: Seuil, 1980), p. 348: "texts which are self-contained rather than being the representation of past actions." All translations are mine.

[6]This phrase is used by Michel Serres in *The Parasite*, trans. Lawrence R. Schehr (Baltimore: Johns Hopkins University Press, 1982), p. 6. The French phrase is "une anthropologie figurée."

In a recent essay, James Clifford refers to the "allegory of salvage," which generally tended to dominate the representational practice of fieldworkers in the era of Boasian anthropology. For these fieldworkers, says Clifford, the preservation of disappearing cultures and vanishing lore was seen as the vital "redemption" of the "otherness" of primitive cultures from a global entropy: "The other is lost, in disintegrating time and place, but saved in the text."[7] This textualization of the object of representation incorporated a move from the oral-discursive field experience of the collector of folklore to his or her written version of that initial intersubjective moment—a transcription that is also a way of speaking *for* the other culture, a kind of ventriloquism. Having been trained under Boas, Hurston was supposed to be going in the field to do just that: to salvage her own "vanishing" Negro culture. Her position of fundamental liminality—being at once a participant in and an observer of her culture—would bring home to her the distorting effects of that problematic shift from orality to fixed, rigid textuality and thus would reinforce her skepticism about the anthropological project, in her assigned role as detached, objective interpreter and translator. Having shared in that rural culture during her childhood in Eatonville, she could not adopt the nostalgic pose common to those Western ethnographies that implicitly lament the loss of an Edenic, and preindustrial past. Instead, her skepticism about the writing of culture would permeate the writing of the self, the autobiography, turning it into the allegory of an ethnographic project that self-consciously moves from the general (the history of Eatonville) to the particular (Zora's life, her family and friends) and back to the general (religion, culture, and world politics in the 1940s). Unlike black spiritual autobiographies, which exhibit a similar threefold pattern of death, conversion, and rebirth, as well as a strong sense of transcendent purpose, *Dust Tracks* does not seek to legitimate itself through appeal to what William L. Andrews has called a "powerful source of authorization," such as religion or another organized system of belief.[8] It is in that sense that *Dust Tracks* is a powerfully an-archic work, not anchored in any original and originating story of racial or sexual difference.

The tone of the work and its rhetorical strategy of exaggeration draw attention to its style and away from what it directly denotes. For example, the statement "There were no discrete nuances of life on Joe Clarke's porch . . . all emotions were naked and nakedly arrived at" (62) describes the men's reactions to instances of adultery (a folksy topic), but it also carries historical

See *Le Parasite* (Paris: Grasset, 1980), p. 13. See also Alexander Gelley, *Narrative Crossings: Theory and Pragmatics of Prose Fiction* (Baltimore: Johns Hopkins University Press, 1987), pp. 79–100, for a useful discussion of "parasitic talk" and narrative agency, cultural norms, and quotidian talk applied to Melville's *Confidence-Man.*

[7]James Clifford, "On Ethnographic Allegory," *Writing Culture: The Poetics and Politics of Ethnography,* ed. Clifford and George E. Marcus (Berkeley: University of California Press, 1986), pp. 98–121 (112).

[8]See William L. Andrews, ed., *Sisters of the Spirit: Three Black Women's Autobiographies in the Nineteenth Century* (Bloomington: Indiana University Press, 1986), p. 13. To say that Hurston is not interested in *organized* resistance to patterns of social injustice is not to imply that she is not strongly critical of injustice. See pp. 336–45.

implications about the pioneer spirit in general, as the sentence that follows it makes clear: "This was the spirit of that whole new part of the state at the time, as it always is where men settle new lands" (62). Similarly, when Zora talks about her unhappy love affair, it is through vivid images that convey, with some irony, the universality of pain rather than deep personal anguish: "I freely admit that everywhere I set my feet down, there were tracks of blood. Blood from the very middle of my heart" (260). Regretting the "halcyon days" of childhood, she bemoans the gravity that pervades adulthood and makes us unable to "fly with the unseen things that soar" (78). And when she is discussing race, her denial—"No, instead of Race Pride being a virtue, it is a sapping vice" (325)—implicates us directly in that seemingly volatile statement instead of pointing us to the obvious historical context of the moment, that is, the rise of fascism, World War II, colonialism, the hypocrisy and self-satisfaction of "the blond brother" (343), and the preponderance of "instances of human self-bias" (281). Clearly, *Dust Tracks* does not gesture toward a coherent tradition of introspective self-examination with soul-baring displays of emotion.

Paradoxically, despite its rich cultural content, the work does not authorize unproblematic recourse to culturally grounded interpretations. It is an orphan text that attempts to create its own genealogy by simultaneously appealing to and debunking the cultural traditions it helps to redefine. Hurston's chosen objects of study, for example, the folktales that come alive during the story-telling, or "lying," sessions she observes, are indeed never "fixed." Their content is not rigid and unchanging but varies according to the tale-telling situation. It is the contextual frame of reference, the situation of the telling, that determines how a tale is reinterpreted by each new teller; hence, for the anthropologist, there is no "essential" quality to be isolated in the content of those tales, but there is a formal structure that can and must be recognized if she is to make sense of, and do justice to, the data gathered. The chapter titled "Research" puts the matter clearly and succinctly:

> I enjoyed collecting folk-tales and I believed the people from whom I collected them enjoyed the telling of them, just as much as I did the hearing. Once they got started, the "lies" just rolled and story-tellers fought for a chance to talk. It was the same thing with the songs. *The one thing to be guarded against, in the interest of truth, was over-enthusiasm. For instance, if the song was going good, and the material ran out, the singer was apt to interpolate pieces of other songs into it.* The only way you can know when that happens, is to know your material so well that you can sense the violation. Even if you do not know the song that is being used for padding, you can tell the change in rhythm and tempo. *The words do not count. The subject matter in Negro folk-songs can be anything* and go from love to work, to travel, to food, to weather, to fight, to demanding the return of a wig by a woman who has turned unfaithful. *The tune is the unity of the thing.* And you have to know what you are doing when you begin to pass on that, because Negroes can fit in more words and leave out more and still keep the tune better than anyone I can think of. (197–98; my italics)

The whole issue of form and content, style and message is astutely condensed here. "Truth" is clearly a matter of degree and can easily be distorted by the over-enthusiasm of the performer. If *over-enthusiasm* can be seen as another word for hyperbole, then Hurston the writer is hereby cautioning her own reader to defer judgment about the explicit referentiality of her text. Why come to it with preconceived notions of autobiographical truth when the tendency to make hyperbolic and over-enthusiastic statements about her subject matter is part of her "style" as a writer? Couldn't we see in this passage Hurston's own implicit theory of reading and thus use it to derive our interpretive practice from the text itself, instead of judging the work according to Procrustean notions of autobiographical form?

Hurston is fully aware of the gaps and discrepancies that can exist between intention and execution, reality and representation, reason and imagination, in short, between the words (or subject matter) and the tune, which is the source of unity for the singers on the porch. For her, too, the flow of creative energy is an imaginative transfiguration of literal truth/content through rhetorical procedures. The resulting text/performance thus transcends pedestrian notions of referentiality, for the staging of the event is part of the process of "passing on," of elaborating cultural forms, which are not static and inviolable but dynamically involved in the creation of culture itself. It is thus not surprising that Hurston should view the self, and especially the "racial self," as a fluid and changing concept, an arbitrary signifier with which she had better dispense if it is meant to inhibit (as any kind of reductive labeling might) the inherent plasticity of individuals.[9] Viewed from such an angle, *Dust Tracks*, far from being a "camouflage" and an "escape," does indeed *exemplify* the "paradoxes of her personality" by revealing a fluid and multidimensional self that refuses to allow itself to be framed and packaged for the benefit of those

[9]This is not the place to engage in a detailed analysis of the methods and assumptions of Hurston's great teacher and mentor, "Papa" Franz Boas. Suffice it to say that as an anthropologist he was a firm believer in "the plasticity of human types": his research for his book *Changes in Bodily Forms of Descendants of Immigrants,* published in 1911, served to convince him that physical and mental characteristics were not simply inherited but profoundly modified by time and environment. Furthermore, the views expressed in his essay "The Race Problem in Modern Society," published in a work that was to be widely influential and of fundamental importance to the field of anthropology, *The Mind of Primitive Man,* could not fail to influence Zora Neale Hurston's own attitudes about the race problem in America, to reinforce her personal tendency toward individualism, and to strengthen her belief that human beings are infinitely variable and not classifiable into distinctive national or racial categories. As Boas puts it, "Our tendency to evaluate an individual according to the picture that we form of the class to which we assign him, although he may not feel any inner connection with that class, is a survival of primitive forms of thought. The characteristics of the members of the class are highly variable and the type that we construct from the most frequent characteristics supposed to belong to the class is never more than an abstraction hardly ever realized in a single individual, often not even a result of observation, but an often heard tradition that determines our judgment" (344) (from a selection from *The Mind of Primitive Man,* 1911, reprinted in Ashley Montagu, *Frontiers of Anthropology* [New York: Putnam's, 1974], pp. 332–44). Boas recognizes the role played by "tradition" and ideology in our construction of the world, and his work paves the way for what I would call Hurston's dynamic and contextual approach to culture and to private forms of behavior.

human, all-too-human mortals, "both black and white who [claim] special blessings on the basis of race" (235).

Indeed, in the case of the folkloric forms she studies, the plasticity of the "subject matter" of songs and tales is corroborated by her research experience in the field; if we can be justified in seeing the "subject" of the autobiography and the "subject matter" of folklore as homologous structures or *topoi* that reflect and mirror each other, then the dialogue between these homologies shapes the autobiographical text while revealing the paradoxes of the genre. This dialogue serves to illuminate Hurston's combined identities as anthropologist and writer as these simultaneously begin to emerge and to converge in *Dust Tracks*. In the process of articulating their differences, she actually establishes their inescapable similarities, prefiguring the practice of such theorists as Clifford Geertz or Victor Turner. As Hemenway rightly points out, "Zora never became a professional academic folklorist because such a vocation was alien to her exuberant sense of self, to her admittedly artistic, sometimes erratic temperament, and to her awareness of the esthetic content of black folklore."[10] But this psychologizing approach does not suffice to clarify the work and to explain Hurston's liminal position, her confident straddling of "high" (academic) and "low" (folk) cultures, the ease with which she brings to the theoretical enterprise of the academic collector of lore the insights and perceptivity of the teller of tales. What makes the autobiography interesting is that it unfolds the structures of meaning—the cultural "topics" that are discussed chapter by chapter (history, geography, mythology, kinship, education, work, travel, friendship, love, religion, politics, philosophy, etc.)—through which the creative artist gives shape to her personal experiences as seen through the "spy-glass" of anthropology.[11]

Moving away from what might be the sterile analyses of a fieldworker to the inspirational language of an artist, Hurston involves herself and her reader in a transformative process. She does not just record, describe, and represent; she transforms and is transformed by her autobiographical performance. To look at life from an aesthetic point of view and to celebrate her ethnic heritage are thus two complementary projects for her. Life is an aesthetic experience, a staged performance, reflected in the autobiography as well as the fictional writings, and literature is a means of recording with what Hemenway identifies as "a studied antiscientific approach" the lives and subjective realities of a particular people in a specific time and place.[12] It is this apparently antagonistic movement between life and literature, reality and its representation, orality and literacy, which informs the structural coherence of *Dust Tracks*,

[10]Robert Hemenway, *Zora Neale Hurston: A Literary Biography* (Urbana: University of Illinois Press, 1980), p. 213.

[11]See Zora Neale Hurston, *Mules and Men* (Bloomington: Indiana University Press 1978), p. 3, hereinafter *MM*; and Barbara Johnson, "Thresholds of Difference: Structures of Address in Zora Neale Hurston," in *"Race," Writing, and Difference*, ed. Henry L. Gates, Jr. (Chicago: University of Chicago Press, 1985), pp. 317–28.

[12] Hemenway, p. 213.

rather than the simply linear progression through the lived life. What the text puts in motion is a strategy of displacement regarding the expectations governing two modes of discourse: the "objective" exteriority is that of the autobiographer whose "inside search" does not bear out its promise of intro-spection, and the "intimate" tone is that of the anthropologist who implicates herself in her "research" by delving into Hoodoo, by performing initiation rites, and in an ironic and clever reversal of the ventriloquism of ethnography, by letting her informants inform *us* about Zora's persona in the field. As Big Sweet puts it, "You ain't like me. You don't even sleep with no mens. . . . I think it's nice for you to be like that. You just keep on writing down them lies" (189).

So, if Hurston sometimes seems to be aspiring toward some kind of "raceless ideal," it is not because she is interested in the "universality" of human experiences. Quite the contrary, she wants to expose, as Hemenway explains, "the inadequacy of sterile reason to deal with the phenomena of living."[13] And "race" in that context is but a reasonable, pseudoscientific category for dealing with a basically fluid, diverse, and multifarious reality: "The stuff of my being is matter, ever changing, ever moving, but never lost" (279). Her philosophical position in *Dust Tracks* is in fact echoed more than twenty years later by Frantz Fanon in *The Wretched of the Earth:* "This historical necessity in which the men of African culture find themselves, that is, the necessity to racialize their claims and to speak more of African culture, than of national culture, will lead them up a blind alley." Warning that the undefined and vague entity "African culture" was a creation of European colonialism, Fanon chose to emphasize local historically and geographically specific contingencies, rather than "race" as a general and abstract concept: "And it is also true that those who are most responsible for this racialization of thought—or at least of our patterns of thought—are and remain those Europeans who have never ceased to set up white culture over and against all other so-called non-cultures [d'opposer la culture blanche aux autres incul-tures]."[14] Similarly, Hurston's interest in the folk communities of Eatonville, Polk County, Mobile, New Orleans, Nassau, Jamaica, and Haiti stemmed from the belief that the universal can only be known through the specific and that knowledge grounded in first-hand experience can yield more insights into the human condition and into the processes of acculturation, differentiation, and historicization to which human beings are subjected. I would thus argue that her unstated aim is identical to Fanon's later formulation: to destroy the white stereotype of black *inculture* not by privileging "blackness" as an oppositional category to "whiteness" in culture but by unequivocally showing the vitality and diversity of nonwhite cultures around the Caribbean and the

---

[13]Ibid.

[14]Frantz Fanon, *The Wretched of the Earth,* trans. Constance Farrington (New York: Grove Press, 1968), p. 214. (I have modified the translation of both quotations.) *Les Damnés de la terre* (Paris: Maspéro, 1968), p. 146. The word *inculture* is practically untranslatable into English.

coastal areas of the South, thereby dispensing completely with "white" as a
concept and a point of reference. Unlike the proponents of the negritude
movement, whose initial thrust was against white racism and prejudice,
Hurston assumes the supremely confident posture of the anthropologist who
need not *justify* the validity of her enterprise but can simply *affirm* by her
study the existence of richly varied black cultures, thus delineating the
semiotics of spaces where, in Houston Baker's words, "white culture's representations are squeezed to zero volume, producing a new expressive order."[15]

What must not be overlooked, therefore, in the passage I quoted from
"Research" is the emphasis Hurston puts on contextual considerations and the
implicit distinctions she then draws between her own position as anthropologist observing the event and the role of the singers directly involved in the
performance. For example, it is important for the anthropologist—and for the
literary critic attempting to model her approach on Hurston's—to know the
"material," that is, to be steeped in the historical, geographical, and vernacular contexts of the "songs" in order to be able to determine where "pieces of
other songs" are "interpolated" and used as "padding" when the original
material "ran out." Does Hurston imply that there is a certain autonomy of the
original text which is violated by the interpolation of fragments of other songs?
It would seem, rather, that as an anthropologist she feels that it is important
to make those kinds of distinctions; yet she recognizes that for the singers the
question is unimportant. The song goes on; the participants collectively "keep
the tune" and do not worry about the singularity or inviolability of a given text
or song. In other words, the question of intertextuality or of hybridization of
content is not significant for the artists (they do not see it as a transgression of
rules of identity), however important it may be for the observer who wants to
be able to determine where one particular song ends and the next one starts.
The question of boundaries is thus raised and examined by the anthropologist
while the artist in her recognizes both the futility of such conceptual distinctions and how severely limiting it is to try to establish the "true" identity and
originality of the subject matter—or of authorial subjectivity, permeated as it
is by the polyphonic voices of the community, which resonate throughout the
text and thereby reflect different narrative stances, different points of view on
life and on Zora herself.[16] Indeed, since "no two moments are any more alike
than two snowflakes" (264), there is no inconsistency in presenting a multi-
tude of personae and being nonetheless sincere. As a folk aphorism puts it,

[15]See Houston A. Baker, Jr., *Blues, Ideology, and Afro-American Literature: A Vernacular Theory* (Chicago: University of Chicago Press, 1984), p. 152.

[16]See Claudine Raynaud, *"Dust Tracks on a Road:* Autobiography as a 'Lying' Session," in *Studies in Black American Literature* (Greenwood, Fla.: Penkevill Annuals, 1988), 111–38. Whereas Raynaud tends to see the autobiography as founding the self in a gesture of appropria-
tion of the perennial proverbs and sayings of the community, I prefer to see in the text a continuing tension between philosophical skepticism about communal values and visionary creation.

"Li'l flakes make de deepest snow," or what appears to be homogeneous is in fact a complicated layering of vastly disparate elements. The chapter "Seeing the World as It Is" emphasizes Hurston's intentions and method: "I do not wish to close the frontiers of life upon my own self. I do not wish to deny myself the expansion of seeking into individual capabilities and depths by living in a space whose boundaries are race and nation" (330). Clearly, race and nation are singled out here as colonizing signs produced by an essentializing and controlling power ("Race Pride" 324–28) external to the inner self and bent on denying her access to "spaces" other than the ones to which she ostensibly belongs by virtue of her concrete situation. Her free-spirited call for "less race consciousness" (326) is to be understood in the context of her unabashed denunciation of "democracy" as just another name for selfish profiteering by the West at the expense of those "others" who live far away from the so-called democratic nations of Europe and America (338). These subversive and politically anarchic statements—which provoked the Procrustean editing of the autobiography—are the logical consequence of the ethnographer's skepticism. Because she remains radically *critical* without proposing positive and totalizing alternatives, she exemplifies a truly philosophical sensibility.[17] Her urge to ask questions rather than to propose solutions invites and provokes her readers to think beyond the commonplaces and received ideas of our cultures, beyond those proverbial voices of the community, the vox populi, *ouï-dire*, Heideggerian *Gerede*, or Barthesian *bêtise*—always rendered in free indirect speech—which enunciate the webs of beliefs that structure local consciousness of self.[18] Reporting those quotidian voices, she establishes cultural context, but by her skeptical detachment, she undermines the gregarious values of the group, whether it is the folk community (involved in "specifying" [186, 304], in "adult double talk" [62], and whose verbal creativity is nonetheless celebrated) or the social consensus that articulates interdictions and contradictions of all sorts ("This book-reading business was a hold-back and an unrelieved evil" [117]; "Not only is the

17It might perhaps be appropriate to add here that Hurston shows a truly "metaphysical" turn of mind on top of her properly "exegetical" talents! See a reference to the debate between Robert Penn Warren and Sterling Brown in Henry L. Gates, Jr., *Figures in Black: Words, Signs, and the "Racial" Self* (New York: Oxford University Press, 1987), p. xix. And indeed, Fanon takes up the same relay: the last words of *Black Skin, White Masks*, trans. Charles L. Markmann (London: Pluto Press, 1986), (hereinafter *BSWM*) are "O my body, make me always a man who questions!" (232). It is not likely that Fanon either knew or read Hurston, although he was familiar with the work of Langston Hughes, but their accomplishments in *Dust Tracks on a Road* and *Black Skin, White Masks* derive from a parallel need to shake off the totalizing traps of historical determinism, and to do so in a style that is its own message, narrative and aphoristic in order to subvert the cultural commonplaces they both abhor. See also Chester J. Fontenot's study of Fanon and his useful discussion of form and content in *Black Skin, White Masks*, "Visionaries, Mystics and Revolutionaries: Narrative Postures in Black Fiction," in *Studies in Black American Literature*, ed. Joe Weixlmann and Chester J. Fontenot (Greenwood, Fla.: Penkevill Annuals, 1983), 1:63–87.

18For a detailed discussion of the philosophical and linguistic implications of the "discours indirect libre," see Gilles Deleuze and Félix Guattari, *Mille plateaux* (Paris: Minuit, 1980), pp. 95–109.

scholastic rating at Howard high, but tea is poured in the manner!" [156]; "If it was so honorable and glorious to be black, why was it the yellow-skinned people among us had so much prestige?" [226]). These "common" values are now made available for parody. She thus opens up a space of resistance between the individual (*auto-*) and the collective (*-ethno-*) where the writing (*-graphy*) of singularity cannot be foreclosed.

Yet, a nagging question remains: how can Hurston's historical, embodied self, subject to the determinants of time and place—an Afro-American woman confronting racism and a world war—represent the site of a privileged resistance to those webs of belief which might encourage resentment and fixation on an unjust and painful past? As she puts it: "To me, bitterness is the under-arm odor of wishful weakness. It is the graceless acknowledgment of defeat" (280). Since both the perpetrators and the immediate victims of slavery are long dead and since she has "no personal memory of those times, and no responsibility for them" (282), she affirms that she would rather "turn all [her] thoughts and energies on the present" (284). This affirmation of life against "the clutching hand of Time" (284) is a creative release from the imposition of origin and the prison of history. Zora becomes a joyful Zarathustra, whose world is no longer limited and bound by the reality principle and who advocates deliverance from the spirit of revenge. But can this visionary posture of the self-portraitist allow for a positive involvement in the shaping of reality, present and future? How can it be reconciled with the anthropological claim to locally specific knowledge and with the historical novelist's success in drawing the suggestive allegorical fresco of a mythic Afro-Mediterranean past in *Moses, Man of the Mountain*?

Since Fanon, too, denounced revenge and fixation on the past as "a crystallization of guilt" (*BSWM* 228), perhaps he can provide some answer to the questions we ask of Hurston. If resentment is the essence of negative potentiality for the self, it is clear why Hurston rejects it outright. She wants the utmost freedom in "seeking into individual capabilities." Her refusal to adopt the "herd" mentality for the sake of solidarity actually places her in a long tradition of thinkers—Heraclitus, Montaigne, Nietzsche, Walter Benjamin, Frantz Fanon, and Roland Barthes—all essayists or masters of hyperbolic aphorisms. Fanon, in particular, was well aware of the peculiarly *racial* dilemma facing the children of the colonialist diaspora: their marginality could not simply be articulated in terms of binary categories of black versus white. Fanon's plea against racialist attitudes thus echoes Hurston's reformulation of freedom and responsibility on a planetary scale:

> I as a man of color do not have the right to hope that in the white man there will be a crystallization of guilt toward the past of my race. (228)

> I find myself—I, a man—in a world where words wrap themselves in silence; in a world where the other endlessly hardens himself. . . .

I am not a prisoner of history. I should not seek there for the meaning of my destiny.

I should constantly remind myself that the real *leap* consists in introducing invention into existence. (229)

It is through the effort *to recapture the self and to scrutinize the self*, it is through the lasting tension of their freedom that men will be able to create the ideal conditions of existence for a human world. (231; my italics)

The wish to "create . . . ideal conditions of existence" is synonymous here with the fight against all petit bourgeois mental habits that tend to favor manifestations of closure. Fanon wants to demythologize history and to prevent it from being used as the source of "reactional" behavior because, as "Nietzsche had already pointed out" and as he himself elaborates, "there is always resentment in a *reaction*" (*BSWM* 222). While severely criticizing his fellow colonized intellectuals for simply reproducing the values of the colonizer in adopting racialist thinking, Fanon did not hesitate to state that the quest for disalienation must be mediated by the refusal to accept the "Tower of the Past" (*BSWM* 226) and the problems of the present as definitive, in other words, by the belief that only the poetry of the future can move and inspire human beings to action and to revolution. Unlike Fanon, Hurston did not develop the visionary perspective into a revolutionary one, but her mystical desire to be one with the universe stems from a similar utopian need for a "waking dream"[19] of the possible which might inspire us to see beyond the constraints of the here and now to the idealized vision of a perfect future, albeit, in *Dust Tracks* [*DT*], a life after death in which the substance of her being is again "part and parcel of the world" and "one with the infinite" (279). Both Fanon and Hurston suggest that we urgently need to retrieve those past traditions that can become the source of reconciliation and wholeness, for it is more important to learn from those traditions than to dwell on pain and injustice.

For Hurston, "the effort to recapture . . . and to scrutinize the self" is a project grounded in the quicksand of linguistic performance and thus inseparable from what Beaujour has called "a type of memory, both very archaic and very modern, by which the events of an individual life are eclipsed by the recollection of an entire culture." As Michael M. J. Fischer has stressed, ethnic memory is not only past- but future-oriented, and the dynamics of interpersonal knowledge within the intercultural strands of memory are inseparable from Hurston's project of self-portraiture, since to recapture the past is literally to create a new field of knowledge within her academic discipline: "If science ever gets to the bottom of Voodoo in Haiti and Africa, it

[19]The phrase is Ernst Bloch's. See Anson Rabinbach, "Unclaimed Heritage: Ernst Bloch's *Heritage of Our Times* and the Theory of Fascism," *New German Critique* 11 (Spring 1977), p. 7. Hurston was familiar with the German philosophical tradition of utopian thinking. She mentions Spinoza for example, *DT* 285. See also my comments in note 25.

will be found that some important medical secrets, still unknown to medical science, give it its power, rather than the gestures of ceremony" (*DT* 205).[20] By suggesting historically valid mythological connections between ancient deities and prophets such as Isis and Persephone, on the one hand, and Damballah, Thoth, and Moses, on the other, and between those figures and the "two-headed" magicians of Hoodoo (191), who know the creative power of words, Hurston leaves the door open for a historical revision both of Hoodoo religion and of antiquity, implying "two-headed" Egyptian and Greek origins for both Euro- and Afro-Americans. Because such a thesis would have been rejected by contemporary scholars, who then followed the "Aryan model" of antiquity, Hurston can only allude to it through literature.[21]

A comparison of the thematic similarities in Hurston's work does show that she was quite consciously using those ancient "personae" as multiple facets of her own self and of her own Afro-Mediterranean genealogy. One of her first published stories, "Drenched in Light," tells the story of Isis Watts, a protagonist who is clearly autobiographical, as is Isis Potts of *Jonah's Gourd Vine*.[22] This same persona is reintroduced in *Dust Tracks* under the name Persephone. The similarity of the protagonists suggests that the three narratives form a triptych: it is only by taking into consideration the mythological background of the protagonists' names that we can accurately understand the process of self-discovery through self-invention which characterizes Hurston's method. Tellingly, this process is a search for familial and maternal connections, for "mirrors" that can reflect positive aspects of the past instead of alienating images of subaltern faces.

It is thus significant that the only events of her "private" life on which Hurston dwells in *Dust Tracks* are those that have deep symbolic and cultural value: the death of the mother and subsequent dispersion of the siblings echo the collective memory of her people's separation from Africa-as-mother and their ineluctable diaspora. That is why Kossola/Cudjo Lewis's story emblematizes her own sense of bereavement and deprivation: "After seventy-five years, he still had that tragic sense of loss. That yearning for blond and cultural ties. That sense of mutilation. It gave me something to think about"

[20]Beaujour, p. 26; see Michael M. J. Fischer, "Ethnicity and the Post-Modern Arts of Memory," *Writing Culture*, pp. 194–233 (201). Fischer uses "ethnic" autobiographical narrative as a means of allowing "multiple sets of voices to speak for themselves" thus effectively marginalizing his anthropological commentary on the ethnic group he studies.

[21]See Martin Bernal's revision of that model in *Black Athena: The Afroasiatic Roots of Classical Civilization* (London: Free Association Books, 1987). For Hurston's use of Damballah, Moses, and Thoth as facets of the same mythological persona, see her *Moses, Man of the Mountain* (Urbana: University of Illinois Press, 1984). See also Karla F. C. Holloway, *The Character of the Word* (New York: Greenwood Press, 1987), chap. 3, for a useful discussion of those figures.

[22]For the passages of *Jonah's Gourd Vine* which are useful here, I shall be quoting from *I Love Myself When I Am Laughing: A Zora Neale Hurston Reader*, ed. Alice Walker (New York: Feminist Press, 1979), pp. 189–96, hereinafter *ILM*. "Drenched in Light" is reprinted as "Isis" in *Spunk: The Selected Stories of Zora Neale Hurston* (Berkeley: Turtle Island Foundation, 1985), pp. 9–18.

(204). Coming at the end of the "Research" chapter, the embedded narrative of Kossola's life serves as a powerful counterpoint to Zora's own story of strife and reconciliation with her brothers (172–73). It is thanks to her research and professional travels that she becomes, like the legendary Isis of Egyptian mythology, the link that reunites, reconnects the dispersed siblings, who can now "touch each other in the spirit if not in the flesh." The imagery that describes the disintegration of the family unit is a clear reminder of the historical conditions of the Middle Passage:

> I felt the warm embrace of kin and kind for the first time since the night after my mother's funeral, when we had huddled about the organ all sodden and bewildered, with the walls of our home suddenly blown down. On September 18th, that house had been a hovering home. September 19th, it had turned into a bleak place of desolation with unknown dangers creeping upon us from unseen quarters that made of us a whimpering huddle, though then we could not see why. But now that was all over. (173)

As private experiences echo collective ones and punctuate the deployment of the self-portrait, a picture of the fieldworker as keeper of important knowledge, as go-between whose role is to facilitate the articulation of collective memory, emerges. By foregrounding the field research as the causal link to an empowering reunion with her scattered siblings, Hurston deploys much broader implications for the social lives of Afro-Americans. She implies that connections to the past must not be severed if we are to regain a sense of what it is like to "touch each other in the spirit" and also that a sense of history must not be allowed to degenerate into the remembrance of paralyzing images. That is why she also remarks that "any religion that satisfies the individual urge is valid for that person" (205). Since ancient traditions such as Hoodoo contain, as Hemenway says, "the old, old mysticism of the world in African terms," they are useful to a "thick description" of cultural nuances, and they help demarcate the historical context relevant to the study of folklore.[23]

Hurston's aim is to maintain the integrity of black culture without diluting it and to celebrate its values while remaining critical of those pressures from within the "family" which can mutilate individual aspirations—as her eldest brother Bob had been guilty of doing to her when she went to live with him, hoping that he would help put her through school, only to find herself playing the role of maid to his wife. It is this de facto lack of solidarity among "brothers" which Hurston observes and which forms the basis for her critique of a blanket endorsement of simpleminded, universal "Race Solidarity" (327) or of the pan-Africanism that in the thirties and forties must have sounded disturbingly like pan-Germanism, whose evil historical consequences were well understood. The text of *Dust Tracks* thus shuttles between appreciation and opprobrium, finding its impetus in the joyful affirmation of its contradic-

---

[23]Hemenway, *Hurston*, p. 249. I use the phrase "thick description" after Clifford Geertz, *The Interpretation of Cultures* (New York: Basic Books, 1973), chap. 1.

tions. To recall the past in order to transcend it, Fanon will also point out, is the only emancipatory stance we can confidently adopt without risk of falling prey to reactionary forces.

Thus, the chapter titled "Religion" reveals Hurston's total indifference to the "consolation" traditional religion affords: "I am one with the infinite and need no other assurance" (279). Her style subverts the need for "organized creeds," which are but "collections of words around a wish" (278) and which Fanon will denounce as the motor of a "closed society . . . in which ideas and people are in a state of decay" (*BSWM* 224).[24] Comfortable in the knowledge that the whole world exists in a Heraclitean flux of becoming, Hurston affirms a principle of eternal change based in her observation of the radical fluidity of inorganic, organic, social, and cultural forces:

> I have achieved a certain peace within myself, but perhaps the seeking after the inner heart of truth will never cease in me. . . .
>
> So, having looked at the subject from many sides, studied beliefs by word of mouth and then *as they fit into great rigid forms, I find I know a great deal about form, but little or nothing about the mysteries I sought as a child.* . . .
>
> But certain things have seemed to me to be true as I heard the tongues of those who had speech, and listened at the lips of books. . . . (277; my italics)
>
> The springing of the yellow line of morning out of the misty deep of dawn, is glory enough for me. I know that nothing is destructible; things merely change forms. (279)[25]

Poetic speech has now replaced the folk idiom, the artist, the anthropologist. The distinction between form and content ("mysteries") is made again but then put under erasure: "things merely change forms," and content is never lost; yet knowledge of content is determined by the "great rigid forms" that structure the universe while veiling the motley appearance of "matter." These allegories of death and rebirth, change and permanence, temporality and eternity, retroactively map the territory of the autobiographical text and the life it attempts to represent. By retracing those ephemeral "dust tracks" whose trajectory the table of contents surveys, Hurston seems to spiral out into infinity and the cosmos: "The cosmic Zora emerges," as she writes in "How It Feels to Be Colored Me" (*ILM* 155). Her journey, like that of the storytellers who never leave the porch, is an itinerary through language, "a journeying by way of narrating," as Alexander Gelley puts it. That is why it is impossible to make, on a theoretical level, "any clear-cut division between theme and form, between journey as geography and journey as narrative."[26]

24See Fontenot, p. 84 for a discussion of "open" and "closed" society as defined by Fanon. I have modified the translation of *BSWM*.

25Hurston's Spinozist philosophy is evident here. See Benedict de Spinoza, *Ethics* (n.p.: Joseph Simon, 1981), pt. 1, proposition 8: "Every substance is necessarily infinite" (p. 32). As S. P. R. Charter puts it in the introduction to this edition, "Spinoza attempted to unite the mind/ body complexity and the realities of existence with the all-embracing actuality of Nature, and to do so organically—that is, without the imposition of man-made religious structures" (p. 3).

26Gelley, p. 31.

The "curve in the road" at which Hurston sees her first "vision" (93) is a mythical point of departure for the global adventure during which she will learn to take distance from the "tight chemise" and the "crib of negroism" (*MM* 3) that have shaped her. Distance alone can enable her to recognize and assemble the fragments of her changing folk culture in the New World, and because she is dealing with familiar territory, she does not run the risk of subjugating the "other" to her self, of making her subjects into marionettes for the benefit of those patrons who are only interested in the static, "primitive" aspects of her research. Engaged in a truly dialogical enterprise and not in the delusions of Boasian "pure objectivity" to which she alludes ironically (174), she can negotiate the terms of her insertion within and without the ethnographic field and can even parody popular beliefs with impunity: the jokes come naturally with the territory of storytelling.

Similarly, the discursive enterprise of self-portraiture is a process of collecting and gathering, of assembling images and metaphors to portray a figural self, always already caught in entropy and in permanent danger of returning to "dust," of becoming again "part and parcel" of the universe. In what follows, then, I would like to examine briefly the textual mechanism that generates the journey of ethnic self-scrutiny, the slippage between particular and universal, individual and collective, daughter and mother(s), the self and its mythologies. In describing these displacements, I want to show how the collective functions as a silverless mirror, capable of absorbing the self into a duplicitous game in which one code, singularity, is set aslant by another, syncretic unity with the universe, thus preventing narrative closure.[27] The tensions at work in *Dust Tracks* between these two sets of expectations (local versus universal knowledge) are not simply resolvable through (ethnographic) narrative. They constitute what Stephen Tyler has called the proper domain of "post-modern ethnography," neither "the upward spiral into the Platonic . . . realm of conscious thought and faceless abstraction" nor the "descent 'beneath the surface' into the Plutonic 'other of separation.' " Hurston's approach to the study of culture indeed prefigures the future trend of the discipline as outlined by Tyler: "The ethnographic text will thus achieve its purposes not by revealing them, but by making purposes possible. It will be a text of the physical, the spoken, and the performed, an evocation of quotidian experience, a palpable reality that uses everyday speech to suggest what is ineffable, not through abstraction, but by means of the concrete. It will be a text to read not with the eyes alone, but with the ears in order to hear 'the voices of the pages.' "[28]

Hurston, too, captures the voices of the people and relays them through

[27]What I call the silverless mirror here is to some extent assimilable to what Houston A. Baker, Jr., associates with the term "black (w)hole": "a *singularly* black route of escape" (p. 155). By analogy, it refers also to the covered looking-glass in the room of the dying mother (*DT* 88), to which I will return.

[28]See Stephen Tyler, "Post-Modern Ethnography: From Document of the Occult to Occult Document," in *Writing Culture*, pp. 133, 136.

the "lips of books," which do not "announce" their purpose but braid "palpable reality" with the incommensurable, the quotidian with the ineffable. She makes it possible to envisage purposive, enabling, and empowering structures of meaning which do not coerce the subject into historically and Eurocentrically determined racial metaphors of the self. She succeeds in tracing a map of her territory—a symbolic geography—by using the same accommodating principles that governed the expedient building of roads over the winding footpath between Orlando and Maitland: the metaphor of the road that curves effortlessly around "the numerous big pine trees and oaks" (7) reinforces a principle of flexibility, a respect for nature rather than the need to dominate it, a pliability connoting the plasticity of human forms, the capacity to undergo mutations, to endure and survive hardships in that middle passage from birth to death, from mud to dust.

The allegory of the voyage that is only a return to one's point of departure is already present in the first chapter, "My Birthplace." The "three frontier-seekers" who embark for Brazil only to return to the United States prefigure Hurston, who journeys through black folklore in order to rediscover the "geography . . . within" (115), the lost community of her childhood in "A pure Negro town!" (9). Her search for an originary plenitude is the universal biblical "return to dust" at the end of the road of life—not the romantic nostalgia for a prelapsarian time of innocence. In that respect, the death of her mother represents the first moment in a chain of destabilizing experiences that forever undermine her sense of belonging to a specific place: "That hour began my wanderings. Not so much in geography, but in time. Then not so much in time as in spirit. Mama died at sundown and changed a world. That is, the world which had been built out of her body and her heart. Even the physical aspects fell apart with a suddenness that was startling" (89). The death scene of the speechless mother becomes the motivation for writing, for the effort of self-fashioning, which is also an effort to stave off death. Hurston's wandering phase will be the result of this experience of absence and loss, which is repeated on different levels throughout the next chapters. The narrator attempts to fill the void of death by journeying *and* by narrating.

That is why it is interesting to note that the description of the mother's death in *Dust Tracks* closely parallels the fictional rendering of that scene in *Jonah's Gourd Vine*. Telling details are repeated almost word for word: "I could see the huge drop of sweat collected in the hollow at Mama's elbow and it hurt me so" (*DT* 88) and "Isis saw a pool of sweat standing in a hollow at the elbow" (*ILM* 195); "I thought that she looked to me (*DT* 86). . . . I think she was trying to say something, and I think she was trying to speak to me" (*DT* 88) and "Isis thought her mother's eyes followed her and she strained her ears to catch her words" (*ILM* 195). Isis is indeed the fictional alter ego Hurston chooses for herself, the name of an ancient Egyptian goddess who wandered the world in search of her dismembered brother, a mythical representation of interiority as experience of death. In Egyptian mythology, her brother, Osiris, is both the god of fertility (like Demeter/Ceres in the Greco-Roman myth) and the king and judge of the dead. He is also the companion of Thoth, god of death and of writing, who presides with him in the underworld. Hurston thus makes an implicit connection between the Osirian mysteries, which were tied to the cult of the dead and of which Isis was the high priestess, and the occult practices of Hoodoo, of which Hurston herself became an initiate. Having flippantly named herself the "queen of the niggerati" in one of her histrionic moments among her New York friends,[29] Hurston then proceeded to develop (in the autobiographical triptych) in a mythically accurate and artistically sensible manner the theme of a life lived in the shadow of Isis/Persephone, queens of the underworld, of the "dark realm" of otherness. The persona Isis—both the goddess and the fictional daughter of Lucy Potts—is like the mirror that figures prominently in the mother's death scene. She is an image of memory and interiority, an "other" who focuses, crystallizes, and gives sharp contours to the project of self-invention. She is an important thread in the process of re-membering one's past and one's own mortality as one pays homage to the dead and departed. Here, the folk custom of veiling the mirror (so that the dead may rest in peace and not trouble the living) is implicitly criticized: the dying mother suggests that the mirror should not be veiled if the past and the faces of our mothers in it are to leave their imprint on the memory of the living so that *we* may live in peace with history and be thus able to "think back through our mothers," as Virginia Woolf believed it was important for women to be able to do.[30]

What the death scene allegorizes, then, is Hurston's subtle and complex view of the relationship of individuals to culture and history: some elements of culture, because they are unexamined traditions, "village custom" (86), "mores" (89) upheld by the voices of patriarchy (the "village dames," or phallic women, and the father, who together prevent her from fulfilling her mother's wishes), are destructive and stultifying. The child's (Isis' and Zora's) experience of anxiety and guilt is the result of those unexamined cultural myths that thwart the mother's desire to remain imprinted on the daughter's memory. As Adrienne Rich has put it, "The loss of the daughter to the mother, the mother to the daughter, is the essential female tragedy."[31] The loss brought about by the patriarchal customs of the "village" is a painful enactment of separation and fragmentation, of lost connections to the mother as symbol of a veiled and occulted historical past. Albert Memmi and Frantz Fanon will both point out that our problem as colonized people (or gender) is that we all suffer from

[29]Holloway, p. 24.

[30]See Jane Marcus, "Thinking Back through Our Mothers," in *New Feminist Essays on Virginia Woolf* (Lincoln: University of Nebraska Press, 1981), pp. 1–30.

[31]Adrienne Rich, *Of Woman Born: Motherhood as Experience and Institution* (New York: Norton, 1976), p. 237. As Sandra M. Gilbert and Susan Gubar have amply demonstrated, the lack of a female tradition in which to insert her own words is the source of a great "anxiety of authorship" for the woman writer. See *The Madwoman in the Attic: The Woman Writer and the Nineteenth-Century Literary Imagination* (New Haven: Yale University Press, 1979), pp. 45–92.

collective amnesia. The self-portrait Hurston draws in *Dust Tracks* is an anamnesis: not self-contemplation but a painstaking effort to be the voice of that occluded past, to fill the void of collective memory.

Indeed, Zora feels that her mother "depended on [her] for a voice" (87), and in *Dust Tracks* she chooses the mythical Persephone as alter ego. The Greek word for voice is *phone* and the scene of the mother's death is symbolic of the daughter's responsibility to articulate her story, to exhume it from the rubble of patriarchal obfuscation. Martin Bernal has pointed out that the Eleusinian story of Demeter searching for Persephone has its roots in the Egyptian myth of Isis and Osiris.[32] By identifying with Persephone in *Dust Tracks,* Hurston makes a brilliant and sophisticated rapprochement between the two myths—a connection, says Bernal, that classicists who follow the "Aryan model" of antiquity have studiously avoided. Hurston approaches Afro-Mediterranean antiquity with the intuitions of the anthropologist who sees connections where traditional classical scholarship had not.

The displacement from Isis to Persephone as objective persona is significant in helping us understand Hurston's feeling of being an orphan, of being cut off from her origins, or *arche.* "Isis" is the wanderer who conducts her research, establishes spatiotemporal connections among the children of the diaspora, and re-members the scattered body of folk material so that siblings can again "touch each other." "Persephone," on the other hand, is not a rescuer but rather a lost daughter whose mother searches for her with passion. She is an ambiguous figure "with her loving and hellish aspects."[33] Ironically, it is Zora's reading of the Greco-Roman myth ("one of [her] favorites" [48]) during the visit of two white women at her school that attracts attention to her brilliance and configures her later "rescue" by other white mentors, friends who become surrogate mothers (like Helen in "Drenched in Light"). If, as Ronnie Scharfman has noted, "mirroring" and "mothering" are twin terms for defining the reciprocal nurturing bonds a female subject needs in order to feel anchored in the tradition linking her to her mother(s), then Zora's vain efforts to prevent the veiling of the mirror in the mother's room must be understood as an allegorical attempt to look into the mirror of her mother's soul, to retain severed connections, to recapture and to "read" the dark face of the mother in the silverless mirror of the past, and to become the voice that bridges generations.[34] Those efforts also prefigure her professional predicament as an adult. Persephone was the queen of Pluto's dark realm of the dead, but she also traveled back and forth between the underworld and "the sunlit earth" (49), like Hurston, who retrieves the voices of her black culture in order to call her readers, in Karla Holloway's words, "back to primal ground." Caught

[32]Bernal, pp. 69–73.

[33]The words Bernal uses to describe Persephone (p. 70).

[34]See Ronnie Scharfman, "Mirroring and Mothering in Simone Schwarz-Bart's *Pluie et vent sur Télumée Miracle,* and Jean Rhys's *Wide Sargasso Sea,*" *Yale French Studies* 62 (1981), 88–106. Scharfman discusses psychoanalytic object-relation theorists. My purpose here is to relate those issues to the larger historical and ethnographical contexts within which I situate *Dust Tracks.*

between the upper and the lower realms, the black and the white world, life and death, she bridges the tragic gap of separation by writing. As Beaujour has explained, "the self-portrait tries to reunite two separate worlds, that of the living and that of the dead."[35]

Her description of a ceremony in New Orleans in which she participates draws the obvious parallels: "I had to sit at the crossroads at midnight in complete darkness and meet the devil, and make a compact. There was a long, long hour as I sat flat on the ground there alone and invited the King of Hell" (192). Since we also know that fasting was an essential part of her initiation, the parallel with Persephone is even more convincing, for Persephone's fate was to be Pluto's queen for three months of each year because "she had bitten the pomegranate" (49). Cleansing by fasting is, of course, a common part of initiatory practices in many religions and underscores Hurston's philosophy of the universal oneness of religious symbols.

When the child's experience of absence in *Dust Tracks* becomes specifically racial, a new and negative dimension is added to the metaphor of the mirror. As Hurston puts it, "Jacksonville made me know that I was a little colored girl" (94). This discovery of the ethnic self as mirrored by the other, the white culture of Jacksonville, functions in the text as another moment of an-archic self-discovery. The image reflected in the mirror of white culture is like the photograph in which Janie, in *Their Eyes Were Watching God,* cannot recognize herself because she does not yet know that she is colored, that for the white family who calls her "Alphabet," she is different because she symbolizes namelessness, darkness, absence, and lack.[36] This is Janie's first experience of difference, seeing her face as a bad photograph, as a "negative" and a flaw in the developed picture she holds in her hand. This scene of nonrecognition, like the deathbed scene, is the primal motivation for the journey of self-discovery through language. Isis, Persephone, Thoth, and Osiris are thus the four poles that mark the perimeter of Hurston's cultural mythology of the self. Thoth's gift links writing to death and to immortality; here the threads of memory and narrative allow Janie to "[pull] in her horizon like a great fish-net" (*TE* 286) in which the fragments of a faceless past are reassembled and given new names, new origins.

When we look at the allegory of the veiling of the mirror in *Dust Tracks* in the context of those similar scenes in the novels, a strong statement about the self and its enabling and distorting mirrors emerges. The idea that a mirror can be the vehicle of a negative self-image (depersonalization and loss) seems to be tied to two cultural myths perceived as destructive and debilitating by the child: the patriarchal folk belief about mirrors and death and the white culture's myths about blackness as radical otherness and absence. In both cases, reflections are void, absent, or distorted because they emanate from a

---

[35]Holloway, p. 113; Beaujour, p. 161.
[36]Zora Neale Hurston, *Their Eyes Were Watching God* (Urbana: University of Illinois Press, 1978), p. 21, hereinafter *TE*.

reductionist context: the realities of a culture's myths about death and otherness become a burden and a distortion of the historical metaphors by which
women must learn to live if we are to recapture the faces of our mothers in
the mirrors of the past. It is by uncovering those mirrors that we can begin to
articulate connections to ancient and empowering symbols of femaleness.
Hence the anguish of the child at not being able to fend off the voices of white
and black patriarchy, which rob her forever of the peace that comes from
seeing the face(s)—and knowing the mythical name(s)—that connect her to a
cultural tradition not grounded only in darkness and silence. Again Beaujour's
formulation is valid: "The self-portrait is constructed around an empty center:
vanished places and disrupted harmonies."[37] The experience of death generates the writing of a self-portrait through which appears, pentimento, the
mother's lost face.

The child who leaves Eatonville after her mother's death experiences
alterity and dislocation, distances herself forever from the illusory possibility
of an unexamined and unmediated participation in the network of relations
which constitutes culture. In effect, her avocation as anthropologist starts
right then and there: her exile from Eatonville is the first step on the nomadic
road of lore collecting, a road on which "the individual looks for soul-mates
while simultaneously affirming [her] absolute difference from all others,"
Beaujour says. That is why the collective voice is so often relayed with irony
and pathos: the self-portrait is the medium of subversion par excellence,
which relativizes the fetishistic recourse to a foundational world beyond its
discourse. It evolves the ethnic reality of which it partakes but, in so doing,
puts into question the mimetic principles of description and classification
which inform its writing. It thus simultaneously demystifies the writing of
both the self (auto) and the culture (ethno) because it involves the self and its
cultural contexts in a dialogue that transcends all possibility of reducing one to
the other. Michel Beaujour expresses it thus: "Mirror of the subject and
mirror of the world, mirror of the 'I' searching for a reflection of its self
through the mirror of the universe: what might first appear as a simple
correspondence, or a convenient analogy, proves under close scrutiny to be a
homologous relation warranted by the rhetorical tradition and the history of
literature."[38] Beaujour's formulation can be applied to *Dust Tracks* with an
important modification: it is not the medieval rhetorical tradition that fur-
nishes the topics of mimesis but the anthropological essay with its system of
categories, which locate culture at the nexus of history and geography,
religion and myth. What this formulation means for the "self-portrait," according to Beaujour, is that writing is engendered primarily by the *impossibility* of
self-presence, by the realization that realist narratives are functionally distorting and that myths are more appropriately evocative and suggestive of a
subject's liminal position in the world of discursive representation.

[37]Beaujour, p. 22.
[38]Ibid., pp. 15, 31.

Here, a myth of ancient Afro-Mediterranean folklore establishes the parameters according to which Hurston will go on performing the role of daughter
after her mother's death and until they can both be syncretically reunited.
The faceless woman encountered on a porch in Jacksonville during a school
walk, "who looked at a distance like Mama" (96), prefigures the last of her
twelve "visions": the two women, one young (herself?), one old (the mother?),
whose faces are averted as they are "arranging some queer-shaped flowers
such as [she] had never seen" (58). This indirect allusion to the funeral
flower—the white narcissus—is also the figure of the self reflected in the pool
of language, the dark ("miroirs d'encre") medium of self-knowledge, the white
symbol of death's attraction. It is an unformulated, unnamed, but richly
suggestive allusion to the desire for the absent mother, which will be reen-
acted both in the bonds of female friendships (the visitors at the school, Big
Sweet, Fannie Hurst, Ethel Waters, the Dahoman Amazons) and in those of
hatred or rivalry with other women (her stepmother and knife-toting
"Lucy").[39] At once Persephone and Narcissus, the autobiographical narrator
attempts to recapture the (m)other in the self and the self through the
(m)other:[40]

> Once or twice I saw the old faceless woman standing outdoors beside a tall plant
> with that same off-shape white flower. She turned suddenly from it to welcome me.
> I knew what was going on in the house without going in, it was all so familiar to
> me.
>   I never told anyone around me about these strange things. It was too different.
> They would laugh me off as a story-teller. Besides, I had a feeling of difference
> from my fellow men, and I did not want it to be found out. (58–59)

Her experiences of singularity and difference are intimately connected to
her visions of death. Not surprisingly, the reference to "Pluto's dark realm"
(48) and to the temporary reunification of Persephone with her mother turns
the circumstances of her life upside down and transforms the past by reorient-
ing it toward an unlived future in which the lost potentialities of love and
daughterhood are given a second chance, and an elusive possibility of peace
and transfiguration: "I stood in a world of vanished communion with my kind,
which is worse than if it had never been. Nothing is so desolate as a place
where life has been and gone. I stood on a soundless island in a tideless sea.

---

[39]For an analysis of the "thematic consistency . . . found in these echoing episodes of female
strength," see Raynaud. On this aspect of the text, I am in complete agreement with Raynaud.
[40]See Beaujour's informative discussion of the associations between Demeter, Persephone, and
Narcissus in Greek mythology and the connections between these divinities and death. His
argument is that narcissism as commonly understood in psychoanalytic terminology is a distorted
and reductive interpretation of the myth and that far from being "narcissistic" in that sense, "the
self-portrait tries to reunite two separate worlds, that of the living and that of the dead. . . .
Through anamnesis, Narcissus . . . performs a poetic invention of 'childhood memories' which
recreates a timeless paradise, at once personal treasure trove and cultural topic" (p. 161). See
especially pp. 156–62.

Time was to prove the truth of my visions . . . bringing me nearer to the big house, with the kind women and the strange white flowers" (59).

If the mother is a figure for the "lost" potentialities of history and for the "dark" continent of Africa, it is not surprising that images of death and decay begin to pervade the daughter's self-recollection during those years of loneliness and wandering in which she feels "haunted" (116). Just like "Lazarus after his resurrection," she cannot experience her own self in a unified way, past and present, mind and body can never coincide completely: "I walked by my corpse. I smelt it and felt it. I smelt the corpses of those among whom I must live, though they did not. They were as much at home with theirs as death in a tomb" (117). Like the Zombies she will later study, she is one of the living dead whose childhood memories of that time—between ten and fourteen years of age—are the undeveloped photographic negative of the singular images of blankness which will keep recurring in later chapters. For instance, her first love affair, although it provides the closeness and warmth she had sorely missed ever since her mother's death, turns into an oppressive relationship that imprisons her in feelings of doubt and unreality that cannot be shared with the husband: "Somebody had turned a hose on the sun. What I had taken for eternity turned out to be a moment walking in its sleep. . . . A wind full of memories blew out of the past and brought a chilling fog" (251).

Numbed by the impossibility to communicate, drained of life, she buries herself in her work. The next time she falls in love, the pattern seems to repeat itself. She is thwarted by the conflicts caused by her career, the man's possessiveness, and his complaints that her "real self had escaped him." She is not permitted to have a life of her own, is restrained by limiting circumstances, "caught in a fiendish trap" (259). Love is never experienced as an empowering force—unlike friendship, this "mysterious and ocean-bottom thing" (321) without which life is not worth much: "To live without friends is like milking a bear to get cream for your morning coffee. It is a whole lot of trouble, and then not worth much after you get it" (248). In contrast to the flatness of her love life, her affective landscape is peopled with many picturesque and vivid portrayals of friends. The topic of "friendship" is a much richer and more satisfying one than "love," and the treatment it receives in *Dust Tracks* bears testimony to the importance self-portraitists have accorded to the interface with an other whose ambivalent companionship may be the spur that compels a writer to articulate the potentialities of his or her vision.[41] "Conversation is the ceremony of companionship" (248), Ethel Waters says to Zora and Zora's self-portrait is this conversation with the past, a ceremony for the dead mother(s), but one that simultaneously empowers the living.

The narrator also experiences singularity as separation from the realm of nature. After her departure to Jacksonville, her introduction to formal education goes together with another deprivation which adds to her grief and

---

[41]Augustine, Montaigne (O un amy!), Gertrude Stein, Christopher Isherwood, Roland Barthes, to name but a few. See Réda Bensmaïa, *The Barthes Effect: The Essay as Reflective Text* (Minneapolis: University of Minnesota Press, 1987), pp. 62–89 especially.

mourning: "the loving pine, the lakes, the wild violets in the woods and the animals [she] used to know" (95) are no longer part of her daily life. Orphaned for a second time when her father asks the school to "adopt" her and she is nonetheless sent home on the riverboat, she experiences a thrilling form of rebirth because she is again part and parcel of nature: "The water life, the smothering foliage that draped the river banks, the miles of purple hyacinths, all thrilled me anew. The wild thing was back in the jungle. The curtain of trees along the river shut out the world so that it seemed that the river and the chugging boat was all that there was, and that pleased me a lot" (109). The floating boat and the trees that "shut out the world" are like the protective layers of a womb; the boat's chugging motor connotes a maternal heartbeat, a reassuring companion that spells the return to an earlier form of peace and harmony. These layered allusions to the archaic times of a prenatal life and to the historical moments of preslavery days in Africa again configurate the mother as the sheltering presence whose disappearance generates the no-madic search for collective meanings that will establish a system of resonance between seemingly heterogeneous entities or "topics," such as daughterhood, friendship, nature, and antiquity—all of which can be seen as so many inaugurating moments of similarity within difference, of self-absorption in an enigmatic mirror, the Augustinian "per speculum in aenigmate," which can be contrasted and paralleled with death itself, the "face that reflects the face of all things, but neither changes itself, nor is mirrored anywhere" (*DT* 87).

Later on, working as a maid for the soprano of the traveling opera company, Zora becomes a kind of mascot for the whole company, and her writing career gets started: "I got a scrapbook . . . and wrote comments under each picture. . . . Then I got another idea. I would comment on daily doings and post the sheets on the call-board. . . . The results stayed strictly mine less than a week because members of the cast began to call me aside and tell me things to put in about others. . . . It was just my handwriting, mostly" (138–39). She becomes the repository of other people's words, a kind of transparent mind or ghost writer. She experiences another form of Zom-biehood, mediated by the acquisition of language, by the absorption of other voices, just like all that "early reading," which had given her "great anguish through all [her] childhood and adolescence" because, as she puts it, "My soul was with the gods and my body in the village. People just would not act like gods" (56). Her experiences at school in Baltimore follow the same pattern: "And here I was, with my face looking like it had been chopped out of a knot of pine wood with a hatchet on somebody's off day, sitting up in the middle of all this pretty" (150–51). Undefined features, "a woman half in shadow," the self-portraitist draws a picture of herself which remains "a figure in bas relief," an intaglio, "the weaving of anthropology with thanatography."[42]

---

[42]The first two phrases are Fannie Hurst's in "A Personality Sketch," reprinted in *Zora Neale Hurston*, ed. Harold Bloom (New York: Chelsea House, 1986), pp. 24, 23; the third is Michel Beaujour's, p. 13. The first one is also the title of Mary Helen Washington's introduction to *ILM*.

These echoing patterns of disfiguration and death give an improvisational rhythm to the text, the ebb and flow of musical counterpoint, and suspend meaning between suggestive similarities the reader is free to associate or not. One subtle parallel the text thus draws is between two gruesome events: the decapitation of Cousin Jimmie, "mother's favorite nephew" (85), unintentionally shot by a white man, who covered up the accident by making it look as though a train had killed him, and the similar fate that had befallen the son of Kossola/Cudjo, David, who was actually beheaded in a train accident. In both cases, it is the grief of the parental figures which resonates in the text, rather than a hypothetical repetition of real-life events. Indeed, framing as they do Hurston's vision of the two faceless women and Kossola's stories of famed Dahoman Amazons who sack cities and carry "clusters of human heads at their belts," the stories underscore a singularly repetitive pattern that would seem to point not to referents beyond the text but to the allegorical disfiguring of generation upon generation of black individuals whose plight is ignored or covered up, except in the memory of those who grieve for them as Cudjo's Takkoi King, beheaded by the Amazons, is mourned by his people (cf. 201).

The ephemeral quality of collective memory itself is reflected in the transient nature of Hurston's "first publication": "On the blackboard . . . I decided to write an allegory using the faculty members as characters" (153). The "allegory" is the source of much entertainment and laughter for her schoolmates, a successful rehearsal for her future tale telling and an important metaphoric hyphen between the immediacy of oral performance and the permanence of the written words. Like these allegorical portraits, which will be erased once they have served their purpose, her twelve visions, which were initially meant to structure the deployment of the autobiography, are soon forgotten because they do not need to be used. The tale teller dynamically reshapes her material as she goes along, the content of the visions becoming irrelevant since the essayistic form of the latter chapters ("My People! My People!," "Looking Things Over," "The Inside Light") spontaneously generates a framework through which to communicate her philosophy.

As she ironically suggests about the experiences told by the religious congregation: "These visions are traditional. I knew them by heart as did the rest of the congregation, but still it was exciting to see *how the converts would handle them. Some of them made up new details. Some of them would forget a part and improvise clumsily or fill up the gap with shouting.* The audience knew, but everybody acted as if every word of it was new" (272; my italics). Inconsistencies are inherent to the performance of traditional cultural forms: it is precisely in the way they individually diverge from the set norms that the converts excite interest in the audience. The "origin" of the tradition must be acknowledged, but acknowledgment does not sanction simple repetition: each new performer "signifies" upon that origin by transforming it, and by allowing for infinite of permutations.[43] To approach a form genealogically, then, is to attempt to retrace its transformations back to an origin—*arche*—that will always prove elusive since every discrete manifestation is the interpellation of a previous one, which sets the stage for the next one, and so on ad infinitum. A particular form acquires value not from its timeless origin or essential qualities but because it is related to practices that inform a mode of life while dynamically shaping reality. Whether Hurston's twelve visions signify upon a particular religious tradition or the vernacular ritual of the "dozens" (cf. 187, 217) or both is of no importance since, in any case, she can make vicarious use of the clichés, parody some of them, ignore the rest, and "tell a story the way [she] wanted, or rather the way the story told itself to [her]" (206). Since "playing the dozens" or "specifying" is a form of invective and name calling that points genealogically to a fictitious origin—"they proceed to 'specify' until the tip-top branch of your family tree has been given a reading" (217)—we can readily infer that this "self-affirming form of discourse"[44] does not require foundational support in reality. It is by virtue of its perlocutionary function that it affirms the underlying gutsiness and creativity of the agent of discourse, drawing a portrait of the self as capable of enduring, diverging, and surviving because it adheres to the formal aspects of a dynamic and improvisational cultural tradition that allows the storyteller to "keep the tune" for the benefit of the collectivity, to lift the veil on the mirror of a different history, to be a "keeper of our memories" (*Moses* 350). Hurston's "exuberant sense of self"[45] allows her to adopt a thoroughly Nietzschean perspective on this "topsy-turvy world" of hers, and to value memory as a viable alternative to oppressive history.

In *Dust Tracks*, we have a powerful example of the braiding, or *métissage*, of cultural forms, since Persephone figures both as the voice of the dead mother and as the boundary crosser who links up two different worlds. Turning the mythical relation between Ceres and her daughter upside down, Hurston invents her own reading of the tradition, "signifying" upon that tradition in a specifically "black" way, diverging from the Greco-Roman text in the only way possible for the Afro-American self-portraitist. To rejoin her mother, Zora/Persephone must travel back to the underworld, to the "dark realm" of her own people, to the friendship with Big Sweet, in order to learn to say what her dying mother could not, in order to name the chain of legendary female figures who can teach her to re-member and to speak the past.

[43]I am using the word *signifies* in the black traditional sense discussed in particular by Henry L. Gates, Jr., "The Blackness of Blackness: A Critique of the Sign and the Signifying Monkey," *Black Literature and Literary Theory* (New York: Methuen, 1984), pp. 285–321.

[44]See Susan Willis, *Specifying: Black Women Writing the American Experience* (Madison: University of Wisconsin Press, 1987), p. 31.

[45]The phrase is Hemenway's in *Hurston*, p. 213.

From Experience to Eloquence:
Richard Wright's *Black Boy* as Art

Charles T. Davis

Native Son[1] is the work for which Richard Wright is best known, but *Black Boy*,[2] an autobiography more or less, may be the achievement that offers the best demonstration of his art as a writer. This idea is not so startling given Wright's special talents—the eye of a skilled reporter, the sensibility of a revolutionary poet, alert to varied forms of injustice, and the sense of symbolic meaning carried by the rituals of ordinary life. The problem up to the present time is not the lack of attention the work has received. Like *Native Son*, *Black Boy* was selected by the Book-of-the-Month Club and was thus assured a wide distribution and a serious if somewhat skewed reading from many critics. In 1970 Stanley Hyman, in reviewing Wright's entire career, assigned *Black Boy* to a period in which Wright's "important writing" occurred—according to his definition, Wright's last years as a resident in America, from 1940 to 1945.[3] But *Black Boy* by itself failed to acquire as an original work of art the reputation it deserves.

It appears now, from the perspective of a generation, that a measure of distortion was unavoidable, given the political temper of the time. The history of the publication of the manuscript entitled *American Hunger*,[4] of which *Black Boy* was a part, encouraged a violent political response. It was well known that "I Tried to Be a Communist," which appeared in the August and September issues of the *Atlantic Monthly* in 1944,[5] were chapters of an

Reprinted with permission from Charles T. Davis, *Chant of Saints*, ed. Robert B. Stepto and Michael S. Harper, 425–39. Urbana: University of Illinois Press, 1979.

[1](New York: Harper, 1940.) Dorothy Canfield Fisher in the introduction writes that the "novel plumbs blacker depths of human experience than American literature has yet had, comparable only to Dostoievski's revelation of human misery in wrongdoing" (p. x).

[2]The full title is *Black Boy: A Record of Childhood and Youth* (New York: Harper, 1945). Dorothy Fisher in the introductory note calls Wright's work "the honest, dreadful, heartbreaking story of a Negro childhood and youth . . ." (p. vii), without referring to its art or even its place in an American literary tradition.

[3]"Life and Letters: Richard Wright Reappraised," *Atlantic Monthly*, 225 (March, 1970), 127–32.

[4]*American Hunger* (New York: Harper & Row, Publishers) was published in 1977. It is not the whole autobiography but the second part, the continuation of *Black Boy*. Michel Fabre in the afterword provides an accurate brief history of the decision to publish only the first section in 1945. See pp. 143–44.

[5]*Atlantic Monthly*, 174 (August, 1944), 61–70; (September, 1944), 48–56.

autobiographical record to be published the following year, even though they were excluded finally with the rest of the matter dealing with the years in Chicago and New York. When *Black Boy* did appear, knowing critics read the book in light of the much-publicized account of Wright's difficulties with the Communist party. Baldly put, the situation for the critic encouraged a form of outside intrusion, a case of knowing too much, of supplying a frame of reference which a reading of the basic text does not support. The board of the Book-of-the-Month Club or Edward Aswell or both,[6] in suggesting a restriction of autobiographical matter to the period before migration to Chicago, exercised a judgment that displayed something more than the good sense of successful editors; indeed, that judgment pointed up the artistic integrity of the work. Someone concluded accurately that the intensity of *Black Boy* came from a concentration upon one metaphor of oppression, the South, and prevented the diffusion of power that would be the consequence of the introduction of a second, the Communist party.

If the political reaction created one kind of distortion in the eye of the examiner, more normal literary expectations created another. *Black Boy* baffled W. E. B. Du Bois, the most impressive black intellectual of his time. His review in the New York *Herald Tribune* states his dilemma: ". . . if the book is meant to be a creative picture and a warning, even then, it misses its possible effectiveness because it is as a work of art so patently and terribly overdrawn."[7] By 1945 Du Bois had published three major works with outstanding autobiographical elements, one of which, *Dusk of Dawn*, was a fully developed autobiography of considerable intellectual distinction,[8] and he could not be accused of responding merely to a sense of affront to his middle-class sensibilities. Du Bois was not prepared to accept Wright's bleak Mississippi; he was appalled not so much by the condition of terror there as by a state of mind that denied the possibility of humanity for blacks and frustrated all black efforts to achieve satisfaction beyond the minimal requirements for life. After all, Du Bois had vivid memories of his experience as a young teacher in rural Tennessee, where he encountered aspiring, sensitive pupils who, though often defeated or betrayed by their environment, were not totally crushed by Southern oppression.[9] Moreover, Du Bois joined, no doubt, a group of critics of *Black Boy* best defined by Ralph Ellison as consisting of readers who complained that Wright had "omitted the development of his own sensibility."[10] But this is to define sensibility in a way

---

6Fabre, "Afterword," *American Hunger*, pp. 143–44.

7W. E. B. Du Bois, "Richard Wright Looks Back," *New York Herald Tribune*, March 4, 1945, sec. 5, p. 2.

8The three are *The Souls of Black Folk: Essays and Sketches* (Chicago: A. C. McClurg, 1903), *Darkwater: Voices from Within the Veil* (New York: Harcourt, Brace, 1920), and *Dusk of Dawn: An Essay toward an Autobiography of a Race Concept* (New York: Harcourt, Brace, 1940).

9Chapter IV, "Of the Meaning of Progress," in Du Bois, *The Souls of Black Folk*, pp. 60–74.

10"Richard Wright's Blues," *Antioch Review*, 5 (June, 1945), 202. Reprinted in *Shadow and Act* (New York: Random House, 1964).

generally understood by the nineteenth century, which is to hold that sensibility is an orderly accretion of the mind and heart within an environment recognizably human, and not to accept Wright's radical equation of the existence of sensibility with survival.

Du Bois did not doubt that autobiography could be art, though more naive critics might. He could not accept the principles of an art as austere as Wright's was, one in which many of the facts of Southern life, so familiar to him, were excluded and in which generalization had been carried to such extreme lengths. After all, the book's title was *Black Boy*, not "A Black Boy,"[11] with an appropriately limiting modifier. Viewed superficially, Richard's odyssey was unique primarily because it had a happy ending—the escape from the hell of the South, where, apparently, all of his black associates (he had no friends in the narrative) were destined to spend the rest of their days. Wright's generalizations about the dehumanizing relationships between whites and blacks and the almost equally unsatisfying connections between blacks and blacks shaped his South, and these assumptions Du Bois thought to be distorted. One sweeping statement by young Wright in Memphis, where he lived from his seventeenth to his nineteenth year and where he committed himself formally to becoming a writer,[12] would certainly extract from Du Bois an expression of disbelief, if not annoyance: "I knew of no Negroes who read the books I liked and I wondered if any Negroes ever thought of them. I knew that there were Negro doctors, lawyers, newspapermen, but I never saw any of them. When I read a Negro newspaper I never caught the faintest echo of my preoccupation in its pages."[13]

Not only Du Bois, but also other blacks, even those lacking the knowledge of black life in America which Du Bois had acquired from his surveys and research projects at Atlanta University,[14] would be appalled at Richard's confession of his cultural isolation. This is a moment when generalization approaches fiction, when we must say that a statement may be acceptable within its context, but that it is questionable as a fact standing on its own, as something that might be supported by the confessions of other black boys, especially those emerging from families with middle-class aspirations and pretensions like Wright's.

Editing the raw matter of life is necessary, of course, to write an autobiography with any claim to art. No one has described this activity better than

[11]Wright wrote Edward Aswell, his editor at Harper's, on August 10, 1944, suggesting *Black Boy* as a title for the book. He added, for emphasis, that *Black Boy* was "not only a title but also a kind of heading to the whole general theme" (Fabre, "Afterword," *American Hunger*, p. 144).

[12]Wright comments on this commitment in *Black Boy:* "I had once tried to write, had once reveled in feeling, had let my crude imagination roam, but the impulse to dream had been slowly beaten out of me by experience. Now it surged up again and I hungered for books, new ways of looking and seeing" (p. 218).

[13]*Ibid.*, p. 220.

[14]Between 1897 and 1915 Du Bois edited fifteen studies on the condition and status of blacks in America. These volumes represented the Proceedings of the Annual Conference on the Negro Problem, organized by Du Bois and held at Atlanta University.

Ellison has in his critical examination of *Black Boy:* "The function, the psychology, of artistic selectivity is to eliminate from an art form all those elements of experience which contain no compelling significance. Life is as the sea, art a ship in which man conquers life's crushing formlessness. . . ."[15] What Ellison did not say is that such editing requires the use of controlling principles that are invariably fictional. This is to say that the organizing ideas are assumptions that are not strictly true according to the most objective criteria. Operating from a strict conception of the truth, we have every right to question the emotional basis for *The Education of Henry Adams,* an especially intense form of self-pity coming from the most widely cultivated American of his time, who, nonetheless, constantly reminds us of his lack of preparation for the nineteenth century, not to mention the twentieth. And in *Black Boy* we are asked to accept Richard's cultural isolation as well as his vulnerability to all forms of deprivation—physical, emotional, social, and intellectual.

Some critics, carried off by the impact of *Black Boy,* tend to treat the autobiography as if it were fiction. They are influenced by the fact that much great modern fiction, Joyce's *Portrait of the Artist as a Young Man,* for example, is very close to life. And the tendency here is reinforced by the fact that the author himself, Wright, is a creator of fictions. Yielding so is a mistake because many of the incidents in *Black Boy* retain the sharp angularity of life, rather than fitting into the dramatic or symbolic patterns of fiction. Richard's setting fire to the "fluffy white curtains" (p. 4), and incidentally the house, is not the announcement of the birth of a pyromaniac or a revolutionary, but testimony primarily to the ingenuity of a small black boy in overcoming mundane tedium. We must say "primarily" because this irresponsible act suggests the profound distress and confusion an older Richard would bring to a family that relied heavily upon rigid attitudes toward religion, expected behavior, and an appropriate adjustment to Southern life. Richard's fire is not Bigger's rat at the beginning of *Native Son,* when the act of killing brings out pent-up violence in the young black man and foreshadows, perhaps, the events of Book Two, "Flight," when Bigger's position becomes that of the cornered rat.[16] Nor does Richard's immodest invitation to his grandmother during his bath (p. 49) offer disturbing witness of the emergence of a pornographer or a connoisseur of the erotic; rather, it points to something more general, the singular perversity in Richard that makes him resist family and the South. In *Black Boy* we exist in a world of limited probability that is not life exactly, because there is an order to be demonstrated, and it does not display the perfect design of a serious fiction. We occupy a gray area in between. The patterns are here on several levels. Though they may not be so clear and tight as to permit the critic to predict, they do govern the selection of materials, the rendering of special emphases, distortions, and the style.

15Ellison, "Richard Wright's Blues," pp. 82–83.
16*Native Son,* pp. 4–5.

We seldom raise questions about what is omitted from an autobiography, yet if we wish to discover pattern, we must begin with what we do not find. The seasonal metaphor in *Walden* (we move from spring to spring) becomes all the more important once we realize that Henry Thoreau lived on the shore of Walden Pond more than two years.[17] Franklin's few "errata"[18] point up the strong aridity of an autobiography that touches so little on the traumas of the heart. Franklin's education, his achievements in business and science, and his proposals for the benefit of society seem at times supported by an emotional sub-structure far too frail. But the purposes of both autobiographies—in *Walden,* to offer the model of a renewed life; in the *Autobiography of Benjamin Franklin,* to sketch a convincing design of a successful life in the new world, one that emphasizes the practical values that most Americans admired and many Europeans envied—were achieved in part because of the shrewdness in excluding truthful, though extraneous matter. So, too, *Black Boy* profits from rigorous and inspired editing.

One function of the omissions is to strengthen the impression in our minds of Richard's intense isolation. This is no mean achievement given the fact that Wright was born into a large family (on his mother's side, at least) which, despite differences in personality, cooperated in times of need. The father, because of his desertion of his mother, was early in Richard's mind, perhaps in the sentiments of other family members, too, an object of hate and scorn. There are no names in the early pages of *Black Boy,* not even that of Richard's brother, Leon Allan, just a little more than two years younger than Richard. When the names begin to appear in *Black Boy,* they tend to define the objects of adversary, often violently hostile relationships—Grandmother Wilson, Aunt Addie, Uncle Thomas. Two notable exceptions are Grandfather Wilson, an ineffectual man capable only of reliving his past as a soldier in the Civil War, and Richard's mother, Ella, a pathetically vulnerable woman of some original strength who, because of continuing illness, slipped gradually into a state of helplessness that became for Richard symbolic of his whole life as a black boy in the South.[19]

The admirable biography of Wright by Michel Fabre suggests another dimension for Richard's opponents in his embattled household. The climax of the violence in the family occurred with the confrontation with Uncle Tom, portrayed as a retired and defeated schoolteacher reduced at the time to

---

[17]Thoreau is precise about the length of his actual stay, despite the fact that the events of *Walden* fall within the design of a single year: "The present was my next experiment . . . for convenience, putting the experience of two years into one." Henry David Thoreau, *Walden,* ed. Sherman Paul (Boston: Houghton Mifflin, 1957), p. 58.

[18]Franklin refers in this way to his neglect of Miss Read, to whom he was engaged, during a period spent in London: "This was another of the great errata of my life. . . ." "Autobiography" in Benjamin Franklin, *Autobiography and Other Writings,* ed. R. B. Nye (Boston: Houghton Mifflin, 1958), p. 38.

[19]See Michel Fabre, *The Unfinished Quest of Richard Wright* (New York: William Morrow, 1973), pp. 1–17.

earning a living by performing odd jobs as a carpenter. Richard resented the fact that he was the victim of Uncle Tom's frustrations, and he responded to orders from the older man by threatening him with razors in both hands and by spitting out hysterically, "You are not an example to me; you could never be. . . . You're a *warning.* Your life isn't so hot that you can tell me what to do. . . . Do you think that I want to grow up and weave the bottoms of chairs for people to sit in?" (p. 140). A footnote from Fabre adds more information about the humiliated uncle:

> The portrait of Uncle Thomas in *Black Boy* is exaggerated. After living with the Wilsons, he moved next door and became a real-estate broker. In 1938, he was a member of the Executive Committee of the Citizen's Civic League in Jackson and wrote a book on the word *Negro,* discussing the superiority complex of the Whites and its effects on the Blacks. At this time Richard put him in contact with Doubleday publishers and the uncle and the nephew were completely reconciled.[20]

Wright includes in *Black Boy* a touching description of meeting his father again after a quarter-century. As the newly successful author looked at a strange black sharecropper in ragged overalls holding a muddy hoe, the old resentment for past neglect faded: "I forgave him and pitied him as my eyes looked past him to the unpainted wooden shack" (p. 30). But *Black Boy* contains no softening reconsiderations of Uncle Tom, or of Aunt Addie, who, like her brother, seems to have possessed some redeeming qualities,[21] or of Granny Wilson for that matter. Their stark portraits dominate the family and define a living space too narrow, too mean, and too filled with frustration and poverty for an imaginative youngster like Richard.

A growing boy, when denied the satisfactions of a loving home, looks for emotional support at school or at play, and if he is lucky, he finds something that moderates domestic discontent. But there is little compensation of this sort in *Black Boy.* The reality of the life away from the family seems to be less bleak than Wright represents it, though his schooling was retarded by early irregularity because of the family's frequent moves, and his play restricted, perhaps, because of the family's desperate need for money and Granny's Seventh Day Adventist scruples. Once again we are struck by the absence of names—of teachers like Lucy McCranie and Alice Burnett, who taught Richard at the Jim Hill School in Jackson and recognized his lively intelligence,[22] or Mary L. Morrison or the Reverend Otto B. Cobbins, Richard's instructors in the eighth and ninth grades of the Smith-Robinson School,[23] to whose dedication and competence, despite personal limitations, Wright paid

---

[20]Fabre, *Unfinished Quest,* p. 533.

[21]Another footnote by Fabre in *Unfinished Quest* suggests an additional dimension for Addie, who, "too, was not spared in *Black Boy.* She reacted rather well to reading the book—she stated that if Richard wrote in that way, it was to support his family . . ." (p. 533).

[22]*Ibid.,* p. 39.

[23]*Ibid.,* p. 48.

tribute elsewhere.[24] There was no question about his marginal status in these institutions, since Richard stood regularly at the head of his class.

Black Boy is singularly devoid of references to rewarding peer associations. There is no mention of Dick Jordan, Joe Brown, Perry Booker, or Essie Lee Ward, friends of this period and so valued that Wright was in touch with several of them ten years later when he was living in Chicago.[25] The fact that a few of Wright's childhood associates did succeed in making their way to Chicago has an amount of interest in itself, serving, as well, to break the isolation that Wright has fabricated so well. Among the childhood activities that went unrecorded were the exploits of the Dick Wright clan, made up of a group of neighborhood boys who honored in the name of their society, no doubt, their most imaginative member. The clan included Dick Jordan, Perry Booker, Joe Brown, and also Frank Sims, a descendant of a black senator during the Reconstruction period, Blanche K. Bruce.[26] What is amply clear, then, is that Wright had a childhood more than a little touched by the usual rituals and preoccupations of middle-class boys growing up in America, but what is also apparent is that reference to them would modify our sense of Richard's deprived and disturbed emotional life, a necessity for the art of the autobiography, rather more important than any concern for absolute accuracy.

Wright has little to say directly about sex. Richard's most serious temptation for sexual adventure comes toward the end of *Black Boy* in Memphis, when he is taken in by the Moss family. Richard succeeds in resisting the opportunity to take advantage of a cozy arrangement with Bess, the daughter whom Mrs. Moss seeks to thrust upon him, with marriage as her ultimate objective (p. 185). There are some indirect references to frustrated, sublimated, or distorted forms of sexual energy—in Miss Simon, certainly, the tall, gaunt, mulatto woman who ran the orphan home where Richard was deposited for a period (pp. 25–28). And there were exposures to white women, all calculated to teach Richard the strength of the taboo prohibiting the thought (not to mention the fact) of black-white sexual relations in the South. But Richard never takes an aggressive interest in sex; the adventures that he stumbles into create traumas when they are serious and unavoidable, or are embarrassing when he can resist participation and control his reactions. Wright, indeed, seems to be even more discreet than Franklin was; by comparison, Claude Brown is a raving sensualist in *Manchild in the Promised Land,* though roughly the same period of growth is involved. It is strange that so little space is given to sexual episodes and fantasies in the record of the gradual maturing of an adolescent—unbelievable, given the preoccupations of the twentieth century. We face the problem of omission again. Wright deliber-

24E. R. Embree describes, in *Thirteen Against the Odds* (New York: Viking, 1944), Wright's attitude toward his education in Jackson: "He [Wright] remembers the Smith-Robinson school with some gratitude. The teachers tried their best to pump learning into the pupils" (p. 27).
25Fabre, *Unfinished Quest,* p. 39.
26*Ibid.,* p. 43.

ately seeks to deprive his hero, his younger self, of any substantial basis for sensual gratification located outside his developing imagination. The world that *Black Boy* presents is uniformly bleak, always ascetic, and potentially violent, and the posture of the isolated hero, cut off from family, peer, or community support, is rigidly defiant, without the softening effects of interludes of sexual indulgence.

Richard's immediate world, not that foreign country controlled by whites, is overwhelmingly feminine. Male contacts are gone, except for occasional encounters with uncles. The father has deserted his home, and the grandfather is lost in the memories of "The War." The uncles tend to make brief entrances and exits, following the pattern of Hoskins, quickly killed off by envious whites in Arkansas, or the unnamed new uncle, forced to flee because of unstated crimes against whites (pp. 48–49, 57–60). Thomas is the uncle who stays around somewhat longer than the others do, long enough to serve as the convenient object for Richard's mounting rebellion. The encounter with Uncle Tom is the culminating episode marking a defiance expressed earlier against a number of authority figures, all women—Richard's mother, Miss Simon, Grandmother Wilson, Aunt Addie. Women dominate in Richard's world, with the ultimate authority vested in Granny—near-white, uncompromising, unloving, and fanatical, daring Richard to desecrate her Seventh Day Adventist Sabbath. The only relief from feminine piety is the pathetic schoolteacher who, in a happy moment, tells an enraptured Richard about Bluebeard and his wives (p. 34). But even this delight, moved in part, no doubt, by Bluebeard's relentless war against females, is short-lived. Granny puts a stop to such sinning, not recognizing, of course, the working out of the law of compensation.

Richard's odyssey takes him from the black world to the white—from the problems of home and family to new and even more formidable difficulties. The movement is outward into the world, to confront an environment that is not controlled by Granny, though it provides much that contributes to an explanation of Granny's behavior. Richard's life among blacks emphasizes two kinds of struggle. One is simply the battle for physical existence, the need for food, clothing, shelter, and protection that is the overwhelming concern of the early pages of *Black Boy*. The second grows out of Richard's deeply felt desire to acquire his own male identity, a sense of self apart from a family that exerts increasing pressure upon this growing black boy to behave properly, to experience Christian conversion, and to accept guidance from his (mostly female) elders. Survival in two senses, then, is the dominant theme, one which does not change when he leaves the black community. The terms are the same though the landscape is new. Richard desperately seeks employment in white neighborhoods and in the downtown business districts in order to contribute to the support of his family. He discovers, when he does so, that the demand to accommodate becomes even more insistent and less flexible than that exerted by his own family.

The difference is that the stakes are higher. Richard thinks he must find a job, any job, to earn a living. This awareness represents a step beyond the simple dependence that moves a small boy to complain, "Mama, I'm hungry" (p. 13). If he does not find work, Richard feels that he has failed his family in an essential way and made its survival precarious. Though his independence in the black world leads to harsh sanctions—threats, bed without supper, whippings—he is not prepared for the infinitely greater severity of the white world. It is cruel, calculating, and sadistic, Richard never doubts that he will survive the lashings received from his mother, Granny, and assorted aunts and uncles, but he does question his ability to endure exposure to whites. The ways of white folks are capricious and almost uniformly malignant. Richard understands that the penalty for non-conformity, down to the way a black boy walks or holds his head, is not simply a sore body, but death. When Richard gives up a good job with an optical company, with a chance, according to his boss, to become something more than a menial worker, he does so because of the opposition exhibited by whites who think he aspires to do *"white man's work."* Richard confides to his boss when he leaves the factory; "I'm scared. . . . They would kill me" (p. 168).

From the woman who inquires of Richard, looking for yet another job, "Boy, do you steal?" (p. 128) to the two young men who attempt to arrange for Richard to fight another black boy for the amusement of an assembly of whites (pp. 209–10), we witness an unrelieved set of abuses. Certainly omission of some mitigating circumstances and artful distortion is involved in this bitter report. Richard is gradually introduced to a white world that grows progressively more dominant, divisive, and corrupting concerning the black life that serves it. Richard understands fully what is expected of him:

> I began to marvel at how smoothly the black boys acted out the roles that the white race had mapped out for them. Most of them were not conscious of living a special, separate, stunted way of life. Yet I know that in some period of their growing up—a period that they had no doubt forgotten—there had been developed in them a delicate, sensitive controlling mechanism that shut off their minds and emotions from all that the white race had said was taboo. (p. 172)

In Wright's South it was unthinkable for a black boy to aspire to become a lens-grinder, much less to harbor the ambition to become a writer. When Richard is thoughtless enough to reveal his true aim in life to one of his white employers, the response is predictable: "You'll never be a writer. . . . Who on earth put such ideas into your nigger head?" (p. 129). Given his difficulties in adjusting to an oppressive Southern system, Richard sustains his interest in writing through a monumental act of will. We are led to the inevitable conclusion that Richard must flee the South if he is to remain alive, and the desire to achieve an artistic career seems less important in light of the more basic concern for life itself.

We have every reason to suspect that the treatment of whites gains a certain strength from artistic deletion, too. Michel Fabre points out that

Wright's relationship with a white family named Wall does not fit the pattern of abuse and brutal exploitation that emerges from the autobiography: "Although *Black Boy* was designed to describe the effects of racism on a black child, which meant omitting incidents tending to exonerate white persons in any way, there is no doubt that the Walls were liberal and generous employers. For almost two years Richard worked before and after class, earning three dollars a week bringing in firewood and doing the heavy cleaning."[27] Fabre adds, with reference especially to Mrs. Wall and her mother, "Since they respected his qualities as an individual, he sometimes submitted his problems and plans to them and soon considered their house a second home where he met with more understanding than from his own family."[28] This is not matter that reinforces a design displaying increasing difficulty for Richard as he moves outward and into contact with white society. Nor does it support Richard's growing conviction that his survival depends upon his escape from the South. The design of *Black Boy* offers an accelerating pattern of confrontations, taking into account both an increase in danger for Richard and a mounting seriousness in terms of society's estimate of his deviations. Like Big Boy, Richard must flee or die.

The narrator of *Black Boy* has three voices. The simplest records recollected events with clarity and a show of objectivity. We may be troubled by an insufficient context surrounding or an inadequate connection linking these episodes until we become aware of the suggestion of a psychological dimension for them. The incidents illustrate basic emotions: the discovery of fear and guilt, first, when fire destroys Richard's house; the experience of hate, directed this time toward the father, in killing the kitten; the satisfactions of violence, in defeating the teenage gang; the dangers of curiosity about the adult world, in Richard's early addiction to alcohol. The psyche of a child takes shape through exposure to a set of unusual traumas, and the child goes forth, as we have seen, into a world that becomes progressively more brutal and violent. Style in this way reinforces the first theme of the autobiography, survival.

It is in hearing the more complicated and lyrical second voice of the narrator that we sense for the first time another theme in the autobiography. This is the making of the artist. The world, we have been told, is cold, harsh, and cruel, a fact which makes all the more miraculous the emergence of a literary imagination destined to confront it. The bleak South, by some strange necessity, is forced to permit the blooming of a single rose. Wright expends upon the nourishment of this tender plant the care that he has given to describing the sterile soil from which it springs.

A third, didactic voice offers occasional explanations of the matter recorded by the other two. It comments at times upon the lack of love among blacks in the South, the distortions in human relationships involving blacks and whites,

[27]*Ibid.*, pp. 46–47.
[28]*Ibid.*, p. 47.

and corruption in the social and economic systems. At other times it advises us of the necessity for secrecy when a black boy harbors the ambition to write, and explains the difficulties which he confronts when he seeks to serve an apprenticeship to his art. Despite formidable opposition and the danger of complete isolation, this ambition lives and forces the growth of Richard's imaginative powers.

We do not begin simply with the statement of the intention to become an artist. We start, rather, as Joyce does in *A Portrait of the Artist*, with the sense experience that rests behind the word. Richard's memory offers rich testimony of the capacity to feel objects of nature, small and large. Not only these. We note that accompanying the record of sensations is the tendency to translate sensation into an appropriate emotion—melancholy, nostalgia, astonishment, disdain. All of the senses achieve recognition in Richard's memory, and all combine to emphasize memories of violent experiences: the killing of the chicken; the shocking movement of the snake; the awesome golden glow on a silent night (pp. 7–8).

Apart from this basic repository of sensation and image, we sense early in Richard two other qualities just as essential to the budding artist. One is detachment, the feeling of being different from others. In two worlds to which he is exposed, that of the family and then the more muddled arena of affairs, he rejects all efforts to moderate his apartness. Though conversion and subsequent baptism apparently point to joining the company of the saved, viewed in the conventional way, damnation is assured by the refusal to deliver the right kind of valedictory at the graduation exercises of his grammar school (p. 153). Barely passing one ritual, he flunks another. He maintains under pressure his status as an alien, so ultimately he will be free to exercise the imagination that faces the cold world.

The second quality is curiosity. His mother tells Richard that he asks too many questions. Our young hero is apparently undaunted by the fact that his insistent prying has led to one of the earliest addictions to alcohol recorded in literature. But another addiction is more serious, to the truth in the appearances about him. "Will you stop asking silly questions!" his mother commands (p. 42). About names, about color, about the relationship between the two. Curiosity constantly leads Richard to forbidden areas more menacing than the saloon, to the mysterious privileged province of whites in Mississippi and the equally mysterious restriction of the blacks.

A neat form of inversion is involved in the development of Richard's artistic talent. We note that the qualities supporting and sustaining the growing boy's imagination are just those preventing a successful adjustment to life in the South. To achieve a tolerable existence, not even a comfortable one, Richard must have firm relationships with the members of his family and with his neighbors and peers; to survive in the larger, white-dominated society he must accept without questioning the inflexible system of Southern mores and customs. Richard, rejecting these imperatives, responds to the demands of his own imagination.

Richard's sensations in nature anticipate a discovery just as valuable and far reaching. This is literature itself. Of the encounter with *Bluebeard* Richard says, "My sense of life deepened. . . ." He recalls, further, a total emotional response, emphasized, no doubt, by the background of an unresponding family, and he realizes that he stands on the threshold of a "gateway to a forbidden and enchanting land" (p. 36). So, early, the opposition is clear. On the one hand is the bleak environment frowning upon any activity of the imagination, whether passive or active, and on the other a determined Richard who will not be turned aside. His reading would be done in secret, a clandestine activity abetted by delivering racist newspapers and borrowing the library card of a compliant white man. There is no evidence that he discussed his reading with anyone, black or white. In Memphis, when he was able to patronize second-hand bookstores and to buy magazines like *Harper's*, *Atlantic Monthly*, and *American Mercury*, his tastes reflected the shape of his early conditioning (p. 198). He admired the great liberators, the destroyers of provincial and private worlds like the one that oppressed him: H. L. Mencken in a *Book of Prefaces and Prejudices*; Sinclair Lewis in *Main Street* and *Babbitt*; Theodore Dreiser in *Sister Carrie* and *Jennie Gerhardt* (pp. 217–19).

It might be said that Richard has the loneliness of a naturalistic hero, of McTeague or of Carrie Meeber. Theirs are worlds in which no one talks to anyone else, worlds entirely given over to the expression of power. One person's drive pitted against that of another, and the consequence of the struggle has more to do with heredity or chemistry than with persuasion. Richard's behavior, much like that of a character created by Frank Norris or Dreiser, though it is not governed by the tight probability of fiction, carries constantly the solemn and overwhelming weight of the universe. He cannot say "sir" without acquiescing to the ever-present power of the white man, and he cannot read Mencken without the satisfaction that he has triumphed over a hostile white South through subterfuge and trickery.

Richard's commitment to write precipitates confrontations. As we have seen, his honest admission of this aspiration to one white lady employer results in bitter ridicule, and Richard feels, despite the pressures of his situation, that his ego has been assaulted. His first publication, "The Voodoo of Hell's Half-Acre," is little more than the crude rendering of the stuff of *Flynn's Detective Weekly*, but Richard discovers that printing it is an act of defiance, further separating him from the world that surrounds him, both black and white (p. 146).

Richard does not intend to restrict his range to any half-acre, though his first is identified as "Hell." His province would be the real world around him. True, it is sometimes not to be distinguished from the subject area defined by his first literary effort. At a very young age Richard sees "elephants" moving across the land—not real "elephants," but convicts in a chain gang, and the child's awe is prompted by the unfortunate confusion of elephant and zebra (p. 52). An inauspicious beginning, perhaps, but the pattern of applying his imagination to his immediate surrounding is firmly set. Later, Richard says more soberly that he rejects religion because it ignores immediate reality. His faith, predictably, must be wedded to "common realities of life" (p. 100), anchored in the sensations of his body and in what his mind could grasp. This is, we see, an excellent credo for an artist, but a worthless one for a black boy growing to maturity in Mississippi.

Another piece of evidence announcing Richard's talent is the compulsion to make symbols of the details of his everyday experience. This faculty is early demonstrated in his tendency to generalize from sensational experience, to define an appropriate emotion to associate with his feelings. A more highly developed example is Richard's reaction to his mother's illness and sufferings, representative for him in later years of the poverty, the ignorance, the helplessness of black life in Mississippi. And it is based on the generalizing process that Richard is a black boy, any black boy experiencing childhood, adolescence, and early manhood in the South.

Richard leaves the South. He must, to survive as a man and to develop as an artist. By the time we reach the end of the narrative, these two drives have merged. We know, as well, that the South will never leave Richard, never depart from the rich imagination that developed despite monumental opposition. We have only the final promise that Richard will someday understand the region that has indelibly marked him.

Richard's ultimate liberation, and his ultimate triumph, will be the ability to face the dreadful experience in the South and to record it. At the end of *A Portrait of the Artist as a Young Man,* the facts of experience have become journal items for the artist.[29] At the conclusion of *Invisible Man,* Ellison's unnamed narrator can record the blues of his black life, with the accompaniment of extraordinary psychedelic effects. Stephen Dedalus is on his way to becoming an artist; Ellison's hero promises to climb out of his hole, half-prepared, at least, to return to mundane life.[30] The conclusion of *Black Boy* is less positive and more tentative. True, Richard has made it; he has whipped the devils of the South, black and white. But he has left us with a feeling that is less than happy. He has yet to become an artist. Then we realize with a start what we have read is not simply the statement of a promise, its background and its development, but its fulfillment. Wright has succeeded in reconstructing the reality that was for a long time perhaps too painful to order, and that reconstruction may be Wright's supreme artistic achievement, *Black Boy.*

---

[29]See James Joyce, *A Portrait of the Artist as a Young Man* (New York: New American Library, 1955), pp. 195–96.

[30]Ellison's narrator states his final position with some care: "Thus, having tried to give pattern to the chaos which lives within the pattern of your certainties, I must come out, I must emerge." *Invisible Man* (New York: New American Library, 1952), p. 502.

Malcolm X and the Limits of Autobiography

Paul John Eakin

When a complex and controversial figure writes a book that has achieved the distinction and popularity of *The Autobiography of Malcolm X*, it is inevitable that efforts will be made to place him and his work in the perspective of a literary tradition. Barrett John Mandel, for example, has identified in Malcolm X's story the paradigm of the traditional conversion narrative. His reading of Malcolm X's autobiography, and it is a characteristic one, assumes that the narrative expresses a completed self.[1] Further, Ross Miller has suggested that such an assumption is central to the expectations we bring to the reading of any autobiography: "The pose of the autobiographer as an experienced man is particularly effective because we expect to hear from someone who has a completed sense of his own life and is therefore in a position to tell what he has discovered."[2] Even Warner Berthoff, who has admirably defined Malcolm X's "extraordinary power to change and be changed" as "the distinctive rule of his life," seems to have been drawn to this sense of the completed self when he attempts to locate the *Autobiography* in a special and limited literary tradition, that of the political testament in which "some ruler or statesman sets down for the particular benefit of his people a summary of his own experience and wisdom."[3] The rhetorical posture of Malcolm X in the last chapter would seem to confirm Berthoff's reading and to fulfill Miller's autobiographical expectations, for it is indeed that of the elder statesman summing up a completed life, a life that has, as it were, already ended:

[1][Barrett John Mandel,] "The Didactic Achievement of Malcolm X's Autobiography," *Afro-American Studies*, 2 (1972), 269–74. For other treatments of the *Autobiography* as a conversion narrative see Warner Berthoff, "Witness and Testament: Two Contemporary Classics," *New Literary History*, 2 (1971), 318, 320; and Carol Ohmann, "*The Autobiography of Malcolm X:* A Revolutionary Use of the Franklin Tradition," *American Quarterly*, 22 (1970), 131–49. Louis E. Lomax has identified Malcolm X as the St. Paul of the Black Muslim movement (see *Malcolm X: The Man and His Times*, ed. John Henrik Clarke [New York: Macmillan, 1969], p. xvii).

[2][Ross Miller,] "Autobiography as Fact and Fiction: Franklin, Adams, Malcolm X," *Centennial Review*, 16 (1972), 231.

[3]Berthoff, 319, 321.

Anyway, now, each day I live as if I am already dead, and I tell you what I would like for you to do. When I *am* dead—I say it that way because from the things I *know,* I do not expect to live long enough to read this book in its finished form—I want you to just watch and see if I'm not right in what I say: that the white man, in his press, is going to identify me with "hate."[4]

If Malcolm X's anticipation of his imminent death confers on this final phase of autobiographical retrospection a posthumous authority, it is nevertheless an authority that he exercises here to defend himself against the fiction of the completed self that his interpreters—both black and white, in the event— were to use against him.[5] Each of his identities turned out to be provisional, and even this voice from the grave was the utterance not of an ultimate identity but merely of the last one in the series of roles that Malcolm X had variously assumed, lived out, and discarded.

Alex Haley's "Epilogue" to the *Autobiography* reveals the fictive nature of this final testamentary stance which Berthoff regards as definitive. Here Haley, Malcolm X's collaborator in the *Autobiography*, reports that the apparent uncertainty and confusion of Malcolm X's views were widely discussed in Harlem during the last months of Malcolm X's life, while Malcolm X himself, four days before his death, said in an interview, "I'm man enough to tell you that I can't put my finger on exactly what my philosophy is now, but I'm flexible" (428). Moreover, the account of the composition of the *Autobiography* given by Haley in the "Epilogue" makes it clear that the fiction of the autobiographer as a man with "a completed sense of his own life" is especially misleading in the case of Malcolm X, for even Haley and the book that was taking shape in his hands were out of phase with the reality of Malcolm X's life and identity. Thus Haley acknowledges that he "never dreamed" of Malcolm X's break with Elijah Muhammad "until the actual rift became public" (405), although the break overturned the design that had guided Malcolm X's dictations of his life story to Haley up to that point. The disparity between the traditional autobiographical fiction of the completed self and the biographical fact of Malcolm X's ceaselessly evolving identity may lead us, as it did Malcolm X himself, to enlarge our understanding of the limits and the possibilities of autobiography.

II

The original dedication of the *Autobiography*, which Malcolm X gave to Haley before the dictations had even begun, places the work squarely in one of the most ancient traditions of the genre, that of the exemplary life:

This book I dedicate to the Honorable Elijah Muhammad, who found me here in America in the muck and mire of the filthiest civilization and society on this earth,

---

[4]*The Autobiography of Malcolm X* (New York: Ballantine, 1973), p. 381. All subsequent references are to this edition and will appear in the text.
[5]E.g., see Reverend Albert Cleage, "Myths About Malcolm X," in Clarke, pp. 13–26.

and pulled me out, cleaned me up, and stood me on my feet, and made me the man that I am today. (387)

This dedication (later cancelled) motivates more than half of the *Autobiography* in its final version. The book would be the story of a conversion, and Malcolm X's statement recapitulates in capsule form the essential pattern of such narratives: in the moment of conversion a new identity is discovered; further, this turning point sharply defines a two-part, before-after time scheme for the narrative; the movement of the self from "lost" to "found" constitutes the plot; and, finally, the very nature of the experience supplies an evangelical motive for autobiography.

What concerns us here, however, is not the much-studied features of conversion and the ease with which they may be translated into the formal elements of autobiographical narrative, but rather the natural and seemingly inevitable inference that the individual first discovers the shape of his life and then writes the life on the basis of this discovery. Some version of this temporal fiction, of course, lies behind most autobiography, and I would emphasize it as a corollary to Miller's definition of the completed self: the notion that living one's life precedes writing about it, that the life is in some sense complete and that the autobiographical process takes place afterward, somehow outside the realm of lapsing time in which the life proper necessarily unfolds. The evangelical bias of conversion narrative is especially interesting in this regard, for it supplies a predisposition for such an autobiographer to accept this supporting fiction as fact, since he believes that conversion works a definitive transition from shifting false beliefs to a fixed vision of the one truth. It is, accordingly, when a new discovery about the shape of one's life takes place during the writing of one's story that an autobiographer may be forced to recognize the presence and nature of the fictions on which his narrative is based. The experience of Malcolm X in his final period did foster such a recognition, and this knowledge and its consequences for autobiographical narrative may instruct us in the complex relation that necessarily obtains between living a life and writing about it. However, before we consider the *Autobiography* from the vantage point of the man who was becoming "El-Hajj Malik El-Shabazz" (Chapter 18), let us look at the *Autobiography* as it was originally conceived by the man whose first conversion in prison had transformed him from "Satan" (Chapter 10) to "Minister Malcolm X" (Chapter 13). This is, of course, the way we do look at the *Autobiography* when we begin to read it for the first time, especially if we are relatively unfamiliar with the life of Malcolm X.

The Malcolm X of these years was firmly in command of the shape of his life, tracing his sense of this shape to the pivotal and structuring illumination of conversion itself.[6] At this point his understanding of the design of his

---

[6]Although Malcolm X's *Autobiography* resembles the traditional conversion narrative in many ways, there are important differences as well. For example, it is somewhat misleading to speak, as

experience, especially his baffled fascination with the radical discontinuity between the old Adam and the new, closely parallels the state of St. Augustine, Jonathan Edwards, and many another sinner touched by gracious affections, so much so that the student of spiritual autobiography is likely to feel himself at home on familiar ground:

> For evil to bend its knees, admitting its guilt, to implore the forgiveness of God, is the hardest thing in the world. . . . When finally I was able to make myself stay down—I didn't know what to say to Allah. . . . I still marvel at how swiftly my previous life's thinking pattern slid away from me, like snow off a roof. It is as though someone else I knew of had lived by hustling and crime. I would be startled to catch myself thinking in a remote way of my earlier self as another person. (170)

If we consider Malcolm X's account of his life up to the time of his break with Elijah Muhammad (in Chapter 16, appropriately entitled "Out"), what we have in fact is a story that falls rather neatly into two sections roughly equal in length, devoted respectively to his former life as a sinner (Chapters 3–9) and to his present life as one of Elijah Muhammad's ministers (Chapters 10–15). This two-part structure is punctuated by two decisive experiences: his repudiation of the white world of his youth in Mason, Michigan, and his conversion to Islam in prison at Norfolk, Massachusetts.

Malcolm X describes the "first major turning point of my life" (35) at the end of the second chapter, his realization that in white society he was not free "to become whatever *I* wanted to be" (37). The shock to the eighth-grade boy was profound, for despite his traumatic childhood memories of the destruction of his family by white society, Malcolm X had embraced the white success ethic by the time he was in junior high school: "I was trying so hard . . . to be white" (31). What follows, in Chapters 3 through 9, is Malcolm X's account of his life as a ghetto hustler, his first "career," just as his role as a Black Muslim minister was to be his second. If Allah preserved him from the fate of an Alger hero or a Booker T. Washington, from a career as a "successful" shoeshine boy or a self-serving member of the "black bourgeoisie" (38), he was nevertheless destined to enact a kind of inverse parody of the white man's rise to success as he sank deeper and deeper into a life of crime.[7] This is the portion of the

Mandel does (272), of Malcolm X's first conversion to the Muslim faith of Elijah Muhammad as the typical "false conversion" of spiritual autobiography. A "false conversion" is usually presented as false by the man who has since found the true faith. This is not Malcolm X's treatment, for in his case the "false conversion" is only partly false, and hence not to be wholly rejected (as the older Jonathan Edwards rejected the miserable seeking of his youth). Again, Mandel pushes these correspondences too far when he identifies the "tension" of the last pages of the *Autobiography* as an expression of the familiar post-conversion fears of "back-sliding" (272–73). Malcolm X knew that Elijah Muhammad had sentenced him to death.

7In "Malcolm X: Mission and Meaning," *Yale Review*, 56 (1966), Robert Penn Warren reads Malcolm X as a success in the Alger tradition (161–162), and he notes that, setting aside the hatred of the Black Muslims for white society, their values of temperance and hard work resemble the virtues that have made the white middle-class what it is (165). Ohmann stresses Malcolm X's story as a "parodic inversion" (136) of the success story, and she adds that Malcolm X himself later recognized it as such (137).

Autobiography that has been singled out for its vividness by the commentators, with the result that the conversion experience and its aftermath in Chapters 10 through 15 have been somewhat eclipsed. It would be possible, of course, to see in the popularity of this section nothing more than the universal appeal of any evocation of low life and evil ways. In addition, this preference may reflect an instinctive attraction to a more personal mode of autobiography with plenty of concrete self-revelation instead of the more formal testimony of an exemplary life. Certainly Alex Haley responded strongly to this narrative, and so did Malcolm X, though he tried to restrain himself:

> Then it was during recalling the early Harlem days that Malcolm X really got carried away. One night, suddenly, wildly, he jumped up from his chair and, incredibly, the fearsome black demagogue was scat-singing and popping his fingers, "re-bop-de-bop-blap-blam—" and then grabbing a vertical pipe with one hand (as the girl partner) he went jubilantly lindy-hopping around, his coattail and the long legs and the big feet flying as they had in those Harlem days. And then almost as suddenly, Malcolm X caught himself and sat back down, and for the rest of that session he was decidedly grumpy. (391)

Haley captures here the characteristic drama of the autobiographical act that the juxtaposition of the self as it is and as it was inevitably generates. Malcolm X's commitment to his public role as "the fearsome black demagogue" conflicts with his evident pleasure in recapturing an earlier and distinctly personal identity, the historical conked and zooted lindy champ of the Roseland Ballroom in Roxbury, the hustling hipster of Small's Paradise in Harlem.

If the *Autobiography* had ended with the fourteenth or fifteenth chapter, what we would have, I suggest, is a narrative which could be defined as an extremely conventional example of autobiographical form distinguished chiefly by the immediacy and power of its imaginative recreation of the past.[8] It is true that this much of the *Autobiography* would usefully illustrate the survival of the classic pattern of conversion narrative in the contemporary literature of spiritual autobiography, but this interest would necessarily be a limited one given Malcolm X's reticence about the drama of the experience of conversion itself. For Malcolm X the fact of conversion is decisive, life-shaping, identity-altering, but unlike the most celebrated spiritual autobiogra-

---

[8]To describe this first part of the *Autobiography* as conventional is by no means to deny the importance of Malcolm X's first conversion as a milestone in the rise of black self-consciousness in America. In the two recent studies of black American autobiography, however, this is not the guiding perspective. Sidonie Smith, in *Where I'm Bound: Patterns of Slavery and Freedom in Black American Autobiography* (Westport Conn.: Greenwood Press, 1974), reads the experience with the Nation of Islam as the third in a continuing series of disillusionments teaching Malcolm X that "his freedom within the community is finally only a chimera" (96–97). In *Black Autobiography in America* (Amherst: University of Massachusetts Press, 1974), on the other hand, Stephen Butterfield places Malcolm X's Black Muslim phase in the larger context of his development as a black revolutionary: "Malcolm X, pimp and drug pusher, convict, Muslim minister, Pan-Africanist, pilgrim to Mecca, lifting himself up to become one of the few men who could have been the Lenin of America before he was cut down by gunfire" (184).

phers of the past he chooses not to dramatize the experience itself or to explore its psychological dynamics.[9]

III

It seems probable that when Malcolm X began his dictations to Haley in 1963 he anticipated that his narrative would end with an account of his transformation into the national spokesman of Elijah Muhammad's Nation of Islam (the material covered in Chapters 14 and 15 of Haley's text). This was not destined to be the end of the story, however, for the pace of Malcolm X's history, always lively, became tumultuous in 1963 and steadily accelerated until his assassination in 1965. In this last period Malcolm X was to experience two events that destroyed the very premises of the autobiography he had set out to write. The most well-known convert to the Black Muslim religion was first to break with Elijah Muhammad (Chapter 16, "Out") and then to make a pilgrimage to Mecca (Chapter 17), where he underwent a second conversion to what he now regarded as the true religion of Islam. The revelation that Elijah Muhammad was a false prophet shattered the world of Malcolm X and the shape of the life he had been living for twelve years:

> I was like someone who for twelve years had had an inseparable, beautiful marriage—and then suddenly one morning at breakfast the marriage partner had thrust across the table some divorce papers.
>
> I felt as though something in *nature* had failed, like the sun or the stars. It was that incredible a phenomenon to me—something too stupendous to conceive. (304)

The autobiographical fiction of the completed self was exploded for good, although Malcolm X, with a remarkable fidelity to the truth of his past, was to preserve the fragments in the earlier chapters of the *Autobiography*, as we have seen.

The illumination at Mecca made Malcolm X feel "like a complete human being" for the first time "in my thirty-nine years on this earth" (365), and he assumed a new name to symbolize this new sense of identity, El-Hajj Malik El-Shabazz. In the final chapters of the book (18 and 19) we see Malcolm X in the process of discarding the "old 'hate' and 'violence' image" (423) of the militant preacher of Elijah Muhammad's Nation of Islam, but before he created a design for the life of this new self he was brutally gunned down on February 21, 1965. In fact, it is not at all certain that Malcolm X would have arrived at any single, definitive formulation for the shape of his life even if he had continued to live. In the final pages of the last chapter he observes:

[9]Ohmann interprets the reticence of Malcolm X on the subjective nature of his conversion experience (139–40) as a manifestation of his "distrust of the inner life, even an antipathy to it" (134).

No man is given but so much time to accomplish whatever is his life's work. My life in particular never has stayed fixed in one position for very long. You have seen how throughout my life, I have often known unexpected drastic changes. (378)

With these words Malcolm X articulates a truth already latent but ungrasped in the autobiographical narrative he originally set out to write in his evangelical zeal: his life was not now and never had been a life of the simpler pattern of the traditional conversion story.

Because this complex vision of his existence is clearly not that of the early sections of the *Autobiography*, Alex Haley and Malcolm X were forced to confront the consequences of this discontinuity in perspective for the narrative, already a year old. It was Haley who raised the issue when he learned, belatedly, of the rift between Malcolm X and Elijah Muhammad, for he had become worried that an embittered Malcolm X might want to rewrite the book from his new perspective, and this at a time when Haley regarded their collaboration as virtually complete ("by now I had the bulk of the needed life story material in hand" [406]). Malcolm X's initial response settled the matter temporarily: "I want the book to be the way it was" (412). Haley's concern, however, was justified, for a few months later, following Malcolm X's journey to Mecca, Haley was "appalled" to find that Malcolm X had "red-inked" many of the places in the manuscript "where he had told of his almost father-and-son relationship with Elijah Muhammad." Haley describes this crisis of the autobiographical act as follows:

> Telephoning Malcolm X, I reminded him of his previous decision, and I stressed that if those chapters contained such telegraphing to readers of what would lie ahead, then the book would automatically be robbed of some of its building suspense and drama. Malcolm X said, gruffly, "Whose book is this?" I told him "yours, of course," and that I only made the objection in my position as a writer. He said that he would have to think about it. I was heart-sick at the prospect that he might want to re-edit the entire book into a polemic against Elijah Muhammad. But late that night, Malcolm X telephoned. "I'm sorry. You're right. I was upset about something. Forget what I wanted changed, let what you already had stand." I never again gave him chapters to review unless I was with him. Several times I would covertly watch him frown and wince as he read, but he never again asked for any change in what he had originally said. (414)

Malcolm X's refusal to change the narrative reflects, finally, his acceptance of change as the fundamental law of existence, and yet, curiously, by the very fidelity of this refusal he secures for the remembered past, and for the acts of memory devoted to it, such measure of permanence as the forms of art afford.[10]

---

[10]In his essay "Modern Black Autobiography in the Tradition," Michael G. Cooke argues that rewriting is an "essential issue for autobiography" and one unaccountably neglected by students of the form (in *Romanticism: Vistas, Instances, Continuities,* ed. David Thorburn and Geoffrey Hartman [Ithaca, New York: Cornell University Press, 1973], p. 259). Cooke concludes that "the distinctive feature of the *Autobiography [of Malcolm X]* is its naturalistic use of time, the

The exchange between the two men poses the perplexing issue of perspective in autobiography with an instructive clarity: to which of an autobiographer's selves should he or even can he be true? What are the strategies by which he may maintain a dual or plural allegiance without compromise to his present vision of the truth? In fact, the restraint of the "telegraphing" does leave the climax intact,[11] and yet Malcolm X's decision not to revise the preceding narrative does not produce the kind of obvious discontinuity in authorial perspective that we might expect as a result. Haley's part in this is considerable, for his contribution to the ultimate shape of the *Autobiography* was more extensive and fundamental than his narrowly literary concerns here with foreshadowing and suspense might seem to suggest. Despite his tactful protest that he was only a "writer," Haley himself had been instrumental in the playing out of the autobiographical drama between one Malcolm X, whose faith in Elijah Muhammad had supplied him with his initial rationale for an autobiography, and another, whose repudiation of Elijah Muhammad made the *Autobiography* the extraordinary human document it eventually became. If the outcome of this drama was formalized in Malcolm X's expulsion from the Nation of Islam, it was already in the wind by the time the dictations began in earnest in 1963. Alex Haley was one to read between the lines.

Haley recalls in the "Epilogue" that at the very outset of the project he had been in fundamental disagreement with Malcolm X about the narrative he would help him write. He reports that Malcolm X wanted the focus to be on Elijah Muhammad and the Nation of Islam: "He would bristle when I tried to urge him that the proposed book was *his* life" (388). At this early stage of the collaboration Haley portrays two Malcolms: a loyal public Malcolm X describing a religious movement in which he casts himself in a distinctly subordinate and self-effacing role, and a subversive private Malcolm X scribbling a trenchant counter-commentary in telegraphic red-ink ball point on any available scrap of paper. Determined to feature this second Malcolm X in the autobiography, Haley lured this suppressed identity out into the open by leaving white paper napkins next to Malcolm X's coffee cup to tap his closed communications with himself. Haley carefully retrieved this autobiographical fall-out, and taking his cue from one of these napkin revelations, interestingly about women, Haley "cast a bait" (389) with a question about Malcolm X's

willingness to let the past stand as it was, in its own season, even when later developments, of intellect or intuition or event, give it a different quality" (274). Francis R. Hart writes, in "Notes for an Anatomy of Modern Autobiography," that "the autobiographer has always had to consider how to manage, and whether to dramatize, the discontinuities inherent in autobiographical recreation," and he sees Malcolm X as facing this problem courageously and creatively (*New Literary History*, 1 [1970], 489, 501).

[11]Malcolm X alludes specifically to the impending crisis in Chapter 12, pp. 197–98, 210; in Chapter 14, pp. 264–65; and in Chapter 15, p. 287. For instances of an undercurrent of retrospective criticism of Elijah Muhammad, see Chapter 10, p. 168 (his false teaching); Chapter 11, pp. 187, 189 (his immorality); Chapter 14, p. 248 (his insecurity); p. 252 (his worth as a leader). These passages, reflecting as they do Malcolm X's altered vision of the man he had formerly worshiped, are presumably interpolations from a later phase of the dictations.

mother. Haley reports that with this textbook display of Freudian savvy he was able to land the narrative he was seeking:

> From this stream-of-consciousness reminiscing I finally got out of him the foundation for this book's beginning chapters, "Nightmare" and "Mascot." After that night, he never again hesitated to tell me even the most intimate details of his personal life, over the next two years. His talking about his mother triggered something. (390–91)

From the very earliest phase of the dictations, then, the autobiography began to take on a much more personal and private coloration than Malcolm X originally intended. What Elijah Muhammad accomplished, autobiographically speaking, when he "silenced" Malcolm X, was to legitimatize the private utterance of the napkins which had already found its way into the mainstream of a narrative initially conceived as an orthodox work of evangelical piety. After his separation from the Nation of Islam, Malcolm X comments that he began "to think for myself," "after twelve years of never thinking for as much as five minutes about myself" (306). Haley reports two napkin messages of this period that signal the consequences of Malcolm X's new sense of himself and his power for the nearly-completed *Autobiography*:

> He scribbled one night, "You have not converted a man because you have silenced him. John Viscount Morley." And the same night, almost illegibly, "I was going downhill until he picked me up, but the more I think of it, we picked each other up." (406)[12]

Not only was Malcolm X rejecting the simple clarity of the original conversion narrative he had set out to tell, but he was no longer disposed to sacrifice to the greater glory of Elijah Muhammad his own agency in the working out of his life story.

IV

In the final chapters of the *Autobiography* and in the "Epilogue," as Malcolm X moves toward a new view of his story as a life of changes, he expresses an impressive, highly self-conscious awareness of the problems of autobiographical narrative, and specifically of the complex relationship between living a life and writing an autobiography. All of his experience in the last packed months, weeks, and days of his life worked to destroy his earlier confident belief in the completed self, the completed life, and hence in the complete life story. Thus he writes to Haley in what is possibly his final statement about the *Autobiography*: "I just want to read it one more time because I don't expect to read it in finished form" (426). As Malcolm X saw

---

[12]The second of the two messages reformulates and repudiates the original dedication of the *Autobiography*.

it at the last, all autobiographies are by nature incomplete and they cannot, accordingly, have a definitive shape. As a life changes, so any sense of the shape of a life must change; the autobiographical process evolves because it is part of the life, and the identity of the autobiographical "I" changes and shifts. Pursuing the logic of such speculations, Malcolm X even wonders whether any autobiography can keep abreast of the unfolding of personal history: "How is it possible to write one's autobiography in a world so fast-changing as this" (408)? And so he observes to Haley, "I hope the book is proceeding rapidly, for events concerning my life happen so swiftly, much of what has already been written can easily be outdated from month to month. In life, nothing is permanent; not even life itself" (413–14).

At the end, then, Malcolm X came to reject the traditional autobiographical fiction that the life comes first, and then the writing of the life; that the life is in some sense complete and that the autobiographical process simply records the final achieved shape. This fiction is based upon a suspension of time,[13] as though the "life," the subject, could sit still long enough for the autobiographical "I," the photographer, to snap its picture. In fact, as Malcolm X was to learn, the "life" itself will not hold still; it changes, shifts position. And as for the autobiographical act, it requires much more than an instant of time to take the picture, to write the story. As the act of composition extends in time, so it enters the life-stream, and the fictive separation between life and life story, which is so convenient—even necessary—to the writing of autobiography, dissolves.

Malcolm X's final knowledge of the incompleteness of the self is what gives the last pages of the *Autobiography* together with the "Epilogue" their remarkable power: the vision of a man whose swiftly unfolding career has outstripped the possibilities of the traditional autobiography he had meant to write. It is not in the least surprising that Malcolm X's sobering insights into the limitations of autobiography are accompanied by an increasingly insistent desire to disengage himself from the ambitions of the autobiographical process. Thus he speaks of the *Autobiography* to Haley time and again as though, having disabused himself of any illusion that the narrative could keep pace with his life, he had consigned the book to its fate, casting it adrift as hopelessly obsolete. Paradoxically, nowhere does the book succeed, persuade, more than in its confession of failure as autobiography. This is the fascination of *The Education of Henry Adams*, and Malcolm X, like Adams, leaves behind him the husks of played-out autobiographical paradigms. The indomitable reality of the self transcends and exhausts the received shapes for a life that are transmitted by the culture, and yet the very process of discarding in itself works to structure an apparently shapeless experience. Despite—or because of—the intractability of life to form, the fiction of the completed self, which

13See Cooke, pp. 259–60, on "the problem of the self and time" in autobiography.

lies at the core of the autobiographical enterprise, cannot be readily dispatched. From its ashes, phoenix-like, it reconstitutes itself in a new guise. Malcolm X's work, and Adams' as well, generate a sense that the uncompromising commitment to the truth of one's own nature, which requires the elimination of false identities and careers one by one, will yield at the last the pure ore of a final and irreducible selfhood. This is the ultimate autobiographical dream.

Maya Angelou's *I Know Why the Caged Bird Sings* and Black Autobiographical Tradition

George E. Kent

Maya Angelou, who spent much of her early life in Arkansas and grew up in California, is the author of three books: the autobiographies *I Know Why the Caged Bird Sings* (1969) and *Gather Together in My Name* (1974); and a volume of poetry, *Just Give Me a Cool Drink of Water 'Fore I Diie* (1971). My concern is with the autobiographies, with primary emphasis upon *I Know Why the Caged Bird Sings.*

I Know Why tells the story of a child's growing to maturity in the small universe of Stamps, Arkansas, in St. Louis, Missouri, and in San Francisco, California. We see Maya (nee Marguerite Johnson) and her brother Bailey shuttled to Grandmother Annie Henderson from the broken home of the mother Vivian Baxter, eventually back to Mother Vivian in St. Louis, then a return to Stamps with Grandmother Henderson, and a final return to California where Maya spends most of her time with her mother but also experiences a calamitous summer with her father, Bailey Johnson, in the southern part of the state. The book is rich in portraits of a wide assortment of blacks, descriptions of the rhythms of their lives and their confrontations with both elemental life and racial relations, and evocations of the patterns of the different environments. Their graphic depiction is always in relationship to the development of the child, but since all the experiences emerge from an imagination which has fully mastered them and, at will, turns them into symbols, they tend to operate on two levels: as mirrors of both the vigor and the unsteadiness of childhood innocence and imagination, and as near independent vibrations of the spirit of black life. The book ends with Maya's having become an unwed mother, a result of a confused move for sexual identity. Since the book ends with a dramatic episode which emphasizes Maya's beginning to face up to the terrors of motherhood, its resolution is somewhat tentative but complete enough to register the movement into a stance toward life beyond that of childhood.

Gather Together in My Name tells the story of the struggles of young

From George E. Kent, *Kansas Quarterly*, 7: 72–78, 1975. Reprinted by permission of the editors of *Kansas Quarterly* and executors of the estate of Mr. George E. Kent.

womanhood to create an existence which provides security and love in a very unstable world; its time is the post–World War II period, and it involves settings in San Francisco, Los Angeles, Stamps, Arkansas, and then again various parts of California. On the one side of the tensions is Maya's combination of resourcefulness, imagination, and compulsive innocence; on the other, the intransigence of the world's obstacle courses which impel her into ill-advised love choices, an assortment of jobs ranging from that of short-order cook to setting up a house of prostitution staffed with two lesbians. Finally, in her quest for love and security, she is inveigled into prostitution by the forty-five year old pimp, L. D. Tolbrook, but forcibly argued out of it by her furious brother. Under the pressures of a loveless existence, she sees the decline of her brother into drug addiction and escapes the temptation herself by her new lover's demonstration of the unromantic degradation drugs have inflicted upon him. The book ends with Maya's statement, "I had no idea what I was going to make of my life, but I had given a promise and found my innocence. I swore I'd never lose it again." Technically, the resolution, again, has both tentativeness and a dramatic completeness. However, the feeling it gives is one of abruptness—the sensational character of it registers more fully than the definition of a new stance which it is supposed to impose.

Like *I Know Why, Gather Together* presents a wide assortment of personalities and conveys sharp and imaginative insights through them. It is a good book, well worth the doing. But it lacks the feeling of the fully mastered experience, the full measure and imaginative penetration, and the illusion of life vibrating as an entity in itself as well as in relationship to the heroine's own development.

It is thus *I Know Why* which I cite for creating a unique place in black autobiographical tradition. What is that tradition? Like American autobiography, in general, black autobiography has variety: the simple success story of John Mercer Langston's *From the Virginia Plantation to the National Capitol; or, the First and Only Negro Representative in Congress from the Old Dominion* (1894); the somewhat psychological analysis of Katherine Dunham's *A Touch of Innocence* (1959); the public memoir of John Roy Lynch's *Reminiscences of an Active Life: The Autobiography of John Roy Lynch* (1970); and a varied assortment of autobiographical statements in connection with literary and public matters.

However, a main strand of black autobiographies takes us on a journey through chaos, a pattern established by the narratives of escaped slaves. The pattern takes shape in the first major black autobiography, Gustavus Vassa, *The Interesting Narrative of the Life of Olaudah Equiano, or Gustavus Vassa, the African* (1789). In relationship to later ex-slave statements, Vassa's account can be seen as emphasizing the instability of the black's relationship to all institutions devised to ward off chaos threatening human existence. And it is this instability of relationship to institutions which gives the particular tone and extremity described in much of black autobiography, those of the ex-slave and those born free. Vassa's and other ex-slave autobiographies required the achievement of tenuously held new identities: Vassa's "almost Englishman" and Christian man and usually, with the ex-slave, the combination of a definition implied by the ideals of the enlightenment and Christianity. Thus it is the temperature of urgencies which increases the root uncertainty of existence reflected by a large number of black autobiographies which eventually move from a reflection of the ambiguous dispensations of institutions of the slavery period to the ambiguous dispensations of post-slavery institutions. The autobiographies of Richard Wright (*Black Boy,* 1945), Anne Moody (*Coming of Age in Mississippi,* 1968), Malcolm X's *The Autobiography of Malcolm X* (1965), and others, will illustrate post-slavery journeys of the twentieth century and the persisting ambiguous relationship of blacks to American institutional dispensations.

Up through the early part of the twentieth century, black autobiographies had usually found grounds for a leap of faith and optimism in the complex of ideas known as The American Dream. Booker T. Washington's *Up From Slavery* (1901) is the classic example; it even fits well into the type of success story established by Benjamin Franklin's autobiography, with its emphasis upon common sense and optimism. James Weldon Johnson's *Along This Way: The Autobiography of James Weldon Johnson* (1933) focuses largely upon the public man and ends with a willed optimism: The Black must believe in the American Dream or destroy much that is of value within him. The optimism of such books can be seen as embracing the after-beat of rhythms picked up from those established by the abolitionist perspective in slave narratives. As weapons in the struggle, the narratives absorbed the tenets of Christianity, the ideals of the Enlightenment and of the American Constitution. Things were terrible, but the Great Day would come when the ideals were actualized.

Today the rhythms of the American Dream ideas run in a parallel pattern with a more serious questioning of the Dream itself. Thus Benjamin Mays's *Born to Rebel* (1971) recounts the encounter with nothingness during Mays's youth, but finds grounds for optimism in the fruits of public service. However, Richard Wright's *Black Boy* was the autobiography which began a questioning which shook the fabric of the American Dream, although the autobiography's ending leaves ground for hope of achieving the Dream in the Promised Land of the North. In the process of Wright's questioning, however, the cultural fabric of the black community is torn to shreds and tends to reflect a people teetering upon the brink of nothingness:

> After I had outlived the shocks of childhood, after the habit of reflection had been born in me, I used to mull over the strange absence of real kindness in Negroes, how unstable was our tenderness, how lacking in genuine passion we were, how void of great hope, how timid our joy, how bare our traditions, how hollow our memories, how lacking we were in those intangible sentiments that bind man to man, and how shallow was even our despair. After I had learned other ways of life I

used to brood upon the unconscious irony of those who felt that Negroes led so
passional an existence! I saw that what had been taken for our emotional strength
was our negative confusions, our flights, our fears, our frenzy under pressure.
(*Black Boy*, p. 33)

Wright was offended by the degree to which he found a black folk tradition
oriented toward mere survival, base submission, and escapism, whereas, as he
states in "Blueprint for Negro Writing" (*New Challenge*, Fall, 1937), he wished
to mould the tradition into a martial stance. With the help of Marxism, he also
wished to create the values by which the race was to live or die, to be not
"only against exploiting whites, but against all of that within his own race that
retards decisive action and obscures clarity of vision." He decried "a cowardly
sentimentality [which had] deterred Negro writers from launching crusades
against the evils which Negro ignorance and stupidity have spawned." Thus,
from his autobiography and from several works of fiction, there emerges the
hero as black rebel-outsider, embattled, particularly after *Uncle Tom's Children*, both with the pretensions of the American Dream and his own folk
tradition.

Ralph Ellison's response to Wright's portrait of black life has been mixed.
In his essay "Richard Wright's Blues" [*Shadow and Act*, 1964], he seems partly
to condone and partly to reinterpret from his own perspective. Among other
things, he notes that the personal warmth of black communal life, in line with
Wright's illustrations, "is accompanied by an equally personal coldness, kindliness by cruelty, regard by malice," that the opposite qualities are quickly set
off "against the member who gestures toward individuality," and that "The
member who breaks away is apt to be more impressed by its negative than by
its positive character." He seems to defend the passage I quoted above from
Black Boy: Wright was rejecting not only the white South in his autobiography but the South within himself—"As a rebel he formulated that rejection
negatively, because it was the negative face of the Negro community upon
which he looked most often as a child." Embattled himself with Irving Howe
in his later essay "The World and the Jug" [*Shadow and Act*, 1964], Ellison at
this time rejected the same quotation as having its source in Wright's attempts
to see the forms of Negro humanity through the lens of Marxism and in
Wright's paraphrase of Henry James's "catalogue of those items of a high
civilization which were absent from American life during Hawthorne's day,
and which seemed so necessary in order for the novelist to function." However, it must be said that Wright's intense rendering of negative images of
black life in such works as *Black Boy* [1945], *Native Son* [1940], *Lawd Today*
[1963], and *The Long Dream* [1958], without precluding assists from James
and Marxism, would seem to require that we accept his negative remarks as
an article of faith and belief. Ellison's earlier remarks, taking into consideration the stance of the rebel, and Wright's own aspiration to launch crusades
against ignorance and stupidity seem to come closer to accounting for the
degree of negativity in Wright's position. Certainly, another embattled rebel,

Anne Moody in *Coming of Age in Mississippi*, seeing black communal life's frequent responses to the incursion of white power, gives off a similar tone of negativity and places beside the American Dream idea a large question mark. Such subsequent landmark autobiographies as Huey P. Newton's *Revolutionary Suicide* [1973] and the earlier *Autobiography of Malcolm X* [1965] seem to complete a rhythm of development away from a middle class consciousness or complex of ideas.

In the attempt to define a major strand of development in a black autobiographical tradition, then, I've outlined the theme of a journey through a highly heated chaos deriving from black life's ambiguous relationship to American institutions, an erosion of faith in the American Dream idea which earlier had provided grounds for optimism, and a controversially developing sense of negativity concerning the quality of black life in America.

I Know Why creates a unique place within black autobiographical tradition, not by being "better" than the formidable autobiographical landmarks described, but by its special stance toward the self, the community, and the universe, and by a form exploiting the full measure of imagination necessary to acknowledge both beauty and absurdity.

The emerging self, equipped with imagination, resourcefulness, and a sense of the tenuousness of childhood innocence, attempts to foster itself by crediting the adult world with its own estimate of its god-like status and managing retreats into the autonomy of the childhood world when conflicts develop. Given the black adult's necessity to compromise with prevailing institutions and to develop limited codes through which nobility, strength, and beauty can be registered, the areas where a child's requirements are absolute—love, security, and consistency—quickly reveal the protean character of adult support and a barely concealed, aggressive chaos.

We can divide the adults' resources, as they appear in the autobiography, into two areas of black life: the religious and blues traditions. Grandmother Henderson, of Stamps, Arkansas, represents the religious traditions; Mother Vivian Baxter, more of the blues-street tradition.

Grandmother's religion gives her power to order her being, that of the children, and usually the immediate space surrounding her. The spirit of the religion combined with simple, traditional maxims shapes the course of existence and the rituals of facing up to something called decency. For Maya and her brother Bailey, the first impact of the blues-street tradition is that of instability: at the ages of three and four, respectively, the children are suddenly shipped to Grandmother when the parents break up their "calamitous" marriage. A note "To Whom It May Concern" identifies the children traveling alone from "Long Beach, California, en route to Stamps, Arkansas, c/o Mrs. Annie Henderson." Angelou generalizes the children's situation as follows: "Years later I discovered that the United States had been crossed thousands of times by frightened Black children traveling alone to their newly affluent parents in Northern cities, or back to grandmothers in Southern towns when the urban North reneged on its economic promises."

Gradually, the children adjust to the new life, becoming an integral part of Grandmother Henderson's General Merchandise Store, Grandmother's church and religion, community school, and general community customs. In Chapters 1–8, we see the techniques by which the author is able to give a full registration of both the beauty and the root absurdity built into the traditions of the folk community. She carefully articulates the folk forms of responding to existence by the use of key symbols and patterns of those involved in religious and blues responses and the joining point between their ways of responding. For example, more than Grandmother Henderson is characterized through the following folk prayer, whose set phrases have accreted through a long tradition of bended knees in homes and small rural churches:

> "Our Father, thank you for letting me see this New Day. Thank you that you didn't allow the bed I lay on last night to be my cooling board, nor my blanket my winding sheet. Guide my feet this day along the straight and narrow, and help me to put a bridle on my tongue. Bless this house, and everybody in it. Thank you, in the name of your Son, Jesus Christ, Amen."

The children are required to avoid impudence to adults, to respect religious piety, and to be obedient. Given the freshness of the childhood imagination, however, many meanings are turned into the absurdity often hovering near the fabric of human rituals. On the grim side, we see the poor giving thanks to the Lord for a life filled with the most meager essentials and a maximum amount of brute oppression. The church rituals create for the poor a temporary transcendence and an articulation of spirit, but their hardships are so graphically awaiting their re-confrontation with the trials of daily existence that the evoked spiritual beauty seems hard-pressed by the pathos of the grotesque. Still, it is from such religious rhythms that Grandmother Henderson possesses the strength to give much order to the children's lives, to set the family in initial order in California, and to provide them with the minimum resources to struggle for a world more attractive. The comic side is reflected through the autonomous imagination of the children: the incongruity between the piety of the shouters and the violence with which the religious gestures of one threatens the minister. Briefly, the author records the joining point between the blues and religious tradition: Miss Grace, the good-time woman, is also conducting rituals of transcendence through her barrelhouse blues for those whose uprush of spirit must have an earthly and fleshly source. The agony in religion and the blues is the connecting point: "A stranger to the music could not have made a distinction between the songs sung a few minutes before [in church] and those being danced to in the gay house."

Despite Grandmother Henderson's strength, the folk religious tradition leaves her with serious limitations. Her giant stature goes to zero, or almost, in any confrontation with the white Southern community, a startling and humiliating experience for the child worshipper of black adult omnipotence. In addition, there is what Ralph Ellison spoke of as a warmth in the folk communal life "accompanied by an equally personal coldness, kindliness by cruelty, regard by malice." It will be recalled that Ellison saw the negative qualities as being activated "against the member who gestures toward individuality." Maya Angelou dramatizes such an action in Chapter 15, a masterful section. Mrs. Bertha Flowers, the town's black intellectual, has ministered to Maya's ever-burgeoning hunger and quest for individuality by giving her a book of poetry, talking to her philosophically about life, and encouraging her to recite poems. Returning to Grandmother Henderson, she happens to say "by the way—." Grandmother gives her a severe beating for using the expression, much to the bewilderment of the child. Later, Grandmother explained that "Jesus was the Way, the Truth and the Light," that "by the way" is really saying "by Jesus," or "by God," and she had no intention of allowing the Lord's name to be taken in vain in her house. In *Gather Together* Grandmother Henderson gives her a severe, protective beating because Maya had endangered her life by responding to whites' abuse of her in the local clothing store by superlative abuse of her own. Thus, regarding folk religious tradition and other aspects of community confrontations with existence, the author imposes the illusion of striking a just balance between spiritual beauty and absurdity.

The confrontation of the self with blues-street tradition takes place while she is with her mother, Vivian Baxter, in St. Louis and California. The author manages the same just balance in portraying it. Because of the different levels of the tradition in which various members of the family are involved, because of the fluid movement some make between it and other traditions, and because of the originality with which the mother's portrait emerges, the exposure is fresh, vivid, lasting. Some of the strict man-woman codes reflected by folk ballads emerge from the character of the mother. Men are able to remain with her only so long as they honor the code, one having been cut and another shot for failure to show proper respect for the mother's prerogatives. In this fast-life area of black tradition, the children receive great kindness and considerable impact from built-in instabilities. Mother Vivian is kind in counseling Maya concerning her sexual confusions, in creating a celebrating atmosphere that children would love, in her matter-of-fact acceptance of Maya's unwed motherhood, and in the strong support she gives to the idea of self-reliance and excellence. She herself is the embodiment of bold aggressiveness and self-reliance. Her philosophy, too, has its brief maxims, involving the acceptance of the chaos swirling through and around "protective" institutions and meeting it with an on-topsmanship derived from the tough and alert self. Thus she believes in preparing for the worst, hoping for the best, and being unsurprised at anything which happens in between. At one point in the sequel autobiography, *Gather Together*, she tells Maya to be the best at anything she chooses to do—even should she choose to be a whore.

But in her fluid existence amidst threatening chaos, one drawback is the requirement of intense absorption in one's own life and in the alertness which makes on-topsmanship possible. Thus, the mother manages well her own relationship to one of her mates, a Mr. Freeman, but Maya finds herself raped by him at the tender age of eight, an act which involves her in ambiguous complicity—but also guilt and lingering shame and confusion. Her sense of innocence is stretched into dubious tenuousness by her instinctual and unconscious complicity. The fast-life tradition, unsatisfied with the actions of the court, provides for Mr. Freeman's murder—and Maya's increased sense of guilt. When she visits her hipsterish father, she suddenly is impelled into a battle with his girlfriend deriving from the girlfriend's jealousy and Maya's ambiguous emotions concerning her mother. In the process, Maya is cut.

Both children are in inner turmoil over their relationship to their beautiful, tough, and coping mother: Maya because of the paradox involved in being the ungainly and awkward daughter of the beautiful mother; Bailey, her brother, because the instability he is put through increases his oedipal ties to her. Chapter 17 is a poignant statement of Bailey's quest for his mother through a movie screen heroine who resembles her. In *Gather Together*, despite his consistent love and protectiveness of his sister Maya, he becomes involved in pimping, and after the loss of a young wife, he begins what seems to be a downward path through drugs. The problem is not that the mother did not love him, but that his earlier hunger was never resolved and her life style and codes helped to prevent his sense of security in relationship to her. Thus *Gather Together* reveals the tough and beautiful mother, who has held her poise in relationship to many men, now attempting to conceal the defeat she experiences in relationship to her son. The tough blues tradition, which is all for individuality, fails precisely where the religious tradition was strong: the provision of stable and predictable conditions.

Thus the author is able to give a just balance to the qualities of both traditions and to reveal the exact point where the universe becomes absurd. A good deal of the book's universality derives from black life's traditions seeming to mirror, with extraordinary intensity, the root uncertainty in the universe. The conflict with whites, of course, dramatizes uncertainty and absurdity with immediate headline graphicness. What intensifies the universalism still more is the conflict between the sensitive imagination and reality, and the imagination's ability sometimes to overcome. Maya and her brother have their reservoir of absurd miming and laughter, but sometimes the imagination is caught in pathos and chaos, although its values are frequently superior. When Grandmother Henderson's response to the insulting rejection by a white dentist to whom she has loaned money is humiliating, Maya finds consolation in the rituals she imagines the Grandmother using. The imaginative reproduction of the preacher's humiliating beating by an overbearing shouter is so productive of laughter that the beating the children receive becomes meaningless. Bailey, the brother, receives a very bitter experience when his imaginative simulation of sexual intercourse with girls while fully clothed suddenly leads to his encounter with a girl who demands reality, inveigles him into an exploitative love affair, and then runs away with a pullman porter.

The major function of the imagination, however, is to retain a vigorous dialectic between self and society, between the intransigent world and the aspiring self. Through the dialectic, the egos maintain themselves, even where tragic incident triumphs. In a sense, the triumph of circumstance for Maya becomes a temporary halt in a process which is constantly renewed, a fact evident in the poetic language and in the mellowness of the book's confessional form.

Finally, since *I Know Why* keeps its eyes upon the root existential quality of life, it makes its public and political statement largely through generalizing statements which broaden individual characters into types: Grandmother Henderson into the Southern mother; Maya into the young black woman, etc. And the after-rhythms of the American Dream can flow in occasionally without gaining the solemnity of a day in court.

The uniqueness of *I Know Why* arises then from a full imaginative occupation of the rhythms flowing from the primal self in conflict with things as they are, but balanced by the knowledge that the self must find its own order and create its own coherence.

After *Black Boy* and *Dusk of Dawn:* Patterns in Recent Black Autobiography

Albert E. Stone

As readers have known since 1945, autobiography is one of the richest, most revealing modes of black expression in present-day America. The date refers, of course, to the publication of *Black Boy*. Its distribution to over 325,000 members of the Book-of-the-Month Club and its enthusiastic critical reception were a landmark in literary history. Even more powerfully than with *Native Son*, Wright caught the consciousness of America at the war's end, compelling it to experience through his memory and imagination the pain, deprivation, and triumph of will of his young Mississippi self. One of his severer critics, however, was W. E. B. Du Bois, whose very different notions of autobiography had been expressed five years earlier in *Dusk of Dawn*. Both books have revealing subtitles. *An Essay Toward an Autobiography of a Race Concept* reflects Du Bois' willing surrender of a purely personal chronicle, just as *A Record of Childhood and Youth* reminds Wright's readers that *Black Boy* is not, after all, a novel but a version of actual events. By example and precept, Du Bois and Wright have helped to define the nature of black autobiography which in the last forty-odd years has come to mirror, criticize, and create wider and wider areas of black life and culture. In the generations since these epochal works, nearly every segment of black life has found a voice through the art of personal history. Male and female, the young and the very old, educated and illiterate, revolutionary and conformist, novelist and singer, scholar and sharecropper, expatriate and ghetto-dweller, have sought, like Du Bois, to repossess their social and historical identities or, like Wright, to dramatize by fictional techniques the truth of their recreated lives. As both history and literature, autobiography has served the expressive aims of many diverse talents. The result is a cultural achievement vastly extending and enriching the tradition Du Bois and Wright themselves inherited from Langston Hughes, Ida Wells Barnett, James Weldon Johnson, Booker T. Washing-

Phylon: "After *Black Boy* and *Dusk of Dawn:* Patterns in Recent Black Autobiography," by Albert E. Stone, copyright 1978 by Atlanta University, Atlanta, Georgia. Reprinted with permission. "Postscript: Looking Back in 1992" by Albert E. Stone was written for this publication and is printed with permission of Albert E. Stone.

ton, and the nineteenth-century slave narrators. The sixties and seventies masterworks of this outpouring are well known, for they have found their way via paperback into the libraries and classrooms, the drugstores and supermarkets of the nation. The autobiographies of Claude Brown, James Baldwin, Malcolm X, W. E. B. Du Bois, Dick Gregory, Maya Angelou, Eldridge Cleaver, George Jackson, Angela Davis, Billie Holiday, and Nate Shaw (Ned Cobb) often outsold the most popular white autobiographies at home and abroad.[1] In the struggle for personal, political, and cultural independence, these and other autobiographies are playing a major role in the communications network linking the black writer to his or her audiences. These narratives also articulate emerging forms of personal identity which pose important new issues for social scientists and philosophers of personality, race, and culture.

Because black autobiography is a powerful force in and a characteristic form of contemporary culture, it has attracted a growing number of critics and commentators. These come at the subject from several perspectives, historical and ideological, literary and philosophical, sociological and psychological. This diversity attests to the genre's complexity, the difficulties in defining its varieties, and the mines of information and insight contained. Historians, black and white, have perhaps been slower than others to extend their investigations of contemporary black life through autobiography as C. H. Nichols and John Blassingame have done with slavery and slave narratives. The necessity of checking generalizations about black history against the recorded experiences of individual men and women should now be plain, given the controversial examples of Ulrich Phillips, Stanley Elkins, and Daniel Moynihan. Yet even sensitive scientists like E. Franklin Frazier, St. Clair Drake, and Lee Rainwater and historians like John Hope Franklin and Kenneth Stampp either shied away from autobiographies or treated them in terms of explicit content, without adequate consideration of language, style, or the psychological aspects of these intimate documents. All autobiography, in fact, communicates on several levels at once; it is simultaneously private history, artful story, and rich outpouring of psychic energies. Perhaps understandably, the literary approach to black lives has provided to date more perceptive readings, since close attention to style and language often alerts the literary critic to basic attributes the historian might miss. Confirmation of

---

[1]Paperback editions of works cited hereafter (with page references noted parenthetically following all quotations) include Du Bois, *Dusk of Dawn: An Essay Toward an Autobiography of a Race Concept* (New York: Schocken, 1968) and *The Autobiography of W. E. B. Du Bois: A Soliloquy on Viewing My Life from the Last Decade of Its First Century* (New York: International, 1968); Wright, *Black Boy: A Record of Childhood and Youth* (New York: Harper, 1969); Claude Brown, *Manchild in the Promised Land* (New York: New American Library, 1965); *The Autobiography of Malcolm X* (New York: Grove, 1965); Angela Davis, *With My Mind on Freedom: An Autobiography* (New York: Random, 1975); Billie Holiday with William Dufty, *Lady Sings the Blues* (New York: Lancer, 1965); Theodore Rosengarten, ed. *All God's Dangers: The Life of Nate Shaw* (New York: Knopf, 1974).

this may be found in two recent full-length studies by Sidonie Smith and Stephen Butterfield, both of which greatly extend and update Rebecca Chalmers Barton's pioneer work.[2] Shorter general essays by John Blassingame, Michael G. Cooke, and Roger Rosenblatt, as well as specific studies of authors and texts by Houston A. Baker, Warner Berthoff, George E. Kent, David Levin, and Carol Ohmann, among others, illuminate from various angles a burgeoning literature. The sons and daughters of Du Bois and Wright are beginning to receive the careful appreciation their works demand as deliberate creations.[3]

Despite this sizable body of valuable commentary, contemporary black autobiographies continue to provoke responses and raise issues which literary critics, historians, and social scientists have not clarified—and probably cannot if each sticks to one discipline's assumptions and methodologies. By its protean nature autobiography escapes formal assumptions and prescriptions, for as James Olney has pointed out, each self and hence each life-history reflects "an unrepeated and unrepeatable being."[4] As multifaceted communication it calls for a flexible, interdisciplinary perspective—for a truly cultural critique. What follows is one reader's attempt to suggest such a cultural approach to modern black life-historians in America.

I

An appropriate critique would begin by assuming that all autobiography, but especially black, is inescapably historical. It is the retrospective account of

[2]S. Smith, *Where I'm Bound: Patterns of Slavery and Freedom in Black American Autobiography* (Westport, Conn.: Greenwood, 1974); S. Butterfield *Black American Autobiography* (Amherst: University of Massachusetts Press, 1974); R. C. Barton, *Witnesses for Freedom: Negro Americans in Autobiography* (New York: Harper, 1948).

[3]See J. Blassingame, "Black Autobiographies as History and Literature," *Black Scholar*, V (Dec. 1973–Jan. 1974), 2–9; M. G. Cooke, "Modern Black Autobiography in the Tradition," *Romanticism: Vistas, Instances, Continuities*, eds. D. Thorburn and G. Hartman (Ithaca: Cornell University Press, 1973), 255–80; R. Rosenblatt, "Black Autobiography: Life as the Death Weapon," *Yale Review*, LX (Summer: 1976), 515–27; H. A. Baker, *Long Black Song: Essays in Black American Literature and Culture* (Charlottesville: University Press of Virginia, 1972), 84–108; and *Singers at Daybreak: Studies in Black American Literature* (Washington: Howard University Press, 1974), 7–16, 81–91; W. Berthoff, "Witness and Testament: Two Contemporary Classics," *Aspects of Narrative*, ed. J. H. Miller (New York: Columbia University Press, 1971), 173–88; G. E. Kent, *Blackness and the Adventure of Western Culture* (Chicago: Third World Press, 1972), 76–97; D. Levin, "Baldwin's Autobiographical Essays: The Problem of Negro Identity," *Black and White in American Culture*, eds. J. Chametzky and S. Kaplan (Amherst: University of Massachusetts, 1969), 372–79; C. Ohmann, "The Autobiography of Malcolm X: A Revolutionary Use of the Franklin Tradition," *American Quarterly*, XXII (Summer: 1970), 131–49; see also A. L. Elmissiri, "Islam as Pastoral in the Life of Malcolm X," *Malcolm X: The Man and His Times*, ed. J. H. Clarke (New York: Collier, 1969), 69–78; Saundra Towns, "Black Autobiography and the Dilemma of Western Artistic Tradition," *Black Books Bulletin*, II, No. 1 (Spring: 1973), 28–35.

[4]J. Olney, *Metaphors of Self: The Meaning of Autobiography* (Princeton: Princeton University Press, 1972), p. 21.

an individual life, or a significant part thereof, within a context of relationships and institutions which have in large part formed the self who remembers and writes. Like other historical narratives, therefore, autobiography invites verification, to see how it fits or challenges other data at the reader's disposal. Thus *Black Boy* should be read against the biographies of Constance Webb and Michel Fabre to determine the reliability of Wright's inclusions and the significance of his omissions. Many present-day black autobiographies are lives of youthful or obscure persons for whom the rest of the record is incomplete, biased, or entirely lacking. This makes testing Claude Brown, Maya Angelou, or Nate Shaw a different task than doing so with Du Bois or Malcolm X. Yet all of these writers recognize themselves as participants in the matrix of modern history. "Them secrets I know—I got by history," Shaw observes. "You ought to look back at it as well as forwards" (521), he says of his life as an Alabama farmer, union member, and prisoner. Du Bois, the sophisticated sociologist, expresses his historical consciousness differently. "In the folds of this European civilization I was born and shall die, imprisoned, conditioned, depressed, exalted, and inspired. Integrally a part of it and yet, much more significant, one of its rejected parts. Crucified on the vast wheel of time" (*Dusk of Dawn*, 3). Malcolm X and Angela Davis, faithful to their ideologies, also acknowledge their deep involvement in history and society, and this is an important motive for their particular kinds of autobiography. "I hope that the objective reader, in following my life," Malcolm X concludes, "the life of only one ghetto-created Negro—may gain a better picture and understanding than he has previously had of the black ghettos which are shaping the lives and thinking of almost all of the 22 million Negroes who live in America" (378–79). Angela Davis presents her experiences as a passionate revolt against the very social and historical "forces that have made my life what it is" (vii). Each enters, therefore, by a different door the house of the past in order to understand it and the self through more or less accurate recreation. This reflection on the ordering of temporal experience is, in the view of Wilhelm Dilthey, the basis of all historical vision, and for this act the German philosopher makes the greatest claim. "Autobiography is the highest and most instructive form in which the understanding of life confronts us."[5]

Most black autobiographers, though perhaps distrustful of such extravagant claims, acknowledge their own historicity. Rosenblatt has noted this insistence on historical authenticity and succinctly accounts for it: "No black American author has ever felt the need to invent a nightmare to make his point" (517). Given racial realities, the past retold is likely to be a nightmare revisited. This confrontation may not free the self from the past, but many black writers and readers agree that personal history as an honest, verifiable account of enslavement, oppression, resistance, escape, defeat, or transcendence, works ultimately for the liberation of all black people. History reveals the self to the self

[5]W. Dilthey, *Pattern and Meaning in History* (New York: Harper, 1961), p. 85.

and to others and serves as moral and political weapon. Thus Malcolm X's passionate outburst is also an historical claim: "I'm telling it like it *is!* You *never* have to worry about me biting my tongue if something I know is truth is on my mind. Raw, naked truth exchanged between the black man and the white man is what a whole lot more of is needed in this country—to clear the air of the racial mirages, clichés, and lies that this country's very atmosphere has been filled with for four hundred years" (273).

However, to aspire to authenticity and to achieve it are not the same. Malcolm X can assert that "raw, naked truth" is his aim, but Alex Haley's Epilogue reveals important suppressions in the story. There may be others. Even less trustworthy as historical narratives are books like *Black Boy* or Maya Angelou's *I Know Why the Caged Bird Sings,* which resemble novels more than biographies. What *historical* truth do such works actually express? Is not memory as much a screen for current desires and fears as it is a faithful mirror of the past? Du Bois, as a professional historian, wrestled long with these questions. From *The Souls of Black Folk* to the final *Autobiography* he experimented with different ways of honestly recording his own and his people's history. "Autobiographies do not form indisputable authorities," he concluded.

> They are always incomplete, and often unreliable. Eager as I am to put down the truth, there are difficulties; memory fails especially in small details, so that it becomes finally but a theory of my life, with much forgotten and misconceived, with valuable testimony but often less than absolutely true, despite my intention to be frank and fair. . . .
>
> This book then is the Soliloquy of an old man on what he dreams his life has been as he sees it slowly drifting away; and what he would like others to believe. (*Autobiography,* 12–13)

What is true for an old writer remains also true in different ways for younger autobiographers like Claude Brown or Maya Angelou. Warnings like this invite all readers of life-histories to assume a stance of skeptical sympathy. Far from undercutting their value, such an approach permits a weighing of autobiography as experience captured from the inside, which may therefore be more complete and accurate than all the newspaper accounts or books in the Library of Congress. Even the omitted fact or outrageous assertion may possess historical significance and a core of essential truth. This skeptical receptivity distinguishes the student of history from the consumer of fiction. Though autobiography gratifies both appetites, its deepest hold upon the imagination derives from allegiance to the reality principle. *Black Boy* must, therefore, be read differently from *Native Son,* for authorial intent and narrative strategy are different. The Richard of *Black Boy* is not identical to the Wright who writes; twenty years' experiences in Chicago, Brooklyn, and the Communist Party, for instance, separate actor and author. But Richard is a part of Wright as Bigger Thomas is not, and readers, sensing this distinction, place themselves in an historical relationship to the later story.

Doing so, readers of historical autobiography are surprisingly tolerant of error in the "small details" Du Bois mentions. As Roy Pascal points out in *Design and Truth in Autobiography,* what commands assent as "true" is not everything which has happened to an individual, but rather those events, relations, ideas, and feelings which in retrospect reveal significance by forming parts of a pattern or shape to life. The discovered design is the central truth of all autobiography.[6] As Dilthey asserts also, pattern is the fundamental feature of historical writing, more significant that minutely accurate facts, footnotes, archival research, or a supposedly impersonal viewpoint. The creation of such coherence engages memory and imagination, attention to what actually happened and what these events have come to mean subsequently. Hence *The Autobiography of Malcolm X* and Robert Fogel and Stanley Engerman's *Time on the Cross* are both historical acts, and the reader's skeptical sympathy must learn to distinguish between the truths created by the two black men late at night in Greenwich Village [Alex Haley and Malcolm X] and those found by Fogel and Engerman's obedient computer. "Between the parts [of an autobiographical narrative] we see a connection which neither is, nor is intended to be, the simple likeness of the course of a life of so many years, but which, because understanding is involved, expresses what the individual knows about the continuity of his life" (86). The words are Dilthey's but express the aims of all but the most pedestrian and unhistorical of autobiographers. Reading Malcolm X or Anne Moody, for example, we follow a man or woman as self-conscious actors in time and society. Precisely because it has been the fate of numerous black Americans to have been systematically prevented from creating history, the impulse to write historical autobiography remains strong in this era of alienation.

Nearly as persistent, too, is the impulse to pattern the chaotic, frequently violent memories of a life into one or two traditional narratives. Each of these recurs so often and powerfully that its fitness for black experience and imagination appears beyond question. Shaping a lifetime around the journey, voyage, or pilgrimage is perhaps the oldest design in Western story-telling. In either its religious or secular forms, the life-as-journey is ubiquitous in American autobiography, from the memoirs of John Woolman and Benjamin Franklin to those of Thomas Merton and Malcolm X. The black versions of the archetype, as Sidonie Smith has shown, derive from often bitter realities of historic trips—the Middle Passage, escape from slavery, the trip northward to Harlem or westward to Watts, exile in Paris or Africa. These flights from oppression toward opportunity provide the content and the images for a new identity. New names and a familiar title for the traveler—James Weldon Johnson's *Along This Way,* Langston Hughes's *I Wonder as I Wander*—are common features of an old tradition which today serves both the most original histories of the self and slicker success stories of black athletes and entertainers.

6See R. Pascal, *Design and Truth in Autobiography* (Cambridge, Mass.: Harvard University Press, 1960), chaps. 1, 5.

There is another, less familiar pattern inherited from black history and literature for framing contemporary lives. As found in classic form in Booker T. Washington's *Up from Slavery*, this design organizes a life not around movement but stability, by depicting the self staying in one spot and confronting the challenges and vicissitudes of minority existence in racist America by remaining in Alabama or Mississippi, say, and forging an identity there. In this perspective, Washington's trek from West Virginia to Hampton is less significant than the youth's meticulous cleaning of the room for Miss Mackie, which both gains him an education and announces his essential mythic identity. Present-day authors whose memories imitate this pattern include Nate Shaw and Anne Moody, but the prison autobiographies of Cleaver and George Jackson also exploit, with irony and bitter pathos, certain possibilities in a rooted or caged life as historic variants of black experience.

These preserved patterns are of course not universal in or unique to black autobiography. But they continue to serve writers because they fulfill three needs of a genuinely historical imagination. Each provides, first, narrative momentum to a life recalled in specific event and concrete detail. They also serve ideological needs which locate the self as part of a social or political program aimed at change in a certain direction. Finally, these patterns of journeying or standing fast fit mythic needs by setting finite experience in a timeless, cosmic context. The cultural critic should take account of these overlapping historical imperatives as found in unique works. How the singular self uses and transforms tradition may be briefly illustrated by *All God's Dangers* and Du Bois' final *Autobiography*, two representative historical narratives and powerful cultural documents.

If one opens Nate Shaw's story skeptical of a collaboration between an aged black Alabama farmer and a young white Harvard historian Theodore Rosengarten, these reservations can be allayed. For Shaw's—in real life, Ned Cobb's—grasp of historical autobiography is intuitive, complete, and completely his own. The historicity of his remarkable story could not have been imposed upon the illiterate narrator by the educated questioner from Cambridge. "As the years come and go it leaves me with a better understanding of history" (37), Shaw remarks early in his book. What follows has been arranged by Rosengarten by year, topic, and personal relationship to make a more coherent story. But this is probably less intervention than that which characterizes many ghost-written autobiographies like those of Sammy Davis, Jr., or Dick Gregory. Shaw commands respect and credence not simply for the astonishing richness and precision of his memory (it is "as though he had kept a mental journal" (xix), Rosengarten marvels) but also by keen awareness of his own and everybody's location in social space and time, and by an unusual sensitivity to each person's "nature" as preserved in word, act, and gesture. Shaw possesses another attribute which links him to Malcolm X: he can suspend present feelings, often bitter and frustrated, to capture freshly the attitudes of the past. Again like Malcolm X, his present self presides over the whole chronicle by suffusing it with the poetry of his vigorous Alabama voice.

Finally, he knows the difference between stories told to entertain and ones told "for the truth" (3). The historian investigating the lives of unlettered rural Americans, but suspicious of authorial bias in books like Du Bois' *The Souls of Black Folk* and James Agee's *Let Us Now Praise Famous Men,* will find *All God's Dangers* a model of inside history.

Shaw's recreated life shows the cultural critic that the rock-bottom relationship between the man and his world is expressed in work. Unremitting labor during seventy years as his father's assistant and then on his own as cotton farmer, lumberman, and basketmaker, defines this man, his outlook, imagination, vocabulary, and his ability to stand on his own feet in the face of all God's dangers. "I come here to work out. I didn't come in this world to rust out" (139), he tells his improvident domineering father. What is fate for the average sharecropper is Shaw's opportunity to "come up from the bottom" (124), become a renter, and gradually accumulate the mules and automobiles which earn him the envy of his neighbors; "this whole country knowed me for my work" (184), he remarks with quiet pride. By sweat and skill he relates to his local world—to nature and animals, tools and guns, to members of his family and fellow blacks, and to the white men who "work" sharecroppers and keep them tied to the land. Industry gives Shaw the chance to follow relatives to the North, but except for a brief trip to Philadelphia he remains in the South. "I don't wash my feet with city water" (521).

This consciousness of his life's overall shape extends also to history and politics, for Shaw's awareness of race and property rights involves him with the Southern Tenantfarmer's Union. This precipitates the decisive act of his life when, in December, 1932, he stands alone against the white sheriffs who come to foreclose unjustly on a neighbor's farm. This unheard-of violence by a black man is punished by twelve years in prison, an ordeal he weathers characteristically through his skill as a basketmaker. But though his career as a mule farmer is virtually closed by prison and the coming of the tractor, he remains proud of his defiance. His own sons cannot see its necessity, for as he observes, "they don't see that deep in regards to their own selves." Shaw himself is not "natured" to submission. "But if you don't like what I have done, then you are against the man I am today," he declares. "I ain't goin to take no backwater about it. . . . Don't nobody try to tell me to keep quiet and undo my history" (573–74). Thus Shaw sees his deed, character, and social circumstance as an intricate combination. Racism and capitalism—"this old 'ism' that's been plunderin me and plunderin the colored race of people" (574)—are forces white men use against poor blacks; "work em to death or don't work em enough, that's how they do around here" (563). Though he understands economics and politics differently from Du Bois and Angela Davis, his sense of participating meaningfully in historical change is as quick as theirs. "I wish my children peace and good will," he concludes. "I wish the way will be clearer for em than ever in history and to know that I had a part in makin it clear—that's the grandest of all" (577).

All God's Dangers, then, embraces with a true historical vision the fundamental nature of Alabama rural life in this century, re-creating it in a vivid idiom and convincing detail. No history book is likely to duplicate, for example, Shaw's description of Mr. Henry Chase's hardware store and the catalogue of gear and goods bought there over the years. Even an outsider as acutely sympathetic as James Agee at the Gudger farm cannot match the precise rhythms of Shaw's voice and style. Furthermore, his narrative is not simply a virtuoso vernacular performance, equal to the best Faulkner tale. Larger ideological issues and psychological insights into black and white minds attest to a keen understanding of society and history. Mythic overtones are also heard in Shaw's religious language and his descriptions of mules, horses, foxes, and the cycle of the seasons. Yet all these facets are parts of a pattern which is the story teller's personal identity; they can be separated only by destroying the imaginative unity of *All God's Dangers* as personal history. The old black farmer clearly perceives that he is the core of the truth of his book. "But I have had my eyes open too long to the facts, and my ears, what I've heard; and what I have touched with my hands and what have touched me is a fact" (581).

Du Bois enjoys, of course, a cultural stature qualitatively outweighing Shaw's, one which depends far less on having written an important historical autobiography. He has, in fact, written two or three, perhaps four, all neatly spaced to cover the twentieth century as his sociological studies of Negro Americans were similarly spaced. The last of these attempts to put his world in order is, I believe, even more successful than *Dusk of Dawn*. *The Autobiography of W. E. B. Du Bois* was completed in 1960 by the voluntary exile in Ghana who was then over ninety. The longevity of this career and the variety of its accomplishments are unmatched by any other black American. Yet the interesting feature of the last autobiography is the fact that geography replaces chronology as the chief means by which design and historical truths are achieved. If *All God's Dangers* celebrates an obscure life of standing fast, Du Bois' *Autobiography* is the representative but nonetheless unique chronicle of continuous, meaningful movement. Like Franklin in the eighteenth century and Henry Adams in the nineteenth, Du Bois is carried on the currents of his age to a new identity. But because his is a black identity and experience, the forces whirling him across the globe are perceived and ordered into a different pattern of coherence than those achieved by the other two Massachusetts-born autobiographers.

This special shape is signaled in the opening chapters which report a very old man's impressions of his latest trip in 1958–59 across Europe and Asia— the fifteenth journey of a peripatetic career. This cosmopolitan self has grown out of European, African, Asian, and American experiences which stretch back to his birth on the day before Andrew Johnson was impeached. Travel is the content, form, and meaning of this life and so must come first in any truthful history. What follows then is Du Bois' conversion to Communism, the ideological outcome not simply of the latest tour but, he asserts, of all that has preceded it. Only after these two basic factors have been set forth can the narrator return to normal beginnings: his birth "by a golden river and in the shadow of two great hills" (61). Great Barrington must be approached by the Great Circle Route, via Prague, Moscow, and Peking.

This dislocation of normal expectations emphasizes that Du Bois sees his life as a long spiral. The moving and ascending line is traced by successive journeys which often traverse terrain previously covered. These returns signal continuity and repetition, for in important respects his experience as a black American does not substantially change; but the line rises and wavers in response to new historical forces sweeping him and everyone into radically different paths. His vision of history is thus both cyclical and linear, and much of the cumulative impact of the *Autobiography* derives from this outlook expressed in appropriate images and patterns of events. As a younger man, he remarks that "the content rather than the form of my writing was to me of prime importance. Words and ideas surged in my mind and spilled out with disregard of exact accuracy in grammar, taste in word or restraint in style. I knew the Negro problem and this was more important to me than literary form" (144).

Now, however, the aged author has found the right form of narrative and apt images for the truth he has lived for nearly a century. Juxtaposing one journey against another to emphasize change and continuity is the simple but effective scheme of this autobiography. Thus the fifteen-year-old youth's first trip to visit his grandfather in New Bedford has several personal and cultural implications. He misses a train connection because of the new standard time and sees his first electric streetlight. More significant, however, than these harbingers are two vividly recollected sights. The first is of his grave, courteous mulatto grandfather raising a glass of sherry to greet a dark visitor. "I had never before seen such ceremony," he explains. "I suddenly sensed in my grandfather's parlor what manners meant and how people of breeding behaved. . . . I never forgot that toast" (98). Unforgotten, too, is the sight of thousands of northern Negroes enjoying an annual picnic at Narragansett Bay. The vision of "the swaggering men, the beautiful girls, the laughter and gaiety, the unhampered self-expression" (99), defines another dimension of black life unfamiliar to the shy New Englander. His adult personality and much of the guarded emotion of his autobiography take their imprint from such contrasting memories. For seventy years, his social self and relations are influenced by imitation of his reserved grandfather and his equally genuine feeling of separation from the easy society of pretty women and backslapping men. Going south to Fisk University confirms his Negro identity and prepares him to experience Harvard, Germany, and later life in ways fundamentally different from those he would have felt and acted had he gone straight into the white intellectual world from Great Barrington. The austere Yankee with the Bismarck goatee who looks out from the covers of his books is the conscious combination of New Bedford and Berlin, Nashville and Cambridge. "To the world in general I was nearly always the isolated outsider looking in and seldom part of that inner life" (283). This characteristic comment applies equally to the shy graduate student in Germany, the indefatigable sociologist in (but not of) the Philadelphia ghetto, and the brusque NAACP official. In each sphere Du Bois lives in deliberate acceptance of the tensions and contradictions of his life as black man and American, scholar and politician, nationalist and integrationist, idealist and cynic, capitalist and socialist. Everywhere the outsider's viewpoint is dramatized by the solitary, ceaseless train trips and steamer voyages which define his outer and inner reality by representing realistically and symbolically a life of change, "lurch and stagger" progress, loneliness, intellectual adventure. European and African perspectives on a narrow American, and an even more circumscribed, black experience provide both an accurate picture of present realities and a utopian vision of the future. These actual and imaginative journeys constitute the work of Du Bois' life as the cotton bales and baskets represent Nate Shaw's very different experiences during the same seven or eight decades. Other men and women, seeking to express the uniqueness and representative truth of their lives in autobiography, utilize similar narrative and image patterns of traveling and standing still. Each attempt creates an individual design which is traditional in outline. The historian's task of assessing the significance of each particular text is facilitated but not solved by comparison with exemplary works like those of Nate Shaw and W. E. B. Du Bois.

II

Though the impulse to affirm one's black identity within history remains predominant today, there are strong pulls in other directions. As a special form of history in which imagination has combined with memory to make patterns of the past, autobiography is inevitably a literary act. No matter how strenuously the author tries to recreate a verifiable self and world, sometimes a narrative is so intensely imaginative as to be almost indistinguishable from fiction. The dramatic scenes and tight emotional focus of *Black Boy* or *Caged Bird*, like the passionate, precious rhetoric of Baldwin's autobiographical essays, often bring the present self at the typewriter before the reader more convincingly than the past actor and thinker. Moreover the overlap and confusion between history and literature increase as mythic aspects of character and event are emphasized. *Up from Slavery*, for instance, shows parallels to a Horatio Alger novel as well as to Franklin's autobiography; these are sometimes stronger than parallels to Washington's own biography as Louis Harlan reconstructs it. Only when personal history is carefully focused on chronology and factual detail within an explicit ideological framework, as in Benjamin Mays' *Born to Rebel*, is one tempted to take the writing itself for granted. Many present-day black autobiographers, whether conscious artists like Wright or Baldwin or natural storytellers like Shaw or Gregory, call attention to the deliberate artistry of their narratives. Hence one must be sensitive not merely to the "eventfulness" of texts, to use Kenneth Burke's useful term, but to their style, structure, and system of metaphors as well.[7] As narrative momentum calls attention to the historicity of remembered experience, so language and imagery emphasize the bedrock fact: an autobiography is a verbal artifact, a self made out of words.

Nonetheless, Du Bois' earlier comment about his youthful disregard of literary form is echoed by many later writers who likewise insist that communicating "the Negro problem" directly is more important than niceties of individual expression. Malcolm X's "raw, naked truth" is widely preferred over Baldwin's richly confessional prose. Yet even "telling it like it is" entails a variety of literary choices and techniques, and Alex Haley is as necessary to the astonishing power of *The Autobiography of Malcolm X* as the preacher-politician. What it feels like inside to be young, black, and sensitive; what the thoughts and emotions are behind stereotypes of ghetto child, hustler, movie star, or athlete; what cultural riches are to be tapped in unlettered lives and untrammeled black speech—these are dimensions of private and cultural experience which often demand special ways of storytelling beyond the limits of normal historical narrative. Experiments in imaginative prose, therefore, are nearly as common as historical chronologies in contemporary black autobiography.

Though possibilities for a completely unique style are as real (and as limited) as for any other writer, the black autobiographer finds certain prototypes readily available as inspiration or admonition. Two of the commonest, most serviceable are novelistic narratives, often by a writer or artist, and the collaboration, created by a well-known figure and an amanuensis. Lines separating the two types are not airtight, of course, but each draws attention to the nature and process of its creation, the one by a suggestive written style and structure, the other by a vernacular narrative which captures an authentic speaking voice. Briefly anatomizing these familiar models may provide a useful catalogue of intentions, techniques, and effects to be found in all kinds of black autobiographies. For these forms have been adapted to private ends and public purposes by a wide range of writers less talented than Wright, Malcolm X, or Alex Haley.

To begin with successors of the novel-like *Black Boy*: the first sign is on the spine. A metaphoric or eponymous title invites the reader to generalize more freely from the author's to others' experiences than with a literal title like Du Bois'. Then, inside the covers one finds a dramatically paced story, often cast in the present tense as well as the first person. This imparts immediacy

[7]Burke's term is elaborated in "Freud—And the Analysis of Poetry," *Philosophy of Literary Form* (Baton Rouge: Louisiana State University Press, 1941), 258–92, esp. 284f.

to a narrative like *Manchild* or *Caged Bird* but sacrifices the more historical interplay between the older, wiser author and the inexperienced actor who is slowly becoming that author. (This is an easy sacrifice for Brown or Angelou since both are less than half Du Bois' age.) The story unfolds like a plot. An exciting, often violent opening scene serves to typify the self and its world with an emotional resonance richer than Du Bois' travel-motif beginning. Thus Brown presents himself first as a thirteen-year-old staggering into a Harlem fish-and-chips joint with a bullet in his stomach. The shape and substance of an entire life in the Promised Land are succinctly evoked: violence, the tight circle of crime, flight and incarceration, the possibility of death at an early age, ineffectual parents, and police who are the adult children as he is the manchild. Scenes like this in the autobiographies of Gregory, Angelou, or Malcolm X capture essences and characteristic gestures as well as begin a chronological narrative. What strikes the middle-class reader is the instant maturity often dramatized. "And when you're poor, you grow up fast," Billie Holiday points out. Brown makes the same point even more explicitly: "I wanted to be as old as they were. All the older cats were using horse. The younger cats were still smoking reefers, drinking wine, and stuff like that. But I didn't want to be young. I wanted to be old" (103).

Two aspects of these novelistic autobiographies help to show the thin line separating them from outright fiction. One is characterization. The personages in a literary autobiography are less developed than in novels. At best they are deft thumbnail sketches. But all face in one direction, toward the self, for each exists chiefly to illuminate the author's developing identity. No Jim or Tom Sawyer appears in an autobiography. Even Dick Gregory's Momma is by comparison static and one-dimensional. Another difference is best typified by *Black Boy*, in which several incidents occur which did not actually happen to Wright. The scene with Uncle Hoskins driving his wagon into the Mississippi River and terrifying Richard was actually told to Wright by Ralph Ellison. The reader who learns this from Fabre may henceforth distrust Wright, calling him a liar or a novelist. Or one may note the autobiographical truth in the borrowed episode: "I never trusted him after that. Whenever I saw his face the memory of my terror upon the river would come back, vivid and strong, and stood as a barrier between us" (62). On another occasion Wright is more explicit. Telling of the old black woman who hid a shotgun in a winding-sheet and killed four white lynchers, Wright remarks, "I did not know if the story was factually true or not, but it was emotionally true because I had already grown to feel that there existed men against whom I was powerless, men who could violate my life at will. I resolved that I would emulate the black woman if I were ever faced with a white mob" (83–84). Here the line between the autobiography and "Bright and Morning Star," a short story, is clear. Readers of literary autobiography should not be misled by occasional scenes which do not dissolve but actually heighten the line between fact and fantasy. The borrowed, even the imaginary, incident exists to dramatize an aspect of a real life, just as imaginary names sometimes hide and reveal the truth. The reader aware of autobiography as both literature and history must search for the submerged connections.

Turning to autobiography by collaboration, one notes at once how many novelistic techniques are also used in narratives like *Nigger* by Dick Gregory or *Ossie: The Autobiography of a Black Woman* by Ossie Guffy. Dramatic scene, dialogue, brisk narrative pace, even the possibility of lifted or imaginary episodes, are all to be found. The issue here is whether the ghost-writer has imposed these as tricks upon the subject or has effaced himself and sought appropriate ways of bringing an inarticulate, illiterate, or too-busy-to-write life onto the page with that self's essential verbal features properly expressed. There are no sure answers, but two of the greatest contemporary collaborations happen to be black autobiographies; each suggests distinctive ways of being a dramatic performance and authentic history. Both *The Autobiography of Malcolm X* and *All God's Dangers* meticulously describe the nature of the collaboration. Rosengarten's Preface is, to be sure, less moving and more scholarly than Haley's Epilogue and, coming at the beginning, sets a different tone and context for what follows. Where Shaw turns his eyes almost wholly upon the past and largely ignores the young white liberal who is his immediate listener, Haley makes his Epilogue integral to his and Malcolm X's story, its structure and emotional fabric. "I trust you seventy percent" (400). This confession by the Muslim leader blurted over the phone to Haley is surely one of the touchstones and a touching moment in a dramatic self-portrait. The major theme is that this man's experience and identity—trusting, distrusting, loving, and being betrayed—are shown to be intimately a part of the process by which the book has been created. Malcolm X's voice and vocabulary are indeed graphically and convincingly created by Haley, but this kind of oral realism is also true of *Nigger* and *Ossie*. Many black autobiographies written by another succeed in evoking an authentic personality by reproducing his or her voice and keeping the actual writer entirely in the background. One reason why the stories of Shaw and Malcolm X make superior cultural documents as well as richer emotional revelations is that the reader has grounds for testing and trusting both partners in the creative process.

Trust is indeed at the heart of all autobiographical transactions between writer and reader. This fact has a special point in black life-histories, whether composed by the self or by a white collaborator, whether read by white or black audiences. The best test of a trustworthy story which is by nature both literal and imaginative is the pattern of images created to represent the self's essential identity. These "metaphors of self," to use Olney's apt term, are the clearest evidence that actual experiences from the past and the words used to recreate and pattern them are originally tied to the deepest emotions and moral character of the living subject. Language thus unites all aspects of human nature in tropes or figures which are as close to the "truth" as memory and imagination can devise. The most significant black autobiographies, whether made by one or two persons, are those in which the metaphors of self can be clearly perceived, critically tested, and emotionally accepted as resonant with the reader's own experiences. My earlier discussion of historical autobiography has already suggested two such patterns: Du Bois' images of himself as constant, cosmopolitan, solitary traveler, and Shaw's pictures of himself as a self-respecting maker of bales and baskets and driver of mules. Even richer, more multifaceted is *Black Boy*, in which Wright's youthful self is evoked throughout in a series of fires: the one he sets as a child to his white grandmother's house; the fire in the grate at his father's cabin; the fires of family hatred and racial strife; the fires in his imagination kindled by stories and, later by the social criticism of H. L. Mencken and Sinclair Lewis; fires which culminate in the incandescent art of *Native Son*. Fire on the inside, icy reserve and suspicion on the outside—this is the essence of Wright's recreated self. Alex Haley and Malcolm X find other patterns of images in the past: a journey from West to East; names and nicknames; clothes and belongings. Maya Angelou draws her identity as a sensitive, vulnerable womanchild in images of a westward-moving life of the caged bird. Her freedom and entrapment are exemplified by her own ungainly body and the beautiful baby it produces, the family store in Stamps, symbolic trips to Los Angeles and Mexico, and finally by the entire city of San Francisco in wartime with which the maturing teenager identifies. Thus each remembered life has its own special pattern, at once real and symbolic, which forms a picture of the past and a blueprint of a future. Many perplexing problems of authorship, audience, and authenticity may be clarified by discovering and interpreting the metaphoric patterns creating the autobiographical self.

III

Metaphor does more than unite actor, author, and audience. Word pictures and patterns organize and interpret memories of an actual, verifiable experience; but they also take the reader deep inside the autobiographer's psyche where the questions of his or her identity are phrased in preconscious as well as conscious terms and where distinctions arise between the social self and the transcendent soul. All autobiographical language is thus overdetermined. It expresses more than one thing at once. When, for instance, Malcolm X visits his mother in the insane asylum, only to find that she does not recognize her own son, his feelings spill forth in a striking simile: "It was as if I was trying to walk up the side of a hill of feathers" (21). Many mixed and contradictory emotions—love, fear, guilt, distrust, longing—find outlet in this vivid image, in which social and racial realities are likewise reflected. Hence the cultural criticism of autobiography cannot be limited to historical and literary interpretation, no matter how sophisticated; psychological, sociological, and metaphysical questions must be considered. Theories of personal identity, today so abundant as to bewilder and bore the nonspecialist, are unavoidable. The issue of a distinctive black identity is particularly thorny, and is being explored from various viewpoints by social scientists like Kenneth Clark, Price Cobbs, Alvin Poussaint, Thomas Pettigrew, Philip Hauser, Robert Coles, and Erik Erikson, among others. Except for Erikson, however, few are systematically examining documents like autobiographies with an eye both to scientific hypotheses and the integrity of individual texts.[8] Erikson's sensitive study of Gandhi's autobiography illuminates the historical, spiritual, political, and psychological strands in the revolutionary leader's personality. Gandhi's *The Story of My Experiments with Truth* should provide important perspectives on the life-stories of Du Bois, King, and Malcolm X. Another comparative angle on black autobiography could come from James Olney's *Tell Me Africa*, which surveys contemporary African literature in autobiographical terms.[9] Contrasting exemplary texts like *Black Boy* and Camara Laye's *The Dark Child*, for example, might suggest revealing insights on black American experience and identity in non-European categories. Clearly these are frontier issues which pose challenges to the cultural critic able to move flexibly not only across disciplinary but also national boundaries as well.

Nevertheless, taking a masterpiece like *The Autobiography of Malcolm X* over scholarly fences, first through the historian's, then the literary critic's, and then the social psychologist's bailiwick, will not guarantee full understanding of its cultural significance. Artistic criteria and scientific hypotheses are equally important and necessary, if private experience is to be accurately translated into public knowledge. Yet the reader of autobiography must also contribute to the translation his or her own intuitions and interpretations. Placing autobiography in cultural perspective, like anthropology, is a participant-observer science and art. Its objective methodologies must be combined with an individual's skepticism and sympathy. Despite the patterns I have discovered in and imposed on modern black autobiography, each of these books stubbornly preserves its own unique shape and flavor. For each is simultaneously a record of black life and culture in the shape of the verbal self-portrait of "an unrepeated and unrepeatable being."

IV   *Postscript: Looking Back in 1992*

One justification for reprinting in the preceding pages the *Phylon* essay of 1978, with but minor changes, is my conviction that its basic taxonomy

---

[8]See, for instance, a pioneering but flawed study by R. K. White, "*Black Boy*: A Value Analysis," *Journal of Social and Abnormal Psychology*, XLII (Oct. 1947), 440–61. An exemplary combination of art and science is E. Erikson's "Gandhi's *Autobiography*: The Leader as a Child," *American Scholar*, XXXV (Autumn: 1966), 632–46.

[9]J. Olney, *Tell Me Africa: An Approach to African Literature* (Princeton: Princeton University Press, 1973).

remains plausible and useful. Indeed, recent historical scholarship and literary criticism indicate that the heavily documented memoir or public performance—for example, Ralph David Abernathy's *And the Walls Came Tumbling Down: An Autobiography* (1989), and the introspective confession or private "fiction" like Audre Lorde's *Zami: A New Spelling of My Name* (1984)—are polar modes of self-representation whose prototypes long predate *Dusk of Dawn* and *Black Boy*.[10] Elizabeth Schultz's terms for these traditional modes are the "testimonial" and the "blues performance."[11] Robert Stepto, in an important work of 1979, *From Behind the Veil: A Study of Afro-American Narrative*, organizes his opening discussion of slave narratives by juxtaposing "authenticating" and "generic" impulses, and then demonstrating their intertwined development in later "revoicings" of twentieth-century black experience and sensibility.[12] Whatever the vocabulary, the black writer's choice between "I was there. This happened to me," and "This is me—in my own words, thoughts, feelings," remains available for telling stories which are at once individual and representative.

However, as the number and variety of recent autobiographies clearly suggest, these modes are seldom separate options. In fact, we need look no further than Abernathy's carefully researched and footnoted reminiscence of the civil rights struggle, with its to some controversial comments about the private affairs of Martin Luther King, Jr., to encounter also the author's fictionalizing impulse at work in the plentiful dialogue, dramatic scenes, and some touchingly frank confessional passages. Conversely, *Zami* expresses its black/lesbian/feminist/poet's ambition to create a "biomythography," which the cover blurb describes as an experimental form combining history, biography, myth, and poetry. What such crossing and mixing indicates is the current willingness of African-American writers to continue to ground personal experience in historical and social circumstances common to other black lives, but to do so increasingly in an unmistakable, individual voice activated through novelistic strategies of discourse.

In what has been called "easily the most comprehensive work on black American autobiography," William L. Andrews' *To Tell a Free Story: The First Century of Afro-American Autobiography, 1760–1865* (1986) offers plausible explanations for this growing practice.[13] Over the generations since Emancipa-

[10]R. D. Abernathy, *And the Walls Came Tumbling Down: An Autobiography* (New York: Harper & Row, 1989); A. Lorde, *Zami: A New Spelling of My Name* (Watertown, Mass.: Persephone Press, 1982).

[11]E. Schultz, "To Be Black and Blue: The Blues Genre in Black American Autobiography," *Kansas Quarterly*, 7 (Summer: 1975), 81–96, reprinted in *The American Biography: A Collection of Critical Essays*, ed. A. E. Stone (Englewood Cliffs, N.J.: Prentice-Hall, 1981), 109–32.

[12]R. B. Stepto, *From Behind the Veil: A Study of Afro-American Narrative* (Urbana: University of Illinois Press, 1979).

[13]W. L. Andrews, *To Tell a Free Story: The First Century Afro-American Autobiography, 1760–1865* (Urbana: University of Illinois Press, 1986). The characterization of Andrews' work is by Joanne M. Braxton in *Black Women Writing Autobiography: A Tradition Within a Tradition* (Philadelphia: Temple University Press, 1989), 8.

tion, he argues, black autobiographies have shared three aims and their transactional pressures. These were and are, first, the truth-telling act of documenting one's historical experience for skeptical or indifferent readers (often white); second, the moral address to these others as fellow believers in personal freedom; and, finally, the literary-psychological activity of re-creating a special self whose truth value ultimately derives from her or his own standards rather than from those of history, community, or ideology. For the black writer, however, truth to self seldom means embracing white male models of autonomous identity, a persona typified in mainstream American autobiography by Benjamin Franklin, Andrew Carnegie, or Lee Iacocca. Both the realities of black oppression and the circumstances of authorship and audience relationships militate against such arbitrary representations of black identity formation. On the other hand, contemporary black autobiographers, male and female, have seldom betrayed their roots and sense of being in the world by buying into fashionable postmodernist arguments which challenge the very possibility of an autobiographical self inscribed in referential relation to an extratextual reality. The separation of literature from society, the "disappearance of the self," and the "death of autobiography" announced by white critics like Paul de Man, Louis Renza, and Michael Sprinker are theoretical postulates few if any black authors have opted to honor.[14]

This is not to say that Andrews (along with fellow critics Stepto, Houston Baker, and Henry Louis Gates, Jr.) ignores relevant contemporary theory. The fact that so much present-day African-American autobiography is at once experimental and traditional, flourishing as a mode of self-liberation under increasingly freer story-telling conditions, fits the broad historical development Mikhail Bakhtin claims for Western narrative discourse: the novelization of all genres. For Andrews, freedom to express both external and internal imperatives of remembered experience and authorial consciousness by means of dialogue and dialect, metaphor, synecdoche and pseudonym, drama and sentimentality, as well as indeterminacy and open-endedness of narrative action, makes black writers partners (indeed, on this continent sometimes leaders) in a worldwide lowering of writerly and readerly barriers separating self and society, history and fiction.

It is, in fact, a common feature not only of Andrews' work but of Stepto's and of a third major critical work of the past decade, Joanne M. Braxton's *Black Women Writing Autobiography* (1989), that this gradual process of self-liberation has occasioned—and perhaps been energized by—a new awareness

[14]See P. de Man, "Autobiography as De-Facement," *Modern Language Notes*, 94 (Dec. 1979), 919–30; L. Renza, "The Veto of the Imagination: A Theory of Autobiography," in *Autobiography: Essays Theoretical and Critical*, ed. J. Olney (Princeton: Princeton University Press, 1980), 268–95; M. Sprinker, "Fictions of the Self: The End of Autobiography," in Olney, *Autobiography*, 321–42. For a spirited defense from a feminist and pro–Afro-American perspective, see Elizabeth Fox-Genovese, "My Statue, My Self: Autobiographical Writings of Afro-American Women," in *The Private Self: Theory and Practice of Women's Autobiographical Writings*, ed. S. Benstock (Chapel Hill: University of North Carolina Press, 1988), 63–89, esp. 67–68.

of the rhetorical subtleties and imaginative complexities of some older black autobiographies. Stepto and Andrews, for example, invite readers to revalorize Frederick Douglass' *My Bondage and My Freedom* of 1855, in the process helping to decanonize his *Narrative* of 1845. Andrews and Braxton show the fuller implications of Jean Fagan Yellin's important scholarship in establishing the authorship of Harriet Jacobs' *Incidents in the Life of a Slave Girl, Written by Herself* (1861). This text has been available since 1987 in a Harvard paperback, which demonstrates beyond doubt Jacobs' mastery of her necessarily fictionalized life story. Braxton and Elizabeth Fox-Genovese argue the central places of Ida B. Wells' *Crusade for Justice* (1970) and Zora Neale Hurston's *Dust Tracks on a Road* (1942) in a black woman's lineage of life-writings. This newly expanded women's tradition, unlike the exclusively male succession of prototypes Stepto examines, conforms closely to conventional definitions and reader expectations. Whereas Stepto constructs a twentieth-century descent from the male slave narrative through Du Bois' *The Souls of Black Folk* to autobiographical fiction like James Weldon Johnson's *The Autobiography of an Ex-Colored Man* and Ralph Ellison's *Invisible Man*, Braxton traces a different literary-historical pattern of representative women's texts, one that reaches Maya Angelou's *I Know Why the Caged Bird Sings* (1969) by way of Charlotte Fortin Grimké's diaries (1854–1892), Wells' *Crusade for Justice*, Hurston's *Dust Tracks*, and Era Bell Thompson's *American Daughter* (1947). In the process, Braxton celebrates the outraged mother and the sassily articulate heroine as longstanding models for a female black self equal in social significance and imaginative power to the singular figures like Douglass, Washington, Du Bois, and Wright, who exemplify male pathways to selfhood via escape, literacy, and public activity. Stepto's "call and response" tradition is thus implicitly questioned not only for its male bias but its devaluation of historiography and memoir.

This interlocking of slave narrative and black women's autobiography is, therefore, a promising feature of recent African-American criticism. A major stimulus to this activity is the new literary and historical scholarship exemplified by re-publication projects like the Schomburg Library of Nineteenth-Century Women Writers under the general editorship of Henry Louis Gates, Jr. *Collected Black Women's Narratives* (1988), edited by A. G. Barthelemy, for instance, brings to present-day attention four neglected autobiographical or fictional life-stories by or about Nancy Prince, Louisa Picquet, Bethany Veney, and Susie King Taylor. Another reprint, *Sisters of the Spirit: Three Black Women's Autobiographies of the Nineteenth Century* (1986), edited by William Andrews, does a similar service of recovery for the spiritual life stories of Jarena Lee, Zilpha Elaw, and Julia A. J. Foote.[15] Literary and

---

[15]*Collected Black Women's Narratives*, ed. A. G. Barthelemy (New York: Oxford University Press, 1988); *Sisters of the Spirit: Three Black Women's Autobiographies of the Nineteenth Century*, ed. W. L. Andrews (Bloomington: Indiana University Press, 1986).

cultural contexts and interpretations of these and other forgotten texts are found in several new studies, including John Sekora and Darwin T. Turner's, *The Art of Slave Narrative* (1982), M. W. Starling's *The Slave Narrative: Its Place in American History* (1981), and Dorothy Sterling's *We Are Your Sisters: Black Women in the Nineteenth Century* (1984).[16]

V

"And so there is no single Afra-American experience, nothing static" (208), Braxton concludes. Her gendered respelling quietly underlines a new departure in critical attention and vocabulary. But her *Black Women Writing Autobiography* stops short of the scope of Andrews' work. Braxton merely mentions without discussing the striking outpouring of two sorts of black women's life stories which has taken place in the past decade and a half. Her decision in 1989 to let *I Know Why the Caged Bird Sings*, a book first issued in 1969, stand for the women's autobiographies of the seventies and eighties is unfortunate, although she does call attention to several of the more widely read titles she is passing over. These include Nikki Giovanni's *Gemini* (1971), Gwendolyn Brooks' *Report from Part One* (1972), two additional installments of Maya Angelou's serial autobiography, *The Heart of a Woman* (1981) and *All God's Children Need Traveling Shoes* (1986), as well as two recent political autobiographies, *Angela Davis: An Autobiography* (1974) and Pauli Murray's *Song in a Weary Throat* (1987).[17] Along with these conventional autobiographical narratives Braxton also mentions the names of some notably autobiographical novelists—Toni Morrison, Gloria Naylor, Shirley Anne Williams, and others—who are so prominently a part of present-day African-American literary production.

Nonetheless, some important writing by more obscure women has been overlooked. For instance, neither Braxton nor Fox-Genovese examines the present-day practice of collaborative autobiography, an experimental mode

16J. Sekora and D. T. Turner, *The Art of Slave Narrative* (Macomb: Western Illinois University, 1982); C. T. Davis and H. L. Gates, Jr., eds. *The Slave's Narrative* (New York: Oxford University Press, 1985); M. W. Starling, *The Slave Narrative: Its Place in History* (Boston: G. K. Hall, 1981); D. Sterling, *We Are Your Sisters: Black Women in the Nineteenth Century* (New York: W. W. Norton, 1984). See also Regina Blackburn, "In Search of the Female Self: African-American Women's Autobiography and Ethnicity," in *Women's Autobiography: Essays in Criticism*, ed. Estelle Jelinek (Bloomington: Indiana University Press, 1980), 133–48; and Thomas Doherty, "Harriet Jacobs' Narrative Strategies: *Incidents in the Life of a Slave Girl*," *Southern Literary Journal*, 19 (1986), 79–91.

17N. Giovanni, *Gemini: An Extended Autobiographical Statement on My First Twenty-Five Years of Being a Black Poet* (Indianapolis: Bobbs-Merrill, 1971); G. Brooks, *Report from Part One* (Detroit: Broadside Press, 1972); M. Angelou, *The Heart of a Woman* (New York: Random House, 1981), and *All God's Children Need Traveling Shoes* (New York: Random House, 1986); A. Davis, *Angela Davis: An Autobiography* (New York: Random House, 1974); P. Murray, *Song in a Weary Throat: An American Pilgrimage* (New York: Harper & Row, 1987).

given popular and critical standing by the striking successes of Malcolm X/ Alex Haley and Nate Shaw/Theodore Rosengarten. This activity, not to be confused with the frankly commercial partnership which produced Billie Holiday's *Lady Sings the Blues,* is, one might suppose, admirably adaptable to women's experience and to womanist ideology. Individual and collective existence especially but not exclusively in domestic and intimate relationships is, for some, admirably re-created by cooperation between more than one memory and imagination. In at least two recent instances, the inspiration of Nate Shaw may be detected. However, neither *He Included Me: The Autobiography of Sarah Rice* (1980) nor *You May Plow Here: The Narrative of Sara Brooks* (1986) is a slavish imitation of *All God's Dangers.* Their common settings in rural Alabama and their subjects' common commitment to unremitting hard work as the road to self-respect and self-awareness are the chief points of similarity to Shaw's autobiography.[18] Pertinent and problematic, too, is the fact that both of these "ordinary" women's lives are recaptured with the assistance of white women writers. This situation, as with Shaw/Rosengarten, raises anew some ticklish issues about language and voice, truth, audience, and exploitation. (These matters have long been debated by ethnographers, so it is perhaps no coincidence that a recent central text in that field was co-created by a white anthropologist and an African woman—Majorie Shostak's *Nisa: The Life and Words of a !Kung Woman.*[19]) Sara Brooks' life story, for instance, was taken down by Thordis Simonsen, who was a little girl in a white Cleveland household where Brooks onced served as cleaning woman. This tie may have facilitated more than complicated the rendering of Brooks' strongly "voiced" performance. Yet as Fox-Genovese points out, all black women's writing must represent the language and gender identification and social gaps existing between blacks and whites as writers, storytellers, and readers. "The account of the black woman's self cannot be divorced from the history of that self or the history of the people among whom it took shape," she observes. "It also cannot be divorced from the language through which it is represented, or from the readers of other classes and races who not only lay claim to it but who have helped to shape it" (82–83). Although Fox-Genovese does not focus her sociological sights in this essay on these obscure Alabama farmgirls who grew up to teach in two-room schools or to clean white women's kitchens, she does emphasize the decisive but troublesome factor of class, a dimension of personal experience and discourse seldom examined with the same care given to race and gender.

Class awareness, although subordinated to race, gender, and family, is very much present in another recent and notable collaboration. *Tight Spaces,* winner of an American Book Award in 1987–88, is (as far as my reading

---

[18]S. Rice, *He Included Me: The Autobiography of Sarah Rice* (Athens: University of Georgia Press, 1980), ed. Louise Westling; S. Brooks, *You May Plow Here: The Narrative of Sara Brooks* (New York: W. W. Norton, 1986), ed. Thordis Simonsen, foreword by R. Coles.

[19]M. Shostak, *Nisa: The Life and Words of a !Kung Woman* (New York: Random House, 1983).

extends) unique in that it represents the imaginative cooperation of three closely related black women who grew up in Detroit.[20] Each has lived her variation of a common pattern of experience. Adolescence or young adulthood during the civil rights upheavals; the struggle for education and economic independence; marriage, motherhood, and divorce; escape to the heady environment of a Big Ten campus where freedom and oppression are mixed differently than in the black world south of Eight Mile Road—these are the shared ingredients of the otherwise quite different lives re-created by Kesho Scott, Cherry Muhanji, and Egyirba High. Of their collaborative act, which made *Tight Spaces* a surprisingly unified history woven of many often-fictional threads, Papusa Molina has observed, "They were black women within the same tight space. Thus they began a journey to capture in writing these common experiences. They sat in a triangle: a mystic formation that draws the spirits. SHE provided the inspiration, the courage, the healing tears which dismissed fears and kept them 'talking real honest' " ("Introduction" to *Tight Places*).

A particularly knotted thread in *Tight Spaces* is the authors' conflicted relationships with husbands and lovers, which often causes more traumatic aftereffects in their lives than their relationships with mothers, fathers, or siblings. That such intraracial gender tensions and stressful emotional adjustments are widely shared among black women autobiographers is also documented in a number of other life stories. Sometimes the turmoil of adult heterosexual or homosexual relationships is depicted against the background of older, stabler family ties, especially with fathers. "I don't know why, but my father never did seem as if he was tired. And, oh, he has been a *good* man cause he always looked out for us," Sara Brooks recalls. "He always wanted us to have, and we never had nothin fine, but we had" (43–44). Having *enough* through a loving father's self-sacrifice was, moreover, not simply a matter of food and clothing. The deeper significance of family, farm, and father in her memory is evoked, simply but sharply, by images of fruit trees. When a hurricane swept away their childhood home, Brooks recalled her father's acute pain. Although her mother's precious sewing machine was lost, she fixes upon other valued things. Nothing was left at home except one pear tree which "my father set out there behind the house. The pear tree still stayed there. I imagine that pear tree may be there now. But I never went back because I didn't want that memory" (194). Securely and symbolically preserved in her memory are the peach and pear trees planted by her father in a long-lost Southern farmyard.

A different dream of the life-sustaining father animates even more powerfully another recent black woman's autobiography. Bebe Moore Campbell's *Sweet Summer* (1989) is a semifictionalized reminiscence of a girlhood split

[20]Kesho Scott, Cherry Muhanji, and Egyirba High, *Tight Spaces* (San Francisco: Spinsters/ Aunt Lute, 1987).

between North Carolina and Philadelphia and the two worlds of father and mother.[21] The story is built around memories of one automobile trip South with her paralyzed but husky, wheelchair-wielding father. "I remembered the sweet North Carolina summers of my childhood, my father's snappy 'C'mon, kiddo. Let's go for a ride'" (20). Her youthful freedom to escape "down home" is protected also by the loving presence of uncles and other older men. Later threatened by her parents' divorce, male sponsorship is followed by subsequent immersion in the female world of her Philadelphia mother, aunts, and teachers. That city life is typified by bubble baths and bathrobes, music and ballet lessons, Sunday School and choir practice. It's recalled as a cloying environment which she satirically dubs "the Bosoms":

> And what did they want from me, these Bosoms? Achievement! . . . Pushing little colored girls forward was in their blood. . . . I was to *do* something. And if I didn't climb willingly up their ladder, they'd drag me to the top. Rap my knuckles hard for not practicing. Make me lift my leg until I wanted to die. . . . they were not playing. "Obey them" my mother commanded. (76)

Although partly a sentimental family drama of rebellion and conformity, *Sweet Summer* is redeemed by Campbell's mature awareness of the complexities in both parents' worlds. The metaphor of "the Bosoms," for instance, suddenly turns tragic when her Aunt Ruth dies of breast cancer in 1972, following a radical mastectomy. The trauma of once glimpsing her aunt's scarred chest is vividly recalled. "Never in my life had I felt so instantly, violently nauseated. I really thought I was going to vomit then and there, but I prayed away the feeling" (258). The story closes with evocation of a happier occasion—her wedding day. This account, too, has an ironic twist, when her uncles threaten the groom with death if he doesn't treat his bride tenderly and respectfully. Looking back to and past that day, she confesses: "But I am lonely. I've come to a space in my life where the old men are too few and far between. . . . I have grown strong and whole from the blessings of many fathers. Everything they gave me—roughness, gruffness, awkward gentleness, the contrast to any female world, their love—is as much a part of me as my bones, my blood" (271–72).

Fond recollections of fathers like Brooks' and Campbell's can, of course, be countered by very differently inflected accounts by Kesho Scott and other rebellious daughters. Readers and critics may find themselves groping for generalizations in this sometimes bewilderingly contradictory literature. Both commonly shared and unique experiences of public and private life are mixed together in abundance in present-day autobiographies, yet as compared with most male life stories, black women's autobiographies often take readers more deeply inside the emotional contradictions and social ambiguities of being black (and a woman) in contemporary America. Still struggling with the

[21] B. M. Campbell, *Sweet Summer* (New York: G. P. Putnam's, 1989).

double bind of race and gender, black women writing autobiography are able
to recapture the pain of powerlessness while celebrating the "survival strategies" of black girls and daughters growing up, more often than not, to become
articulate, independent, loving adults.

The rich ambiguities of this personal literature which is helping to change
American stereotypes and simplifications of black life and culture is nowhere
better exemplified than in Audre Lorde's *Zami*. As the second personal
narrative of this talented poet's life, this recent autobiography builds upon its
predecessor, *The Cancer Journals* (1980).[22] Together, the two stories answer
Lorde's poignant question, one which readers (white and black) often refuse to
confront in our homophobic society: *"To whom do I owe the power behind my
voice, what strength I have become, yeasting up like sudden blood under
the bruised skin's blister?"* (3). Lorde's immediate explanation is not simply
lesbian but familial as well. "I have always wanted to be both man and
woman, to incorporate the strongest and richest parts of my mother and father
within/into me" (7). The father in her Grenadian immigrant family is the
easier source to characterize, if not overcome; his was the "silent, intense
unforgiving" presence, a "distant lightning" (3) in the sky of her girlhood. But
her mother remains Lorde's first model of the self-possessed black woman
whose physical and psychic force masks, in a racist culture, less social power
than her children supposed. Her puzzling compound of secret poetry and
hidden anger remains a vital legacy for the author, one of whose precious
memories are of a little girl's treasured Saturday morning moments in her
mother's bed, "feeling my mother's quiet body . . . the smooth deep firmness
of her breasts against my shoulders. . . . I nuzzle against her sweetness" (34).
This primal image of togetherness and separation proves a central motif in
Zami. The author's lesbian identity and adult relationships are frequently
evoked through resonating images of breasts. For readers of 1982 familiar with
The Cancer Journals, such references are ironic and poignant, inasmuch as
they tacitly assume knowledge of Lorde's later loss of her own breast in a
mastectomy. This body blow, vastly more devastating than Campbell's horri-
fied recollection, hovers in the background as the author tells of Eudora, her
white lover in Mexico, who reluctantly consents to expose her postoperative
scars and welcome Lorde's tender kisses.

Society's valuation of heterosexuality and conventional feminine beauty are
threatening but not insuperable obstacles to Lorde's identity formation. Her
declaration of independence is expressed in terms which occasionally anticipate Campbell's, although always with different implications. She writes near
the end of *Zami*,

[22]A sensitive feminist reading of *The Cancer Journals* is provided by Jeanne Perreault in " 'that
the pain not be wasted': Audre Lorde and the Written Self," *a/b: Auto/Biography Studies*, 4 (Fall:
1988), 1–16.

In a paradoxical sense, once I accepted my position as different from the larger society as well as from any single sub-society—black or gay—I felt I didn't have to try so hard. To be accepted. To look femme. To be straight. To be proper. To look "nice." To be liked. To be loved. To be approved. What I didn't realize was how much harder I had to try merely to stay alive, or rather, to stay human. How much stronger a person I became in that trying.

But in the plastic, anti-human society in which we live, there have never been too many people buying fat black girls born almost blind and ambidextrous, gay or straight. Unattractive, too, or so the ads in *Ebony* and *Jet* seemed to tell me. Yet I read them anyway, in the bathroom, on the newsstand, at my sister's house, whenever I got the chance. It was a furtive reading, but it was an affirmation of some part of me, however frustrating. (181)

Lorde's candidly acknowledged "furtive reading" flowers into far from furtive writing about the complexities of black and female character and the consequent contradictions of social role. She has achieved a different brand of freedom—a writer's freedom—different from that known by the great majority of her ancestors and sisters and brothers in the black autobiographical tradition. Furthermore, it is a subtly different freedom from the ones Andrews, Braxton, and Fox-Genovese discuss. The silence—or careful selectivity—of much present-day literary and cultural criticism on the subject of (black) gay or lesbian life stories (extending to the current neglect of James Baldwin) is but one indication that the ideal of an inclusive social and cultural approach to American history, literature, and autobiography, an integration called for by David Levering Lewis, Paul John Eakin, and others, remains far from reality as the nineties unfold.[23] In the face of texts like *Incidents in the Life of a Slave Girl, Dust Tracks on a Road,* and *Zami,* cultural historians need to move beyond one-dimensional discussions of matrilinearity, patriarchy, gender, class, family, and community—basic categories of both black and Euro-American experience and consciousness which are considerably more complicated in individual lives and stories than in sociology textbooks.

[23]See D. L. Lewis, "Radical History: Toward Inclusiveness," *Journal of American History,* 76 (Sept. 1989), 4–72; P. J. Eakin, "Reference and the Representative in American Autobiography: Mary McCarthy and Lillian Hellman," in *Identita e scrittura: Studi sull' autobiografia Nord-Americana,* eds. A. L. Accardo, M. O. Marrotti, and I. Tattoni (Rome: Bulzoni Editone, 1988), 21–47; A. E. Stone, "Modern American Autobiography: Texts and Transactions," in *American Autobiography: Retrospect and Prospect,* ed. P. J. Eakin (Madison: University of Wisconsin Press, 1991), 95–120.

West Indian Autobiography

Sandra Pouchet Paquet

West Indian autobiography is varied and complex. It includes slave narratives like *The History of Mary Prince, A West Indian Slave, Related by Herself* (1831). There are letters, journals, diaries, and, most important to an understanding of the region's cultural identity, oral histories—some of them recently collected and edited in publications like *The Still Cry* [1985], and others transformed into a text for dramatic performance as in *Lionheart Gal: Life Stories of Jamaican Women* [1986]. There are formal autobiographies by a few politicians, sportsmen,[1] and writers. On the periphery of these autobiographical forms are innumerable fictive autobiographies, some of them thinly disguised autobiographies, like Michael Anthony's *A Year in San Fernando* [1965] and, more recently, Vidia Naipaul's *The Enigma of Arrival* [1987]. However, the canonized texts of West Indian autobiography are the works of major creative writers such as George Lamming, Derek Walcott, and Vidia Naipaul.[2]

As a way into the complex issues of self-representation in West Indian autobiography, I would like to distinguish between autobiographies by West Indians who were, or are, active in nonliterary occupations and the autobiographical works of creative writers, chief among them: George Lamming's *In the Castle of My Skin* (1953), C. L. R. James's *Beyond the Boundary* (1963), Derek Walcott's *Another Life* (1973), and Vidia Naipaul's *Finding the Center* (1984). These key texts define the character of West Indian autobiography on which I would like to focus. Problematically, this short list suggests that West Indian autobiography is a male enterprise.[3] Oral histories, journals, and even Jean Rhys's *Smile, Please* [1979] belie this assumption, as do the many fictive autobiographies published by writers such as Jamaica Kincaid, Merle Hodge, and Zee Edgell. Nonetheless, these texts are a convenient point of departure

Reprinted with permission from Sandra Pouchet Paquet, *Black American Literature Forum*, 24 no. 2 (Summer 1990), 357–74.

[1]For example, Eric Williams's *Inward Hunger: The Education of a Prime Minister* (London: Deutsch, 1969), and others by the famous cricketers Learie Constantine and Garfield Sobers.

[2]The Eighth Annual Conference on West Indian Literature at the University of the West Indies, Mona, Jamaica (18–21 May 1988), on "The Written Life: Biography and Autobiography in West Indian Literature," focused primarily on the works of creative writers from Claude McKay to Jamaica Kincaid and Erna Brodber.

[3]See Sidonie Smith's chapter on "Autobiography Criticism and the Problematics of Gender" (3–19). [Note: References cited in the footnotes are listed in full at the end of this reading.]

for examining issues surrounding the balance between the self-expressive, generic function, and other functional aspects of the autobiographical text in contemporary West Indian literature (Bruss 10–11).[4] They reveal an intense and creative struggle with the conventions of autobiography, and engage directly with the social and political issues that have preoccupied West Indian culture and society over the past fifty years. Published ten years apart [over a thirty-year period], these texts are radically different. Yet a distinctive pattern emerges. All four works reveal an organizing concern with defining a West Indian cultural and political reality. In each of these very different texts, issues of self-identity merge with issues of West Indian identity. The individual predicament of the writer as autobiographical subject illuminates the collective predicament of an island community. The autobiographical act emerges as a means to an end rather than as an end in itself.

In *In the Castle of My Skin,* an autobiographical novel, Lamming juxtaposes first-person with third-person narrative, and in the process, self-revelation is subsumed by larger issues of cultural appraisal. In *Beyond a Boundary,* James makes his lifelong obsession with cricket the substance and the occasion for intellectual history and cultural assessment. Despite the book's explicit autobiographical content, James warns in his Preface: "This book is neither cricket reminiscences nor autobiography." His theme, he explains, is the genesis of the West Indian personality, Caliban's attempt to establish his own identity. Walcott's long autobiographical poem *Another Life* uses the poet's growth and development as an artist in a similar way. Walcott, like James, stresses a value other than autobiography. In describing the genesis of the poem, he states that in *Another Life* he abandoned autobiography for elegy and intellectual history.[5] In *Finding the Center,* Vidia Naipaul also rejects the idea that he is writing autobiography, though "Prologue to an Autobiography" is explicitly autobiographical. In the Author's Foreword, he explains that it "is not an autobiography, a story of a life or deeds done. It is an account of something less easily seized: my literary beginnings and the imaginative promptings of my many-sided background" (vii). Naipaul, like Lamming, James, and Walcott before him, clearly intends "Prologue to an Autobiography" to be something other than autobiography. The autobiographical act unfolds as a quest for the familial and ethnic roots of his creativity in colonial Trinidad.

For these writers, self-inquiry is self-imaging and self-evaluation, but it is also cultural assessment.[6] In each of these texts, there is a clearly defined tension between the autobiographical self as a singular personality with

---

[4]Bruss writes: "Definitions of what is appropriate to the autobiographical act are never absolute: they must be created and sustained" (14).

[5]Derek Walcott was talking informally at the University of Pennsylvania to my graduate class in Caribbean literature in the fall of 1987.

[6]Gunn proposes a useful approach to the autobiographical text: "Rather than starting from the private act of a self writing, I begin from the cultural act of a self reading" (8).

psychological integrity and the self as a way into the social and political complexities of the region. Autobiography gives the writer direct access into his privileged relationship to the West Indian community as an insider, and, additionally, it gives him the opportunity to define the quality of his relationship to that community in ideal terms.[7] Self-revelation becomes a way of laying claim to a landscape that is at once geographical, historical, and cultural. In this fashion, the writer is privileged to write himself into the symbolic systems that make up West Indian literature and culture. In the process, the autobiographical self as subject is transformed into a cultural archetype, and autobiography becomes both the lived historical reality and the myth created out of that experience. Personal experience and historical events alike are transformed into autobiographical myth (Cooper vi). In the hands of Lamming, James, Walcott, and Naipaul, autobiography emerges as a compelling way to embody the collective West Indian experience.[8] Naipaul's is a more individual configuration, but, for all four writers, autobiographical modes create an exemplary space for the reconstruction of self and community that accompanies the withdrawal of the British Empire, a totalitarian institution, from the region.

George Lamming's *In the Castle of My Skin* is a useful place to begin departure in a discussion of West Indian autobiography for several reasons. In the absence of an established West Indian literary tradition in mid-century, it represents a dramatic point of entrance for West Indian literature as a distinct body of writing, as opposed to peripheral status as a poor relation of either African-American literature or the literature of Great Britain.[9] West Indian literature, as we know it today, was created by the efforts of writers such as George Lamming, Derek Walcott, Vidia Naipaul, Wilson Harris, Sam Selvon, and Roger Mais in the fifties. This is not to say that West Indian literary history begins with these writers. A literary tradition was already in place, however unrecognized, in the oral literature of the folk, and in the accomplishments of Mary Prince, Mrs. Seacole, Eric Walrond, George Campbell, Claude McKay, and C. L. R. James, to name but a few. But the emergence of a distinguished group of West Indian writers in the fifties became the focal point for the recovery and development of oral and written literature in the West Indies.

In the Castle of My Skin is among the most influential of literary texts published in the fifties. It is a seminal work that continues to exercise a shaping power over a developing West Indian literary tradition, as one of the primary articulators of the symbolic systems that make up contemporary West

---

[7]See Gunn on autobiographical perspective as a mode of self-placing (16).

[8]Autobiographical acts for a purpose that is collective rather than individual invite comparison with the self-expressive function of African-American autobiography (see Butterfield 3).

[9]As Derek Walcott writes in *Another Life*: "I had entered the house of literature as a houseboy, / filched as the slum child stole, / as the young slave appropriated / those heirlooms temptingly left / with the Victorian homilies of *Noli Tangere*" (12.ii).

Indian literature. This is true not only of the autobiographical texts under scrutiny here. From Merle Hodge to Michael Anthony to Erna Brodber and the fictive autobiographies that have proliferated in the English-speaking Caribbean, West Indian writers seemingly have written for or against *In the Castle of My Skin* as a working model.[10] In West Indian literature, *In the Castle of My Skin* has emerged as a paradigm for any number of themes and literary constructs, among these, the use of childhood and adolescence, the quest for selfhood and perspective, and spiritual reconnection with the poor and oppressed as the definitive posture of the West Indian writer in relation to the regional community. Finally, it was *In the Castle of My Skin* that established certain ground rules for the fictionalizing of the self and the construction of the autobiographical self in literary discourse.[11] Not only does it combine two modes of discourse, autobiography and fiction, in a unique way, but its unconventional structuring of content and situating of narrative perspective allows insight into core issues of identity in the reading and writing of self, in the last stages of British colonial rule in the Caribbean.

In describing the genesis of *In the Castle of My Skin*, Lamming explains in retrospect: "In the desolate, frozen heart of London, at the age of twenty-three, I tried to reconstruct the world of my childhood and adolescence. It was also the world of a whole Caribbean reality" (xii). It is this perception of the collective dilemma of the colonial Caribbean, embodied in his individual human predicament, that organizes this autobiographical narrative, structurally and thematically. *In the Castle of My Skin* is set in Creighton's Village, a fictive Barbadian community that is a composite of the Carrington Village and the St. David's of Lamming's boyhood.[12] It describes the author's gradual separation from the landscape and the community that engendered him. Yet, in this structurally challenging autobiographical text, Lamming also describes the dissolution of village life as he knew it, in the context of political changes wrought by the development of organized labor in the Caribbean in the 1930s and 1940s. By the end of the narrative, the village emerges as a metaphor for the evolution of colonial society in the West Indies, and, in turn, the author emerges as a representative figure whose childhood and adolescence are charged with broad social significance.[13] *In the Castle of My Skin* is thus the record of the parallel development of the writer as a young man and of political life in the colonial Caribbean. It is a reconstruction both of the world of childhood and adolescence and of a broader Caribbean reality. Lamming accomplishes this through a combination of fictive and autobiographical

[10]I have in mind Henry Louis Gates, Jr.'s theory that "black writers read and critique other black texts as an act of rhetorical self-definition" (290).

[11]See Houston A. Baker, Jr.'s comments on the intersection of these two worlds of discourse and the nature of black narrative (51–52).

[12]I discuss this aspect of the text in some detail in *The Novels of George Lamming* (13–29).

[13]Lamming explains that he wanted to make Creighton's Village "applicable to Barbados, to Jamaica, and to all of the other islands. I wanted to give the village that symbolic quality" (Munro and Sander 8).

modes, and by splitting [the] narrative point of view between first-person and third-person narration.

The autobiographical element of the text is readily identifiable in Lamming's use of the character G. as first-person narrator of a major portion of the narrative, and in the many correspondences between Lamming's own childhood and the characters and events that shape life in Creighton's Village. The articulation of the text's political themes is the explicit concern of the third-person narrator, though these are continually affirmed and verified by the text of G.'s personal narrative. *In the Castle of My Skin* begins and ends with G.'s narrative as one in which the collective experience is sharply individualized. For example, in the opening scenes of the novel, as G. weeps over his ninth birthday, parallels are established with a devastating flood outside. The flood that ruins his birthday wreaks havoc in Creighton's Village. Similar parallels are carefully established and maintained, however unevenly, throughout the narrative. At the end, G.'s departure for the island of Trinidad is paralleled by the dispossession and dislocation of the villagers, as Creighton sells the land on which the village is built, and the feudal structure of village life gives way to the interests of a newly emergent class of native politicians and entrepreneurs. Thus G.'s growth from childhood to young manhood acquires an emblematic quality as his development is measured against changes in his environment (Paquet 14).

The parallel between the growing alienation of the enigmatic G. and the dislocation of the village is convincingly engineered in two structurally distinct voices and modes. Yet Lamming's characterization of the village in the third-person narrative is complementary to the self-representation of the first-person narrative, and contributes obliquely to the representation of G. For the village is the historical and political and sociological reality that both explains and mirrors G.'s ambitions, insecurities, and uncertainties. At the end of the novel, the village as a physical entity ceases to exist. Its population is scattered by the vagaries of landlessness. G. emerges as a surviving fragment of the whole community and, conversely, as a representative figure in whom the future of the village is subsumed. The novel's ending is open. The conclusion suggests that the disintegration of the village is a beginning and not an end. G.'s impending departure from Barbados for Trinidad affirms the ongoing process of the author's life and the beginning of a quest for autonomy. By virtue of G.'s structural function in the narrative, as a correlative to the village's poverty and ignorance and also to the villagers' curiosity about the world, an evolutionary pattern of continuing growth and development, beyond innocence and dependence, is factored into the ending for the island community as well.

The split in [the] narrative point of view juxtaposes chapters of straight autobiography with chapters of third-person narrative that have as their focus not self-revelation, but an examination of the village and island world in which G. grows up. The immediate impact of Lamming's manipulation of the genre is to raise questions about whose story is being told. The autobiographical center of the book is obscured in the fragmentariness and discontinuities of the narrative point of view. The structural design suggests a conscious repression of G.'s voice.

In his introduction to the 1983 Schocken edition of *In the Castle of My Skin*, Lamming gives one explanation for this elaborate architecture: "The book is crowded with names and people, and although each character is accorded a most vivid presence and force of personality, we are rarely concerned with the prolonged exploration of an individual consciousness. It is the collective human substance of the village that commands our attention" (x). Though Lamming overstates the case for the village as central character, his suppression of autobiography in the fashioning of *In the Castle of My Skin* is clear in the text. Instead of the fuller intimacy and deeper psychology expected of autobiography, self-representation is fragmented; it is muted and elusive, as the society that shaped G.'s values and sensibility undergoes radical change. The third-person narrator characterizes G.'s village as a community in the specific terms of characters, acts, events, and dialogues. But, since that community as an historical reality dissolves to be reconstructed by memory and artistic design, it is G.'s individual consciousness, anxious and anguished by his impending departure and the changing social and political reality of the island, that dominates the end of the text.

The emblematic value of G. is largely accomplished by the third-person narrator, who acts as a foil to G.'s innocence and incomprehension. The authoritative voice in the text is that of the omniscient narrator, who understands the significance of historical events, both private and public, from the vantage point of the author at age twenty-three in London, in a way that is unavailable to the younger G., who is departing for Trinidad at the end of the narrative. Tonally, the third-person narrator's voice is much older than twenty-three, and much is gained by the dramatic contrast between G.'s egocentric and, at times, lyrical voice and the detachment and objectivity of the third-person narrator. The author as third-person narrator writes authoritatively about his island world, distancing himself effectively from G. as an enduring metaphor of a consciousness that senses its environment feelingly but is incapable of an organizing perspective. The juxtaposition of G.'s first-person narrative with third-person narrative reflects the author's spatial, temporal, and artistic distance from his childhood and adolescence in Barbados at the time of writing. The text as a dialogue between two structurally and tonally distinct voices dramatizes Lamming's search for a narrative strategy. The double level of discourse is itself a metaphor for the author's growth and development as an artist. It registers the author's transition from a purely egocentric point of view to a more impersonal point of view, from a lyrical voice to a more objective rendering of Caribbean reality.

After the complexities of [the] narrative point of view in *In the Castle of My Skin*, [C. L. R. James'] *Beyond a Boundary* appears very direct and calculated in its use of personal material. Written entirely in the first-person, *Beyond a Boundary*'s authoritative voice is the voice of the mature James, recalling the past selectively and evaluating it in the context of nation building. Here the fractured consciousness and split sensibility of Lamming's *In the Castle of My Skin* is made whole. The vision changes with James and, with it, the situating of narrative perspective and the structuring of content. The self-parody inherent in an autobiography that traces a pattern of growth and development is more smoothly integrated here. Published when he was sixty-two, the novel records James's personal development, from British intellectual to West Indian nationalist, and provides him and his readers with a means of understanding the social, political, and cultural transition from colonialism to independence. With all the authority and persuasiveness he can funnel into his first-person narrative, James chronicles the parallel development of cricket from a ritual of colonial dominance into ritualized resistance and, finally, a ritual celebration of independent selfhood. He writes: "What interests me, and is, I think, of general interest, is that as far back as I can trace my consciousness the original found itself and came to maturity within a system that was the result of centuries of development in another land, was transplanted as a hot-house flower is transplanted and bore some strange fruit" (50). James's tone is confident and celebratory of West Indian selfhood beyond the conflicting legacies of colonialism. Genius subverts and transforms the structures that were meant to confine it. The evidence lies in the double text: James's subversion of a model British public school education into an instrument of revolutionary social change from colony to nationhood, and the cricketer's subversion of cricket into an instrument for the assertion of national spirit.

Beyond a Boundary is explicitly autobiography in the service of something more than the story of a life and deeds done. It begins as a journey back into childhood and village community, the cultural act of the self reading the society that engendered him. James explains exactly what he is not doing in the Preface and in the text itself: "This book is neither cricket reminiscences nor autobiography." Actually, he is doing both these things simultaneously and something more. His theme is social relations, politics, and art. The subject of his text is the self reading cricket. Autobiography is a framework for his ideas about the growth of nationalism in the colonial Caribbean, ironically, nurtured by the very structure of values Britain used to impose its colonial will. *Beyond a Boundary* is about the genesis of a West Indian identity through years of participation in, and observation of, the game of cricket, a popular national sport in its country of origin, Great Britain, and in the West Indies, formerly colonial territories of Great Britain. This is accomplished by integrating two levels of experience, the public and the private. The public arena is the cricket field: "a stage on which selected individuals played representative roles which were charged with social significance. I propose now to place on record some of the characters and as much as I can reproduce (I remember everything) of the social conflict" (72). The private arena is James's own intellectual development up to the time of writing, from child prodigy to political activist and committed nationalist: "A British intellectual before I was ten, already an alien in my own environment among my own people, even my own family. Somehow, from around me I had selected and fastened on to the things that made me whole" (28).

As with *In the Castle of My Skin*, [in *Beyond a Boundary*] autobiography serves a double function. For, while autobiography personalizes history and politics, conversely, autobiography is depersonalized when individual experience is identified as part of a cultural pattern. The individual predicament merges with the collective, and self-definition is achieved in representative terms. James writes himself into the text as witness and participant. His primary concern with the self as autobiographical subject is with the self as an authoritative and reliable way into the collective experience. He continually reidentifies himself in the text as exceptional and, paradoxically, as representative West Indian, colonial, and one of the populace.[14]

Published ten years after *Beyond a Boundary* and twenty years after *In the Castle of My Skin*, [Derek] Walcott's *Another Life* is yet another reformulation of the distinctive nexus between self and colonial history that is at the core of the earlier texts, in which the autobiographical self is used as a vehicle for exploring the collective dilemma. In *Another Life*, the developing artist's self doubles as text for the cultural development of a region. Autobiography is reconceived as the story of others who, conversely, acquire emblematic value not only as aspects of the environment, but as aspects of the self. It is a process in which the individual is defined and subsumed in others. In *In the Castle of My Skin*, Lamming describes self and society in seemingly tangential episodes like the stories of Bots, Bambi, and Bambina (133–41) and Jon, Jen, and Susie (122–25). The same is true of Walcott's cameo portraits of Castries folk from Ajax to Zandoli (3.ii) and his retelling of "The Pact" (4). It is characteristic of James's narrative that he explains the value of childhood heroes like Matthew Bondman and Arthur Jones—how these men "ceased to be merely isolated memories and fell into place as starting points of a connected pattern" (17). Self acquires meaning through the lives of others, and, in the process, the collective reality is transformed into autobiographical myth.

In an early draft of *Another Life*, Walcott isolates an event in his childhood as the appropriate point of departure for an autobiographical text that is charged with social significance. With a boldness of conception that characterizes all three autobiographical texts under scrutiny so far, Walcott's personal history is conceived as the spiritual history of the region: "So, from a green

---

14A troubling silence in this text that abhors racialism is the marginalization of the Indian experience of cricket in Trinidad and Tobago. This is partially explained by the autobiographical nature of the text.

book held in the hands of an astigmatic master, in those mornings of my life when I imagined myself a painter, the spiritual history of this region begins."[15] The text is designed from the outset as autobiography that will serve the multiple functions of self-definition and collective history. It is a portrait of the artist, but it is also cultural assessment, with the artist as a representative figure in the journey from childhood to maturity. It is a mental journey of epic proportions, as Walcott characterizes his childhood in terms of the antithetical values of the colonial Caribbean, then traces the painful process of recovery and restoration of self beyond the disillusionments of post-colonial politics.

The four books of *Another Life* represent distinct phases in Walcott's artistic development. They are organized chiefly around themes and key figures in Walcott's formative years in St. Lucia rather than as chronologically structured events, although each book represents a chronological development in age and experience. The first three books are set in St. Lucia and, like *In the Castle of My Skin*, selectively reconstruct the world of the author's childhood and adolescence up to the point of his departure from the island at the age of eighteen. But the fourth book is another matter: The author/narrator is resident in Trinidad, and in returning to St. Lucia for a short visit, he steps out of the frame of a reconstructed past in St. Lucia into the author/narrator's present and into another world spatially and temporally.

Like James, Walcott is a self-conscious narrator who takes the reader into his confidence about what he is doing. In *Another Life*, Walcott as poet/narrator casts himself in the role of reader of his book-like life. The metaphor is of the ocean, and the poet is seer and reader:

> Verandahs, where the pages of the sea
> are a book left open by an absent master
> in the middle of another life—
> I begin here again,
> begin until this ocean's
> a shut book, and, like a bulb
> the white moon's filaments wane. (i)

From the outset, the author as narrator asserts his authority over the text and frees himself to function openly as reader of the book of Caribbean life. Janet Varner Gunn explains: "As the reader of his or her life, the autobiographer inhabits the hermeneutic universe where all understanding takes place. The autobiographer serves, by this habitation, as the paradigmatic reader; and the autobiographical text, embodying this reading, becomes, in turn, a model of possibilities and problems of all interpretive activity" (22). *Another Life* is explicitly the cultural act of a self reading. Humbly, the author/narrator acknowledges the limitations of his recollections in tranquility, of memories shaped by artistic vision:

---

[15]This manuscript is in the library of the University of the West Indies, Mona, Jamaica.

They have soaked too long in the basin of the mind,
they have drunk the moon-milk
that x-rays their bodies,
the bone tree shows
through the starved skins,
and one has left, too soon,
a reader out of breath (iv)

Walcott makes the nature of his authorial voice, the authority he assumes and its limitations, part of the text he is reading:

three lives dissolve in the imagination,
three loves, art, love and death,
fade from a mirror clouding with this breath,
not one is real, they cannot live or die,
they all exist, they have never existed:
Harry, Dunstan, and Andreuille. (iv)

Historical reality is transformed by the imagination into the reconstructed reality of autobiographical myth. The artist's life acquires context and coherence, not simply as the central character in his own life story, but as a vehicle for narrating the lives of others.

Walcott's autobiographical narrator employs a variety of narrative styles that Edward Baugh calls novelistic (231), ranging from lyric density to conversational nonchalance, to dialogue, and stream-of-consciousness. Having drawn attention to the nature of the text, Walcott, to register shifts in perspective and autobiographical function, changes narrative point of view at will, moving from first to third person and from past to present tense. This manipulation of autobiographical point of view gives Walcott the freedom of a third-person narrator to characterize his childhood in the broad cultural and political terms of colonial servitude. This element of self-parody, as in Lamming's text, dramatizes the autobiographical text as the self in dialogue with earlier versions of the self. In Book One alone, Walcott can be "the student" or "the child" or "I" or "we." Thus, Walcott, as reader and writer of the book of Caribbean life, is able to bridge the gap between different points of view that fracture *In the Castle of My Skin* and to sustain this unity of vision through the four books of *Another Life*.

This process is facilitated by the lyric organization of observation, thought, memory, and feeling as part of a single process. Walcott's assertion that in *Another Life* he abandoned autobiography for elegy and intellectual history appears the logical outcome of the merging of lyrical and autobiographical modes. In fact, when Walcott abandoned the original prose narrative inspired by "Leaving School—VII," the value of the autobiographical "I" changed radically. The shift from prose to verse in the merger of lyrical and autobiographical modes creates an ideal textual environment for both using and transcending the autobiographical self as subject. It reconceives the lyrical voice of Lamming's G. structurally and tonally. Walcott's lyrical voice, like

James's, has final authority over the text. Its pastoral and elegiac values are pronounced as Walcott shapes the text to mourn the suicide of his mentor, Harold Simmons, a representative West Indian artist and intellectual in whom "the fervor and intelligence / of a whole country is found" (20.iv). James had shaped his text to honor Frank Worrell, the victorious first black captain of a West Indian cricket team. His joy is untempered by the bitterness Walcott feels about the neglect suffered by fellow artists in the Caribbean. This bitterness is nonetheless quite distinct from the anguish and uncertainty that characterizes G.'s farewell at the end of *In the Castle of My Skin.*

Another Life makes explicit a continuing dialogue among West Indian writers who seek to establish the foundations of their selfhood in a Caribbean reality. Theirs is the privilege of naming a world in terms that do justice to its deprivations and humiliations and also to its creative potential. When Lamming referenced a youthful Walcott's definition of West Indian selfhood in the title of *In the Castle of My Skin,* he made it clear that his autobiographical work was intended as a critique of Walcott's definition of self in relation to a "brittle china shepherdess," in *Epitaph of the Young:* "You in the castle of your skin, I the swineherd."[16] James continues the autobiographical discourse on West Indian selfhood by critiquing Lamming's text and, by extension, Walcott's early poem, in an authoritative definition of West Indian selfhood as a blend of African and European cultures embodied in James himself and in West Indian cricket. The great cricketer Learie Constantine is a prince on the cricket field (107). Frank Worrell is "crowned with the olive" (251). Walcott's *Another Life* reenters the discourse to state the case for the artist as representative West Indian due to the interdependence of the artist and community. Interestingly, the creative act begins with the community:

> People entered his understanding
> like a wayside church,
> they had built him themselves.
> It was they who had smoothed the wall
> of his clay-colored forehead,
> who made of his rotundity an earthy
> useful object
> holding the clear water of their simple troubles,
> he who returned their tribal names
> to the adze, mattock, midden and cookingpot. (20.iv)

Walcott abandons the descriptive language of castles and princes altogether. The artist is fashioned by the folk, shaped by them into an object that serves their needs.

Vidia Naipaul's *Finding the Center* (1984) stands in sharp contrast to the

---

[16]Lamming misquotes Walcott's line at the end of *The Pleasures of Exile:* "You in the castle of your skin, I among the swineherd" (228). Subsequently, he substitutes *swine* for *swineherd* (228) and effectively rewrites young Walcott's line of verse.

texts of Lamming, James, and Walcott. Yet, in its strenuous attempt to remain self-focused rather than representative, *Finding the Center* reveals an important aspect of East Indian cultural separatedness within a West Indian cultural milieu. *Finding the Center* brings together two previously published narratives, "Prologue to an Autobiography" and its companion piece "The Crocodiles of Yamoussoukro," with a brief Author's Foreword.[17] As an autobiographical text, the book is fragmentary and discontinuous. There are three distinct voices, each reflecting a different aspect of the self. In the Author's Foreword, the first-person narrator is the authoritative interpreter of the two personal narratives that follow. In "Prologue to an Autobiography," the narrator is the self in search of a symbolic landscape that is familial, ethnic, and colonial. In "The Crocodiles of Yamoussoukro," the narrator as traveler is on a sociopolitical mission of self-validation beyond the autobiographical framework described in "Prologue to an Autobiography."

There is much in *Finding the Center* to suggest that Naipaul is writing out of the context established by Lamming, James, and Walcott and is, in a formal sense, critiquing the antecedent texts as a West Indian and a colonial. The narrative voice in the Foreword is that of a mature and accomplished Naipaul reading the texts he has created, an "imperial self" telling the reader how to interpret the narratives that follow (Gunn). Like James before him, Naipaul uses the Foreword to announce that " 'Prologue to an Autobiography,' is not an autobiography, a story of a life or deeds done. It is an account of something less easily seized: my literary beginnings and the imaginative promptings of my many-sided background" (viii). Yet, like *Beyond a Boundary*, it is autobiographical, with specific references to family, friends, places, and events. Naipaul is just as careful about dates, names, and details. "The Crocodiles of Yamoussoukro," he explains, is complementary to the first narrative. It is intended to show "this writer, in his latest development, going about one side of his business: traveling, adding to his knowledge of the world, exposing himself to new people and new relationships" (viii). This self-placement in relation to the reader anticipates the location of the self, structurally and tonally, in the two narratives that follow, as one who revisits his past not to affirm his sense of connection to the landscape of his birth so much as to confirm an enduring sense of alienation and exile.

In "Prologue to an Autobiography," as in its antecedent West Indian texts, Naipaul lays claim to a specific cultural landscape as a way into himself. Self-definition necessitates a return to one's beginnings: "To become a writer, that noble thing, I had thought it necessary to leave. Actually, to write, it was necessary to go back. It was the beginning of self-knowledge" (34). Naipaul explains that his ambition to be a writer is a legacy from his father; self-

---

[17]"Prologue to an Autobiography" originally appeared in *Vanity Fair* Apr. 1983: 51–59, 138–56. The text is dated July–Oct. 1982. "The Crocodiles of Yamoussoukro" originally appeared in *The New Yorker* 14 May 1984: 52–119. The text is dated Nov. 1982–July 1983.

definition necessitates the definition of his father's world. Thus Naipaul's account of his beginnings as a writer is also an account of his family's journey from colonial India to the British colony of Trinidad and Tobago, where they were settled as indentured laborers, in response to a perceived need for a dependable source of labor after the abolition of slavery. The growth and development of the writer are described in terms of a specific cultural context. Naipaul names the collective reality in order to know himself. Self-exploration is an exploration of the Indian experience of Trinidad and the New World: "a story of discovery and growing knowledge" (viii). While the self is not projected as representative of the ethnic experience, Naipaul's experience of that world becomes a point of access into the ethnic experience of several generations. Self-definition is accomplished obliquely by defining his ancestry. He is both subject of this text and vehicle for narrating the experience of others. The individual writer's experience acquires meaning in the context of the collective experience of East Indians in Trinidad as Naipaul makes his extended family representative of the core aspects of the Indian immigrant experience.

Naipaul's attempt to understand his growth and development as a writer is necessarily an attempt to discover the meaning of self in community, to know the self through the stories of others. For example, Naipaul explains that his search for a narrative strategy ends in the story of Bogart, a peripheral figure in his extended family, who fled to Venezuela and was the inspiration of his first book, *Miguel Street*. Naipaul recovers Bogart from the shifting sands of isolated memories as a way of clarifying his own relationship, in voluntary exile, to the community that engendered him: "For all its physical wretchedness and internal tensions, the life of the clan had given us all a start. It had given us a caste certainty, a high sense of the self. Bogart had escaped too soon; still passive, he had settled for nullity" (44). Naipaul sees himself in Bogart, and Bogart becomes the focal point for restarting a narrative of return that Naipaul had begun eight years previously and abandoned: "My narrative ran into the *sands*. It had no center" (vii).

The metaphor of shipwreck, of running "into the sands" is particularly interesting as the description of a narrative without a center, as a failure of creativity that is an absence of perspective. At the end of "The Crocodiles of Yamoussoukro," Naipaul uses sand as a metaphor for his own sense of cultural insecurity as an Indian from Trinidad, where the ancestral connection is fragile and imperfectly known (174–75). The idea of sand is a charged one in the context of Lamming's *In the Castle of My Skin* and Walcott's *Another Life*. In *In the Castle of My Skin*, there are the shifting sands of the beach where the children playfully reenact apocryphal British history (117–19) and where Boy Blue is nearly drowned while trying to catch crabs (151–53). The sand is where G. hides his pebble and is distraught at being unable to recover it (213–15). In *Another Life*, sand is a metaphor for the book of life, where the ocean continually writes and erases the experience of a New World (22.i). The image is of a subterranean history revealed and erased continuously; a metaphor for the poet's and the island's obscured beginnings, for the poet's creative response to the unwritten history of people and place. To both Lamming and Walcott, sand is a metaphor for the colonial condition and the occasion for a creative response that is *In the Castle of My Skin* and *Another Life*. In *Finding the Center*, sand is a metaphor for the Hindu idea of illusion that comes from the contemplation of nothingness (175). It is the existential terror that is the loss of ancestral roots; it is the terror of a New World identity where traditional India is unavailable as an alternative to experiments in cultural fusion.

The existential void of a New World identity is a recurring theme in Naipaul's work, but "The Crocodiles of Yamoussoukro" demonstrates the centrality of the existential nothing to the author's world view. Naipaul is unable to escape the boundaries of the self as traveler and writer. Adding to his knowledge of the world does not mean expanded vision. For Naipaul, the traveler sees only reflections of himself, evidence of his own neurosis. Autobiographical narrative reflects and validates the existential angst of the writer as subject and author. In "Prologue to an Autobiography," Naipaul identifies a fear of extinction as something he inherited from his father, who for years was unable to see himself in a mirror (71). Naipaul makes a vital connection between this inherited fear of extinction and his vocation as a writer: "The fear could be combated only by the exercise of the vocation" (72).

In this context, the self-authenticating, self-defining function of *Finding the Center* seems utterly self-focused. In both its narratives, the world is seen as a series of metaphors of the self, as opposed to the projection of the self in the contours of the world in *In the Castle of My Skin, Beyond a Boundary*, and *Another Life*. In *Finding the Center*, people encountered and situations described mirror and confirm the self's relationship with the world: "I do believe—especially after writing 'Prologue to an Autobiography'—that I would have found equivalent connections with my past and myself wherever I had gone" (ix). Here, Naipaul's autobiographical voice couldn't be further from Walcott's vision, in "The Muse of History," of "the poet carrying entire cultures in his head, bitter perhaps, but unencumbered" (3). There is a singlemindedness to *Finding the Center* that makes for extraordinary clarity. Perhaps, this is the difference between a writer like Naipaul, who "after a time carries his world with him" (viii–ix), and writers like Walcott and James, who carry entire cultures in their heads as they traverse the cultural landscape that is the Caribbean.

The image of the writer as one who writes the self into a specific Caribbean landscape through a process of self-discovery and creation is inverted in *Finding the Center* to become a movement out of that landscape. "The Crocodiles of Yamoussoukro," as a travel narrative, returns the author as narrator to the world he occupies at the time of writing, and it is no particular place. Self-placement is realized exclusively in the context of the writer's perspective and the ritual act of writing. Self-placement is not realized in a particular landscape, but in a cultural space that is New World Hindu and colonial. The author as narrator is the outsider, one whose heightened understanding of his origins in the West Indies exacerbates rather than ameliorates the detachment he feels. Travel, Naipaul writes, "became the substitute for the mature social experience—the deepening knowledge of a society—which my background and the nature of my life denied me. My uncertainty about my role withered: a role was not necessary. I recognized my own instincts as a traveler and was content to be myself, to be what I had always been, a looker. And I learned to look in my own way" (x). His function as a writer is not to serve the community that engendered him. Here Naipaul distinguishes himself from his father, for whom writing "was a version of the pundit's vocation" (54). Naipaul rejects the role of writer as pundit in favor of writing out of a private encounter with the world. In their autobiographical texts, Lamming, James, and Walcott assume the ancestral function of the poet as chronicler of the national experience, as cultural mediator and griot. In *Finding the Center,* Naipaul's autobiographical impulse is a private act of self-definition and self-affirmation.

Despite differences in political and artistic vision, self-definition is contingent on mapping some aspect of the Caribbean social reality in each of these sample texts. For Lamming, writing out of the colonial Caribbean, it is the dismantling of a deeply entrenched but nonetheless corrupt structure of power. For James, writing and publishing ten years later in an independent Trinidad and Tobago, colonialism is a point of departure, not an imprisoning political reality. His text is a personal account of the genesis of a distinctively West Indian style of cricket. Epic in scope and frame of reference, this "cricketer's *Iliad,*" as Walcott describes it (Review 36), celebrates the movement from colonialism to independent statehood as a personal victory and a national one as well. For Walcott, like Lamming and James before him, personal history is conceived as a spiritual history of the region. The inner life of one man dramatizes the character of regional life. For Naipaul, self-definition takes the form of family history in its multifarious parts, and his family history is representative of the Indian immigrant experience in Trinidad across several generations. The ancestral experience is resurrected in terms that are both personal and collective. In each of these texts, the autobiographical self, however discontinuously, is projected in ideal or symbolic terms in relation to a Caribbean landscape that is at once geographical, historical, and cultural. Each text can be read as a successive attempt to create a new narrative space for the representation of self as West Indian (Gates 295). The landscape changes with the angle of vision, and a distinctively West Indian world is illuminated by the discontinuities of autobiographical response in each successive attempt to locate the self in a Caribbean reality.

Works Cited

Baker, Houston A., Jr. *The Journey Back: Issues in Black Literature and Criticism.* Chicago: U of Chicago P, 1980.

Baugh, Edward. "The Poem as Autobiographical Novel: Derek Walcott's 'Another Life' in relation to Wordsworth's 'Prelude' and Joyce's 'Portrait.' " *Awakened Conscience: Studies in Commonwealth Literature.* Ed. C. D. Narasimhaiah. New Delhi: Sterling, 1978. 226–35.

Bruss, Elizabeth. *Autobiographical Acts: The Changing Situation of a Literary Genre.* Baltimore: Johns Hopkins UP, 1974.

Butterfield, Stephen. *Black Autobiography in America.* Amherst: U of Massachusetts P, 1974.

Cooper, Philip. *The Autobiographical Myth of Robert Lowell.* Chapel Hill: U of North Carolina P, 1970.

Gates, Henry Louis, Jr. "The Blackness of Blackness: A Critique of the Sign and the Signifying Monkey." *Black Literature and Literary Theory.* Ed. Gates. New York: Methuen, 1984. 285–321.

Gunn, Janet Varner. *Autobiography: Towards a Poetics of Experience.* Philadelphia: U of Pennsylvania P, 1982.

James, C. L. R. *Beyond a Boundary.* London: Hutchinson, 1963.

Lamming, George. *In the Castle of My Skin.* 1953. New York: Schocken, 1983.

———. *The Pleasures of Exile.* London: Michael Joseph, 1960.

Munro, Ian, and Reinhard Sander, eds. *Kas-Kas.* Austin: African and Afro-American Research Institute, U of Texas at Austin, 1972. 5–21.

Naipaul, V. S. *Finding the Center: Two Narratives.* New York: Knopf, 1984.

Paquet, Sandra Pouchet. *The Novels of George Lamming.* London: Heinemann, 1982.

Smith, Sidonie. *A Poetics of Women's Autobiography: Marginality and the Fictions of Self-Representation.* Bloomington: Indiana UP, 1987.

Walcott, Derek. *Another Life.* New York: Farrar, 1973.

———. *Epitaph for the Young.* Barbados: Advocate, 1949.

———. "Leaving School—VII." *London Magazine* 5 (1965): 4–14.

———. Review of *Beyond a Boundary. New York Times Book Review* 25 Mar. 1984: 36.

———. "The Muse of History." *Is Massa Day Dead?* Ed. Orde Coombs. New York: Anchor, 1974. 1–27.

The Value of Autobiography
for Comparative Studies:
African vs. Western Autobiography

James Olney

"The Value of Autobiography for Comparative Studies: African vs. Western Autobiography"—thus my subject.[1] For texts I have chosen two books with but one title: [Camara] Laye's *L'enfant noir* or *Black Boy* and Richard Wright's *Black Boy* or *L'enfant noir*. Before I reach those two single-titled texts, however, I think it would be useful to say something about autobiography itself, and the first thing that needs saying is that autobiography is not one thing but many. There are, indeed, almost as many senses for the word "autobiography" as there are autobiographies, for every instance of the mode tends to establish its own ad hoc and sui generis conditions and form. This is naturally very troubling for the literary critic who would make of autobiography a literary genre like any other: if every autobiography tends to be sui generis, then of course the critic cannot establish any generic rules or requirements that will fit all the diverse books to which we would agree to give the large and loose title of autobiography. This is the literary critic's problem (or one of his many problems); a different problem besets the historian, or besets anyone who would take autobiography for history and for a resource in the writing of history rather than for literature. Even when autobiography is not outright apologia, there is nevertheless an element of apologetics inevitably present in the writing of it. The very act of writing a life down constitutes an attempt on the writer's part to justify his life, and implicit in every act of autobiography is the judgment that his life is worth being written down. Moreover, the autobiographer always knows the end of his story—or rather, he *is* the end of his story at the moment of writing. And these two inescapable facts about autobiography—that it contains an element

From James Olney, *Comparative Civilizations Review* 2 (1979), 52–64.

[1]This essay was prepared for delivery in a colloquium on "Biographies and Autobiographies as Civilizational Texts" at the eighth annual meeting of the International Society for the Comparative Study of Civilizations. I have not attempted to remove from the essay all signs that it was originally intended for oral presentation.

of apologetics and that the writer is ever aware of where the story is going because he is situated there at the end—make it a body of writing hardly more manageable by the historian than by the literary critic.[2]

But matters are still a good deal more complicated than I have so far suggested. It is my experience that everyone knows what autobiography is— but that no two people agree about what it is. This failure to agree, I believe, is at least partly—perhaps largely—due to differences in understanding the three elements that go to form the word and the concept of autobiography: *autos, bios, graphein; autos,* "the self" or "himself," *bios,* "life," and *graphein,* "to write."[3] Now each of these elements or terms is in itself sufficiently complex, and in the interplay set up by throwing them together in a single word and single act they become vastly more complex. Consider the central term *bios:* this could signify the historic past, whether from the beginning of memory (and earlier) up to the present, or a piece of that past large or small, or even no more than a moment of the past; it could signify the writer's present life—his psychic configuration as he writes; it obviously could be, and no doubt often is, a combination of life as history and life as present quickness; again, it could be life not as an individual property and possession, but life as the mythic history and the psychological character of a whole people—that communal life that gives its impress to the life of every individual within the group; and finally—though this is not really "finally" since there are other possible senses of *bios*—it could signify, as in C. G. Jung's *Memories, Dreams, Reflections* it does signify, psychic development, or what Jung calls the story of the process of self.

I want to pause here a moment to consider what happens to autobiography when one takes *bios* in this last sense. Jung, to whom I will return later, is my best example. In *Memories, Dreams, Reflections* we are presented with the story of Jung's evolving self told by his presently achieved self, and for that kind of involuted and reflexive exercise, in order to distinguish it from other varieties of autobiography, I should like to suggest the name *autoautography.* The word sounds reasonably well on the lips, I think, and it serves to point up the highly individual and individualistic, inturned and self-centered, self-centering nature of Jung's book and of Western autobiography more generally. In Jung's "autoautography" we find a typically Western way of conceiving of life or *bios* with this single difference that Jung's psychiatric profession and his

---

[2]On autobiography as literature, history, and anthropology, see two brilliant essays by George Gusdorf: "Conditions et limites de l'autobiographie," most easily accessible in Philippe Lejeune's *L'Autobiographie en France* (Paris: A. Colin, 1971), and "De l'autographie initiatique à l'autographie genre littéraire," *Revue d'histoire littéraire de la France,* 75 (1975): 957–994. The first of these essays, translated as "Conditions and Limits of Autobiography," . . . appear[s] in a volume from Princeton University Press, *Autobiography: Essays Theoretical and Critical,* ed. James Olney [1980].

[3]Cf., my essay, "Autos*Bios*Graphein," *South Atlantic Quarterly,* 77 (1978): 113–123, and the introduction to *Autobiography: Essays Theoretical and Critical* as well as a separate essay in that volume ("Some Versions of Memory/Some Versions of Bios: The Ontology of Autobiography").

notion of "individuation"[4] rather intensified these general Western tendencies to take the life of the self to be the true life, the real life, the life about which an autobiography should be written.

Now I would like to return to a point I introduced a moment ago and then dropped: the extremely problematical nature of autobiography for literary critics and historians. What I would say is that those very qualities of autobiography that make it so problematic as literature or history conversely make it a uniquely valuable kind of writing for anyone concerned with the comparative study of civilizations. That there are so few or no conventions guiding and constraining the autobiographer may distress the literary critic in search of a corner of literature that he can define in generic terms and can appropriate as his own special area of expertise; but this openness, this freedom, this flexibility of the mode—lending itself to every sort of variation in form and substance—this is very much to the purpose of students of comparative civilization, for the assumptions, the preconceptions, and the preoccupations of a culture will determine to a very great extent the shape of the story that individual members of that culture tell about themselves and their lives. The same is true of those qualities in autobiography that the historian must be wary of—the comparativist will positively rejoice in them. Of course there is an element of apologetics in every autobiography, and the comparativist will find an autobiographer revealing in that which he seems to feel the need for apology—and perhaps even more in that in which he does *not* feel the need for apology. Likewise, that the autobiographer is ever aware of where his story is going because he is situated at the end of it, is a virtue rather than a defect for the investigator of cultural similarities and differences. *Bios,* as I have already remarked, may or may not refer to an historical past, but it must inevitably, willy-nilly reflect and reveal the present time of writing: it cannot fail to reflect and reveal the autobiographer as he is and understands himself to be and wishes himself to be as he sets pen to paper. Hence in autobiography the student of civilizations normally has dual access to the cultural matrix in which the autobiographer locates himself: access by way of what the autobiographer reveals, for the most part consciously, of the past, access by way of what he reveals, for the most part unconsciously, of the present.

With these remarks by way of general background, and before getting at my two central texts, I want to offer what I take to be some classic statements of Western autobiography, its tendencies and motives, and then, for comparison and contrast, some classic statements of African autobiography. I imagine that for many of us the first group of these statements will seem so natural that we will unconsciously assume that "of course this is what autobiography is all about; this is what it must be—by definition." But those who do make this

---

[4]On Jungian "individuation" see these passages in *The Collected Works of C. G. Jung,* 20 vols. (Princeton University Press/Bollingen, 1960–1979): "Conscious, Unconscious, and Individuation," vol. IX, part 1; *Aion,* vol. IX, part 2, paragraphs 408–411; "Answer to Job," vol. XI, paragraphs 755–756; and *Psychological Types,* vol. VI, paragraphs 755–762.

unconscious assumption are leaning on a definition that is not really there (I have never encountered a definition of autobiography that was really adequate to the existing fact) and again those who make this unconscious assumption will be doing no more than showing themselves children of a particular time and place—that is children of the postsixteenth-century Western world. I have chosen as representative of the Western vision—that is to say as representative of the instructured philosophical/psychological presuppositions of Western autobiographers—passages from Montaigne in the sixteenth century, from Rousseau in the eighteenth century, and from Jung in the twentieth century. These three are by no means the same as men or as autobiographers but in them we find certain key phrases or words that seem to echo from the sixteenth to the eighteenth to the twentieth century and that no doubt reveal something of the essential quality of the act of autobiography in the West.

In the essay "Of Presumption" Montaigne says: "The world always looks straight ahead; as for me, I turn my gaze inward [je replie ma vue au dedans], I fix it there and keep it busy. Everyone looks in front of him; as for me, I look inside of me [je regarde dedans moi]; I have no business but with myself; I continually observe myself, I take stock of myself, I taste myself. Others always go elsewhere . . . ; as for me, I roll about in myself [moi je me roule en moi-même—moi/me/moi-même]."[5] In the essay "Of Giving the Lie" Montaigne writes of the reflexive, reciprocal, and (as he calls it) "consubstantial" process of self creation and book creation: "In modeling this figure upon myself, I have had to fashion and compose myself so often to bring myself out, that the model itself has to some extent grown firm and taken shape. Painting myself for others, I have painted my inward self with colors clearer than my original ones. I have no more made my book than my book has made me—a book consubstantial with its author, concerned with my own self, an integral part of my life."[6] And finally Montaigne begins the great essay "Of Repentance" thus: "Others form man; I tell of him, and portray a particular one, very ill-formed, whom I should really make very different from what he is if I had to fashion him over again. But now it is done. . . . I set forth a humble and inglorious life; that does not matter. You can tie up all moral philosophy with a common and private life just as well as with a life of richer stuff. Each man bears the entire form of man's estate [chaque homme porte la forme entière de l'humaine condition]."[7] Critics have complained to me that Montaigne not be called an autobiographer—that he wrote essays not autobiography. My answer must be that in passages like these Montaigne is unquestionably what I earlier called an "autoautographer" and that "autoautography" is as legitimate a variety of autobiography as any other. Before leaving Montaigne I want

---

[5]*The Complete Essays of Montaigne*, tr. Donald M. Frame (Stanford: Stanford University Press, 1958), p. 499. The French is from *Les Essais de Michel de Montaigne*, ed. Pierre Villey, 3 vols. (Paris: Felix Alcan, 1922), II: 443. The spelling of the French has been modernized.
[6]*Complete Essays of Montaigne*, p. 504.
[7]*Complete Essays of Montaigne*, pp. 610–611; *Les Essais de Michel de Montaigne*, III: 26–27.

to point out that his subject is regularly stated in two ways: it is on the one hand this particular man and it is on the other hand, "Man," general and uppercase: Michel de Montaigne on the one hand and in him on the other hand that paradoxical composite of body and soul which is the human condition. But between the particular and the universal there is for Montaigne no intermediate abstraction—nothing really about being Gascon or French, and precious little about being de Montaigne. This again is specifically Western and, as we shall discover, quite different from the view of human existence implicit in African autobiography.

From Rousseau I am going to quote the famous opening of *The Confessions* where, as I say, there are all sorts of echoes from Montaigne, but besides these echoes there are significant differences as well—as it were Western tendencies in autobiography intensified over the two centuries between Montaigne and Rousseau. For in his version of it, Rousseau, drawing his own portrait, discerns only himself and his singularity, not any likeness to other men or any likeness to the entire species.

> I have resolved on an enterprise which has no precedent, and which, once complete, will have no imitator. My purpose is to display to my kind a portrait in every way true to nature, and the man I shall portray will be myself.
> Simply myself. I know my own heart and understand my fellow man. But I am made unlike any one I have ever met; I will even venture to say that I am like no one in the whole world. I may be no better, but at least I am different. Whether Nature did well or ill in breaking the mould in which she formed me, is a question which can only be resolved after the reading of my book.
> Let the last trump sound when it will, I shall come forward with this work in my hand, to present myself before my Sovereign Judge, and proclaim aloud: "Here is what I have done. . . ." I have displayed myself as I was, as vile and despicable when my behaviour was such, as good, generous, and noble when I was so.[8]

"The man I shall portray will be myself. Simply myself." In the original this is "et cet homme, ce sera moi. Moi seul"[9]—or in another manuscript version, intensifying the singularity and emphasizing the isolate uniqueness of himself and his enterprise, it is "ce sera moi. Oui, moi, moi seul."[10] And what the "moi" principally signified for Rousseau he makes perfectly clear at the beginning of Part II of the *Confessions:* "I may omit or transpose facts, or make mistakes in dates; but I cannot go wrong about what I have felt, or about what my feelings have led me to do; and those are the chief subjects of my story. The true object of my confessions is to reveal my inner thoughts

[8]*The Confessions of Jean-Jacques Rousseau*, tr. J. M. Cohen (Harmondsworth, Middlesex: Penguin, 1953), p. 17.
[9]*Oeuvres complètes de Jean-Jacques Rousseau*, eds. Bernard Gagnebin and Marcel Raymond, 3 vols. (Paris: Bibliothèque de la Pléiade, 1959), I: 5.
[10]From the Neuchâtel ms. Cf. *Oeuvres complètes*, I: 1232, note 3, and "Ébauches des Confessions," *Oeuvres complètes*, I: 1149.

exactly in all the situations of my life. It is the history of my soul that I have promised to recount, and to write it faithfully I have need of no other memories; it is enough if I enter again into my inner self [il me suffit . . . de rentrer au dedans de moi]."[11] Yes, me, me alone—a bundle of emotions and sentiments, an acute sensibility rubbed to the quick by the paranoid feeling that his enemies were omnipresent. How utterly different from the temperate moderation, the security, the serenity, the maturity of Montaigne; and yet Montaigne, no less than Rousseau, rolled in himself and turned his gaze endlessly and only "dedans moi."

Listen likewise to Jung in the "prologue" to his autobiography: "My life is a story of the self-realization of the unconscious. . . . I cannot employ the language of science to trace this process of growth in myself, for I cannot experience myself as a scientific problem. . . . Thus it is that I have now undertaken, in my eighty-third year, to tell my personal myth. I can only make direct statements, only 'tell stories.' Whether or not the stories are 'true' is not the problem. The only question is whether what I tell is *my* fable, *my* truth."[12] Behind the words of this prologue one hears the ghostly echo of Montaigne's saying "Others form man; I tell of him, and portray a particular one" and of Rousseau's "Oui, moi, moi seul." On the penultimate page of his book Jung in effect returns to the beginning and to the essential rationale of his "autoautography": "I am satisfied with the course my life has taken. . . . Much might have been different if I myself had been different. But it was as it had to be; for all came about because I am as I am."[13] There is, I think, a nice balance in Jung of the serenity of Montaigne and the anxiety of Rousseau, but in Jung's "I am as I am" do we not have the great I AM that is the whole logic of the *Essays*, of the *Confessions*, and of *Memories, Dreams, Reflections*? Indeed, is not the great I AM or I AM THAT I AM, the whole logic of autobiography wherever and whenever written?

No, is the answer to the question; no, it is not. "Autoautography" is one kind of autobiography, but not the only one, and if we look to Africa we will find plenty of autobiography—of a special variety for which I shall propose a name in a minute—but we will find scarcely a single instance of "autoautography." "I was thankful," Noni Jabavu writes in her autobiographical book [*The*] *Ochre People*, "that we were each brought up to feel ourselves a symbol, 'a representative of a group' not of a family only, and not as a private person. . . . 'A person is a person (is what he is) because of and through other people.' "[14] This feeling the Xosa have about the real reality of human existence is as far removed from Montaigne's "dedans moi" or Rousseau's

---

[11]*Confessions*, tr. Cohen, p. 262; *Oeuvres complètes*, I: 278.
[12]C. G. Jung, *Memories, Dreams, Reflections*, recorded and edited by Aniela Jaffe, tr. Richard and Clara Winston (New York: Vintage, 1965), p. 3.
[13]*Memories, Dreams, Reflections*, p. 358.
[14]Noni Jabavu, *The Ochre People: Scenes from a South African Life* (New York: St. Martin's Press, 1963), p. 69.

"Oui, moi, moi seul" or Jung's "I am as I am"—as far removed as the civilization of the Xosa or Zulu people is from the civilization of France or Switzerland. The whole logic of African autobiography and the nature of the *bios* around which African autobiography forms itself are there in the notion that "a person is what he is because of and through other people" or in the notion that the Sonjo people (as reported by John Mbiti) hold: "I am because we are, and since we are, therefore I am."[15] An autobiography that takes its orientation in this premise will not say, as Jung's book says, "I am as I am" but will say instead, "I am as we are." For this latter variety of autobiography I promised a new name, replacing *bios* with a different word that should indicate more precisely what the African autobiographer would mean by the "life" that provides the subject of his book. For *bios* I suggest *phyle* which a Greek-English lexicon defines as "*a union among the citizens* of a state, *a class or tribe* formed according to blood, *a class* or *caste*. 2. later, *a union according to local habitation, a tribe*"; and for the variety or autobiography specific to Africa I propose "autophylography." For the life-portrait that the African autobiographer executes is not the portrait of "moi, moi seul," where the subject makes a claim of absolute uniqueness and imagines that his experience is unrepeated and unrepeatable; instead the African autobiographer executes a portrait of "nous, nous ensemble," and the life shared by the group now—by the phyle—is one lived countless times before, shaped by the ritual stages of birth and naming, initiation, marriage, parenthood, eldership, and death that have given form to the life of this people for as far back as the legendary, mythic memory of the people extends. Thus even memory, the chief faculty of the man who would write his own life, is not a personal faculty but a collective one for the African autobiographer, and about the myth that he tells—the myth that is the formative fact of his *bios*—there is nothing of what Jung means by "my *personal* myth." [italics added]

This is the logic according to which two Gikuyu autobiographers, Charity Waciuma and R. Mugo Gatheru—or shall I call them two Gikuyu autophylographers?—begin their books, in striking contrast to the beginning of Rousseau's *Confessions* or Jung's *Memories, Dreams, Reflections*. Charity Waciuma starts her book, significantly titled *Daughter of Mumbi*, with a chapter called "Names" and, after explaining why she was named Wanijiku instead of Waithira as she should have been as the third daughter, she goes on to say: "These are both names of daughters of Gikuyu and Mumbi, the legendary founders of my people. . . . In our country names are not chosen haphazardly; they are vitally bound up with being the sort of person you are. Any name includes many people who are now dead, others who are living, and those who are still not born."[16] As Noni Jabavu would have it—"A person

---

[15]John Mbiti, *African Religions and Philosophy* (Garden City, N.Y.: Doubleday and Co., 1970), p. 152.

[16]Charity Waciuma, *Daughter of Mumbi* (Nairobi: East African Publishing House, 1969), pp. 7–8.

is indeed what he is because of and through other people." A few pages later, Charity Waciuma says, "We are the clan of Achera, which is also called Giceri, and we are the descendents of Njeri, the daughter of Gikuyu."[17] So the life or the *bios* of Charity Waciuma's book begins not with the birth of "moi, moi seul" but with the founding of clans and tribe by Gikuyu and Mumbi, the father and the mother of the Gikuyu people. In thus using collective memory to trace the line back through history and legend to learn the very beginning, Charity Waciuma does the same thing as half a dozen other Gikuyu autobiographers[18]—and she does what no autobiographer in the Western world has ever done or will do: that is, begin the writing of his or her own life with Adam and Eve and the Garden of Eden. Hers is myth in the proper sense—collective myth, not Jungian personal myth. Like Charity Waciuma, Mugo wa Gatheru begins with a name—a name shared from generation to generation as the life has been shared from generation to generation: "My name is Mugo, which in the language of my fathers means 'Man of God.' I come from a long line of men who have borne this name, a line stretching far, far back into time."[19] Two pages later Mugo tells the story of "The Children of Mumbi and Kikuyu"; he names his clan and legendary ancestor (Warigia, eighth of the nine daughters); and he thus locates his life in the life of his people. Mugo wa Gatheru's book—he calls it *Child of Two Worlds*—becomes something different when he goes to America and England, but here at the beginning and in its original premise about the nature of human existence, it is clearly an instance of that special African mode that I have named autophylography.

This brings me at last to my two crucial, mono-titled texts, *L'enfant noir* and *Black Boy*. I have chosen these two books for a number of reasons: not only because, while bearing a single title they are radically different in manner and matter, but also because they are both typical and a-typical of, respectively, African autobiography and Western autobiography. What I mean is that *L'enfant noir* is autophylography—but it is a variation on the pure African type; *Black Boy* is autoautography—but it too is a variation, on the pure Western type. And I think that holding the two books up together might shed considerable light on the value of autobiography for comparative studies.

L'enfant noir and *Black Boy* share not only a title but a number of other features as well: both are by black men writing of a people and an experience in one way or another threatened by a white world; both were written at a considerable distance—in time, in place, in environment—from the experiences recounted; both begin in early childhood—Camara Laye five years old, Richard Wright four years old; and both conclude with the "I" of the narrative

---

[17]*Daughter of Mumbi*, p. 13.
[18]See James Olney, *Tell Me Africa: An Approach to African Literature* (Princeton: Princeton University Press, 1973), chapter II, "Children of Gikuyu and Mumbi."
[19]R. Mugo Gatheru, *Child of Two Worlds* (London: Routledge and Kegan Paul, 1964), p. 1.

leaving the place where he grew up and leaving the world that determined the nature of that growing up. With all these things in common, the books are about as different the one from the other as they could well be. Both narratives begin with what the authors take to be significant and determinative events in their childhood—but while Camara Laye starts with himself playing around his father's hut and learning something about the mysterious snake that is said to be the guiding spirit both of his father and his people,[20] Richard Wright starts with himself burning the house down and receiving from his mother a terrific beating that, in his own words, "came close to killing me."[21] In these two opening scenes Camara Laye and Wright establish the respective tones that their narratives will exhibit throughout: the one depicting a world of mystery, but a world also of warmth and security where the individual is embraced by the family, where the boy hardly distinguishes his own being from the being of his parents—especially his mother—and where man and nature are not at odds, but are, as it were, enacting different roles in one and the same drama of religious mystery; the other—Wright's—is a world of fear, of violence, and of racial insecurity, a world where the only warmth is from the burning house and the consequent beating and where the chief desire of the boy is to flee from his parents and from all that they and his childhood represent. It is typical and telling of the differences between the two books that Wright's intention in telling his story is to distance himself from his bitterly unhappy childhood experiences as much as possible while Camara Laye's intention is to recreate those experiences and in the telling to relive those better, happier days of childhood. Likewise, at the end of his narrative, when Camara Laye leaves Guinea for France, he feels it as "un affreux déchirement,"[22] a terrible tearing apart, as if his very being and the fabric of existence were being torn to shreds when he parts from that family of which he could say, "I am because we are, and since we are, therefore I am"; on the other hand, Wright concludes his narrative, as he leaves the South for Chicago, with the remark, "This was the culture from which I sprang. This was the terror from which I fled. The next day . . . I was already in full flight—aboard a northward bound train. . . ."[23] What for Camara Laye was "un affreux déchirement," something dreaded in both prospect and in retrospect, was for Wright an almost unimaginable good, flight from terror to freedom—or so he thought—freedom to become the writer he felt he was destined to be. Now one might say that these dissimilarities are a consequence of merely incidental differences in the immediate worlds in which Camara Laye and Wright grew up; but I don't think this is sufficient. I think the two writers hold radically different concepts of the self and that these

---

[20]Camara Laye, *L'enfant noir* (Paris: Librairie Plon, 1954).

[21]Richard Wright, *Black Boy: A Record of Childhood and Youth* (New York: Harper and Row, 1966), p. 133. *Black Boy* was first published in 1945.

[22]*L'enfant noir*, p. 253.

[23]*Black Boy*, p. 281.

radically different concepts of the self lead to radically different notions of what constitutes the proper *bios* of autobiography. To turn the matter around: if we examine the *bios* that each realizes in autobiography, we will have some insight into the different concepts of self and life maintained typically by Africa and the West. There are many possible scenes in which one could examine these matters, but the best, I think, will be the scene of Camara Laye's initiation and the scene of Richard Wright's reluctantly agreeing to be baptized.

Again there are certain similarities between the two scenes—naturally, for initiation and baptism after all have much the same ritual significance about them. In both accounts there is the group of uninitiated, unbaptized boys on the one hand, and on the other, the whole people, the unified tribe, the community of believers waiting to receive the boys now reborn into young manhood. But how different the two accounts are in tone and texture and how widely separate they are in the social, psychological, and cultural significance they bear. Camara Laye's description of intitiation, although of course it comes out of the personal experience of going through circumcision, is for the most part cast in the first person *plural: we* did thus and so, and this and that was done to *us*. This is the "we" of the boys, which after the ceremony will become the "we" of the Malinké people. "We had to be 'big' in every sense of the word, and that meant we had to become men," he says at the outset of his account. "My companions felt the same; like myself they were prepared to pay for it with their blood. Our elders before us had paid for it thus; those who were born after us would pay for it in their turn. Why should we be spared? Life itself would spring from the shedding of our blood."[24] And over against the boys, waiting for them to come through, is the whole body of the people, anticipating the new access of life that will come from the ritual shedding of blood. "The whole town danced with us!" Camara Laye says: "The whole town came, because the test, so very important to us, had much the same importance for all. No one could be indifferent to the fact that this second birth, our real birth, would increase the population of the town by a new group of citizens."[25] One thing that helps to bring the boys successfully through their ordeal is the sure knowledge that this is not a unique experience, either in their time or in the generations before and after, and the sure sense also that no one of the boys or anyone else in the community exists as "moi, moi seul." Of the last moments before the actual circumcision Camara Laye says, "The whole town stayed awake and danced all through the night. . . . If we had not been urged on, carried away by the tom-tom beat. . . . But it urged us on, carried us away!"[26]—as if it were the heartbeat

[24]*L'enfant noir*, pp. 143, 145. There are two translations of *L'enfant noir* in English, one by James Kirkup alone, *The African Child* (London: Collins, 1959), the other by Kirkup with revisions—quite badly done—by Ernest Jones, *The Dark Child* (New York: Noonday Press, n.d.). This passage occurs on pp. 93–94 of *African Child*, on pp. 111 and 113 of *Dark Child*.

[25]*L'enfant noir*, p. 146; *African Child*, p. 95; *Dark Child*, p. 114.

[26]*L'enfant noir*, p. 160; *African Child*, p. 102; *Dark Child*, p. 122.

of the village, the heartbeat of the boys becoming men, the heartbeat of the whole people who at the very end retire to their huts to await "the ceremonial shots that would announce to all that one more man, one more Malinké, had been born."[27] When the ritual is accomplished, messengers rush to the families of the boys shouting "Truly your son has been very brave"—"And indeed," Camara Laye adds, "we had all been very brave. We had all concealed our fear very carefully."[28]

With Richard Wright it is not fear that must be concealed—though his book is full of violence and fear—but rather his disgust and bitter anger as an individual at being forced and violated by the community or, as he calls it, "the tribe"; and the result of his forced submission to the enemy—for that is pretty much what the community was for Wright—was that after the fact he felt not (like Camara Laye) more of a man but less than one. When the revival came to town, Wright says, "My mother tried to persuade me to join, to save my soul at last, to become a member of a responsible community church,"[29] and Wright reluctantly agreed to attend the revival meeting, where he and the other unbaptized boys—to Wright's profound dismay and disgust—were quickly moved up in front of the congregation. "Some part of me was cursing," he says, and one has the sense that it was a very large part, if not indeed the whole of him that thus cursed the situation he was in. When the preacher calls the mothers, including Wright's crippled mother, to join him in his emotional blackmail of the boys, this is how Wright describes the scene: "The mothers knelt. My mother grabbed my hands and I felt hot tears scalding my fingers. I tried to stifle my disgust. We young men had been trapped by the community, the tribe in which we lived. . . . The tribe, for its own safety, was asking us to be at one with it."[30] As the pressure on the lone individual increases and the blackmail intensifies, the preacher calls out, "Now, I'm asking the first mother who really loves her son to bring him to me for baptism!" and Wright's silent reaction is highly typical:

Goddamn, I thought. It had happened quicker than I had expected. My mother was looking steadily at me.

"Come, son, let your old mother take you to God," she begged. . . .

This business of saving souls had no ethics; every human relationship was shamelessly exploited. In essence, the tribe was asking us whether we shared its feelings; if we refused to join the church, it was equivalent to saying no, to placing ourselves in the position of moral monsters. One mother led her beaten and frightened son to the preacher amid shouts of amen and hallelujah.[31]

Other boys, weaker than Wright, less individualistic than he, and so more

[27]*L'enfant noir*, p. 160; *African Child*, p. 102; *Dark Child*, p. 123.
[28]*L'enfant noir*, p. 162; *African Child*, p. 104; *Dark Child*, p. 124.
[29]*Black Boy*, p. 167.
[30]*Black Boy*, p. 169.
[31]*Black Boy*, p. 170.

vulnerable to the overwhelming, insidious pressure put on them by the community, give in one by one and defect to the enemy; only Wright holds out to the bitter end, but even he is finally beaten and surrenders, but one could hardly say that it is with a good grace.

> "Don't you love your old crippled mother, Richard?" my mother asked. "Don't leave me standing here with my empty hands," she said, afraid that I would humiliate her in public.
>
> It was no longer a question of my believing in God; it was no longer a matter of whether I would steal or lie or murder; it was a simple, urgent matter of public pride, a matter of how much I had in common with other people. If I refused, it meant that I did not love my mother, and no man in that tight little black community had ever been crazy enough to let himself be placed in such a position. My mother pulled my arm and I walked with her to the preacher and shook his hand, a gesture that made me a candidate for baptism. There were more songs and prayers; it lasted until well after midnight. I walked home limp as a rag; I had not felt anything except sullen anger and a crushing sense of shame.[32]

It was a question, Wright says, "of how much I had in common with other people"—and the answer to the question must be "precious little." For it is not what he has in common with the community that makes him shake the preacher's hand—on the contrary, it is the simple, superior, brute strength of that community—a strength that is altogether alien to Wright, not something he shares—that forces him to submit. And surely the "sullen anger" and "crushing sense of shame" Wright experiences are a result of his feeling that he has violated—or has allowed the community to violate—his private, individual, isolate self: his *real* self, not his social self, his "moi, moi seul," which only he knows and only he could know and which his autobiography— in certain ways his autoautography—is dedicated to realizing for Wright and his reader alike.

This, I think, is enough to say about *L'enfant noir* and *Black Boy*, about African and Western autobiography, and about the value of autobiography for comparative studies. Here at the conclusion it occurs to me that the title of my paper should have been "Two Varieties of Autobiography: Autophylography and Autoautography"—but I didn't know that until I had finished writing the paper.

---

[32]*Black Boy*, p. 170.

Chronology of Important Dates

1619	First Africans brought to North America
1661	First legal recognition of slavery in a North American colony (Virginia)
1700	*The Selling of Joseph*, by Samuel Sewall, first antislavery pamphlet in North America
1760	*A Narrative of the Uncommon Sufferings, and Surprizing Deliverance of Briton Hammon, a Negro Man*, the first African American autobiography
1770	*A Narrative of the Most Remarkable Particulars in the Life of James Albert Ukawsaw Gronniosaw, an African Prince*
1776	*Declaration of Independence* of the United States from Great Britain
1789	*The Interesting Narrative of the Life of Olaudah Equiano, or Gustavus Vassa, the African, Written by Himself*, first internationally best-selling African American autobiography
1808	Prohibition of the African slave trade by the U.S. Congress
1831	Nat Turner's Insurrection in Southampton, Virginia
	Founding of the New England Anti-Slavery Society, headed by William Lloyd Garrison
1845	*Narrative of the Life of Frederick Douglass, an American Slave, Written by Himself*
1855	Frederick Douglass, *My Bondage and My Freedom*
1861	Harriet Jacobs, *Incidents in the Life of a Slave Girl*
1896	"Separate but equal" doctrine of segregation upheld by the U.S. Supreme Court
1901	Booker T. Washington, *Up from Slavery*
1931	Death of Ida B. Wells
1942	Zora Neale Hurston, *Dust Tracks on a Road*
1945	Richard Wright, *Black Boy*
1953	George Lamming, *In the Castle of My Skin*
1954	Segregation in public schools outlawed by U.S. Supreme Court; Camara Laye, *L'enfant noir*

1965	*The Autobiography of Malcolm X*
1968	*The Autobiography of W. E. B. Du Bois*
1969	Maya Angelou, *I Know Why the Caged Bird Sings*
1970	Ida B. Wells, *Crusade for Justice*
1973	Derek Walcott, *Another Life*
1974	Theodore Rosengarten, *All God's Dangers: The Life of Nate Shaw*
1982	Audre Lorde, *Zami: A New Spelling of My Name*
1987	Kesho Scott, Cherry Muhanji, Egyirba High, *Tight Spaces* (American Book Award)

Notes on Contributors

WILLIAM L. ANDREWS is Joyce and Elizabeth Hall Professor of English at the University of Kansas. He is the author of *To Tell a Free Story: The First Century of Afro-American Autobiography, 1760–1865* (1986), the editor of *Sisters of the Spirit: Three Black Women's Autobiographies of the Nineteenth Century* (1986), and general editor of Wisconsin Studies in American Autobiography, published by the University of Wisconsin Press.

JOANNE M. BRAXTON is Frances L. and Edwin L. Cummings Professor of American Studies and English at the College of William and Mary. She is the author of *Black Women Writing Autobiography: A Tradition within a Tradition* (1989) and co-editor (with Andree N. McLaughlin) of *Wild Women in the Whirlwind: The Renaissance in Contemporary Afra-American Writing* (1990).

HAZEL V. CARBY is Professor of English and Afro-American Studies at Yale University. She has written *Reconstructing Womanhood: The Emergence of the Afro-American Woman Novelist* (1987) and has edited *The Empire Strikes Back: Race and Racism in Seventies Britain* (1982).

CHARLES T. DAVIS, (d. 1981) was Professor of English and Afro-American Studies at Yale University. He was the author of *Black Is the Color of the Cosmos* (1982) and co-editor (with Henry Louis Gates, Jr.) of *The Slave's Narrative* (1985).

PAUL JOHN EAKIN is the author of *Fictions in Autobiography* (1985) and *Touching the World: Reference in Autobiography* (1992), and the editor of *American Autobiography: Retrospect and Prospect* (1991). He is Professor of English at Indiana University.

HENRY LOUIS GATES, JR., is the W. E. B. Du Bois Professor of Humanities at Harvard University. Among his best known works are two critical studies: *Figures in Black: Words, Signs, and the "Racial" Self* (1987) and *The Signifying Monkey: A Theory of Afro-American Literary Criticism* (1988).

GEORGE E. KENT (d. 1982) was Professor of English at the University of Chicago and the author of *Blackness and the Adventure of Western Culture* (1971).

FRANÇOISE LIONNET is Associate Professor of French and Comparative Literature at Northwestern University and the author of *Autobiographical Voices: Race, Gender, Self-Portraiture* (1989).

DEBORAH E. MCDOWELL is Professor of English at the University of Virginia. A contributor to many collections of criticism, she is the editor of the Black Women Writers Series, published by the Beacon Press, and is co-editor (with Arnold Rampersad) of *Slavery and the Literary Imagination* (1989).

JAMES OLNEY is Voorhies Professor of English at the Louisiana State University. Among his books are *Metaphors of Self: The Meaning of Autobiography* (1972) and an edited collection, *Autobiography: Essays Theoretical and Critical* (1980).

SANDRA POUCHET PAQUET is the author of *The Novels of George Lamming* (1982) and other essays on Caribbean literature. She is Associate Professor of English at the University of Miami.

ROBERT B. STEPTO is Professor of English, American Studies, and Afro-American Studies at Yale University. He has authored *From Behind the Veil: A Study of Afro-American Literature* (1979) and has edited *The Selected Poems of Jay Wright* (1987).

ALBERT E. STONE is Professor of American Studies and English at the University of Iowa. His books include *Autobiographical Occasions and Original Acts* (1982) and *The Return of Nat Turner: History, Literature, and Cultural Politics in Sixties America* (1992).

Bibliography

Books

Andrews, William L., ed. *Critical Essays on Frederick Douglass*. Boston: G. K. Hall, 1991.

——. *To Tell a Free Story: The First Century of Afro-American Autobiography, 1760–1865*. Urbana: University of Illinois Press, 1986.

Andrews, William L., and Nellie Y. McKay, eds. *Twentieth-Century African-American Autobiography*. Special issue of *Black American Literature Forum* 24 (Summer 1990): 197–413.

Barton, Rebecca Chalmers. *Witnesses for Freedom: Negro Americans in Autobiography*. New York: Harper, 1948.

Bloom, Harold, ed. *Richard Wright's* Black Boy. New York: Chelsea House, 1988.

Braxton, Joanne M. *Black Women Writing Autobiography*. Philadelphia: Temple University Press, 1989.

Brignano, Russell C. *Black Americans in Autobiography*. Durham, N.C.: Duke University Press, 1984.

Butterfield, Stephen. *Black Autobiography in America*. Amherst: University of Massachusetts Press, 1974.

Costanzo, Angelo. *Surprizing Narrative: Olaudah Equiano and the Beginnings of Black Autobiography*. Westport, Conn.: Greenwood, 1987.

Davis, Charles T., and Henry Louis Gates, Jr., eds. *The Slave's Narrative*. New York: Oxford University Press, 1985.

Dudley, David L. *My Father's Shadow: Intergenerational Conflict in African American Men's Autobiography*. Philadelphia: University of Pennsylvania Press, 1991.

Foster, Frances Smith. *Witnessing Slavery: The Development of Ante-bellum Slave Narratives*. Westport, Conn.: Greenwood, 1979.

McPherson, Dolly A. *Order Out of Chaos: The Autobiographical Works of Maya Angelou*. New York: Peter Lang, 1990.

Nichols, Charles H. *Many Thousand Gone: The Ex-Slaves' Account of Their Bondage and Freedom*. Leiden: E. J. Brill, 1963.

Sekora, John, and Darwin T. Turner, eds. *The Art of Slave Narrative*. Macomb, Il: Western Illinois University, 1982.

Smith, Sidonie. *Where I'm Bound: Patterns of Slavery and Freedom in Black American Autobiography*. Westport, Conn.: Greenwood, 1974.

Starling, Marion Wilson. *The Slave Narrative: Its Place in American History*. Boston: G. K. Hall, 1981.

Sundquist, Eric, ed. *Frederick Douglass: New Literary and Historical Essays*. Cambridge, England: Cambridge University Press, 1990.

Substantive Treatments in Books

Baker, Houston A., Jr. *Blues, Ideology, and Afro-American Literature*. Chicago: University of Chicago Press, 1984.

———. *The Journey Back: Issues in Black Literature and Criticism*. Chicago: University of Chicago Press, 1980.

———. *Long Black Song: Essays in Black American Literature and Culture*. Charlottesville: University Press of Virginia, 1972.

Cooke, Michael G. *Afro-American Literature in the Twentieth Century*. New Haven: Yale University Press, 1984.

Dixon, Melvin. *Ride Out the Wilderness: Geography and Identity in Afro-American Literature*. Urbana: University of Illinois Press, 1987.

Evans, Mari, ed. *Black Women Writers (1950–1980)*. New York: Doubleday, 1984.

Fisher, Dexter, and Robert B. Stepto, eds. *Afro-American Literature: The Reconstruction of Instruction*. New York: Modern Language Association, 1979.

Franklin, H. Bruce. *Prison Literature in the United States: The Victim as Criminal and Artist*. New York: Oxford University Press, 1989.

Gates, Henry Louis, Jr. *Figures in Black: Words, Signs, and the "Racial" Self*. New York: Oxford University Press, 1986.

———. *The Signifying Monkey*. New York: Oxford University Press, 1988.

Gwin, Minrose C. *Black and White Women of the Old South*. Knoxville: University of Tennessee Press, 1985.

Harper, Michael S. and Robert B. Stepto, eds. *Chant of Saints: A Gathering of Afro-American Literature, Art, and Scholarship*. Urbana: University of Illinois Press, 1979.

Hull, Gloria T., Patricia Bell Scott, and Barbara Smith, eds. *But Some of Us Are Brave: Black Women's Studies*. Old Westbury, N.Y.: Feminist Press, 1982.

Jackson, Blyden. *A History of Afro-American Literature: The Long Beginning, 1746–1895*. Baton Rouge: Louisiana State University Press, 1989.

Loggins, Vernon. *The Negro Author: His Development in America to 1900*. New York: Columbia University Press, 1931.

Olney, James. *Tell Me Africa: An Approach to African Literature*. Princeton: Princeton University Press, 1973.

Smith, Sidonie, and Julie Watson, eds. *De/Colonizing the Subject: The Politics of Gender in Women's Autobiography*. Minneapolis: University of Minnesota Press, 1992.

Smith, Valerie. *Self-Discovery and Authority in Afro-American Narrative*. Cambridge: Harvard University Press, 1987.

Stepto, Robert B. *From Behind the Veil: A Study of Afro-American Narrative*. Urbana: University of Illinois Press, 1979.

Stone, Albert E. *Autobiographical Occasions and Original Acts*. Philadelphia: University of Pennsylvania Press, 1982.

Yellin, Jean Fagan. *Women and Sisters: The Antislavery Feminists in American Culture*. New Haven: Yale University Press, 1989.

Essays and Articles

Adams, Timothy Dow. "Richard Wright: 'Wearing the Mask,' " 69–83. In *Telling Lies in Modern American Autobiography*. Chapel Hill: University of North Carolina Press, 1990.

Andrews, William L. "Reunion in the Postbellum Slave Narrative: Frederick Douglass and Elizabeth Keckley." *Black American Literature Forum* 24 (Spring 1989): 5–16.

———. "The 1850s: The First Afro-American Literary Renaissance," In *Literary Romanticism in America*, 38–60. Baton Rouge: Louisiana State University Press, 1981.

———. "Toward a Poetics of Afro-American Autobiography." In *Afro-American Literary Study in the 1990s*, ed. Houston A. Baker, Jr., and Patricia Redmond, 78–91. Chicago: University of Chicago Press, 1989.

Bigsby, C. W. E. "The Public Self: The Black Autobiography." In *The Second Black Renaissance*, 182–206. Westport, Conn.: Greenwood, 1980.

Blassingame, John W., ed. Introduction. *Slave Testimony*, xcii–lxv. Baton Rouge: Louisiana State University Press, 1977.

Burger, Mary W. "I, Too, Sing America: The Black Autobiographer's Response to Life in the Midwest and the Mid-Plains." *Kansas Quarterly* 7 (Summer 1975): 43–57.

Cooke, Michael G. "Modern Black Autobiography in the Tradition." In *Romanticism*, ed. D. Thorburn and G. Hartman, 255–80. Ithaca: Cornell University Press, 1973.

Cox, James M. "Autobiography and Washington." In *Recovering Literature's Lost Ground*, 121–43. Baton Rouge: Louisiana State University Press, 1989.

Cudjoe, Selwyn R. "Maya Angelou: The Autobiographical Statement Updated." In *Reading Black, Reading Feminist*, ed. Henry Louis Gates, Jr., 272–306. New York: Penguin, 1990.

Ellison, Ralph. "Richard Wright's Blues." *Antioch Review* 3 (1945): 198–211.

Foster, Frances Smith. "Adding Color and Contour to Early American Self-Portraitures: Autobiographical Writings of Afro-American Women." In *Conjuring*, ed. Marjorie Pryse and Hortense J. Spillers, 25–38. Bloomington: Indiana University Press, 1985.

———. "African American Progress-Report Autobiographies." In *Redefining American Literary History*, ed. A. Lavonne Brown Ruoff and Jerry W. Ward, Jr., 270–83. New York: Modern Language Association, 1990.

———. " 'In Respect to Females . . .': Differences in the Portrayals of Women by Male and Female Narrators." *Black American Literature Forum* 15 (Summer 1981): 66–70.

Fox-Genovese, Elizabeth. "My Statue, My Self: Autobiographical Writings of Afro-American Women." In *The Private Self*, ed. Shari Benstock, 63–89. Chapel Hill: University of North Carolina Press, 1988.

Gibson, Donald B. "Reconciling Public and Private in Frederick Douglass's *Narrative*." *American Literature* 57 (December 1985): 549–69.

Hedin, Raymond. "The American Slave Narrative: The Justification of the Picaro." *American Literature* 53 (January 1982): 630–45.

———. "Paternal at Last: Booker T. Washington and the Slave Narrative Tradition." *Callaloo* 2 (1979): 95–102.

Johnson, Barbara. "Thresholds of Difference: Structures of Address in Zora Neale

Hurston." In *"Race," Writing, and Difference*, ed. Henry Louis Gates, Jr., 317–28. Chicago: University of Chicago Press, 1985.

Kinnamon, Kenneth. "Call & Response: Intertextuality in Two Autobiographical Works by Richard Wright and Maya Angelou." In *Belief vs. Theory in Black American Literary Criticism*, ed. Joe Weixlmann and Chester J. Fontenot, 121–34. *Studies in Black American Literature*, vol. 2. Greenwood, Fla.: Penkevill, 1986.

Lionnet, Françoise. "Con Artiste and Storytellers: Maya Angelou's Problematic Sense of Audience." In *Autobiographical Voices: Race, Gender, Self-Portraiture*, 130–66. Ithaca: Cornell University Press, 1989.

McKay, Nellie Y. "Race, Gender, and Cultural Context in Zora Neale Hurston's *Dust Tracks on a Road*." In *Life/Lines: Theorizing Women's Autobiography*, eds. Bella Brodzki and Celeste Schenck. Ithaca: Cornell University Press, 1988.

———. "The Souls of Black Women Folk in the Writings of W. E. B. Du Bois." In *Reading Black, Reading Feminist*, ed. Henry Louis Gates, Jr., 225–43. New York: Penguin, 1990.

Miller, R. Baxter. " 'For a Moment I Wondered': Theory and Symbolic Form in the Autobiographies of Langston Hughes." *Langston Hughes Review* 3 (1984): 1–6.

Moody, Joycelyn K. "Ripping Away the Veil of Slavery: Literacy, Communal Love, and Self-Esteem in Three Slave Women's Narratives." *Black American Literature Forum* 24 (1990): 633–48.

Rampersad, Arnold. "Biography, Autobiography, and Afro-American Culture." *Yale Review* 73 (Autumn 1983): 1–16.

Reagon, Bernice Johnson. "My Black Mothers and Sisters; or, On Beginning a Cultural Autobiography." *Feminist Studies* 8 (Spring 1982): 81–95.

Rosenblatt, Roger. "Black Autobiography: Life as the Death Weapon." *Yale Review* 65 (June 1976): 515–27.

Schultz, Elizabeth. "To Be Black and Blue: The Blues Genre in Black American Autobiography." *Kansas Quarterly* 7, no.3 (1975): 81–96.

Sekora, John. "Black Message/White Envelope: Genre, Authenticity, and Authority in the Antebellum Slave Narrative." *Callaloo* 10 (Summer 1987): 482–515.

Sekora, John, and Houston A. Baker, Jr. "Written Off: Narratives, Master Texts, and Afro-American Writing from 1760 to 1945." *Studies in Black American Literature* 1 (1984): 43–62.

Stone, Albert E. "Identity and Art in Frederick Douglass's *Narrative*." *CLA Journal* 17 (1973): 192–213.

Taylor, Gordon O. "Voices from the Veil: Black American Autobiography." *Georgia Review* 35 (1981): 341–61.

Walker, Peter. "Frederick Douglass: Orphan Slave." *Moral Choices: Memory, Desire, and Imagination in Nineteenth-Century American Abolition*, 207–61. Baton Rouge: Louisiana State University Press, 1978.